CROSS-CURRICULAR
TEACHING AND LEARNING
IN THE SECONDARY SCHOOL

ENGLISH

What is the purpose of the curriculum in a secondary school? Is it to teach a set of subject knowledge and skills, learning in a way that is faithful to long-standing subject cultures and pedagogies? Or is there another way to consider how the curriculum and the notion of individual subjects and teachers' pedagogy could be constructed?

Cross-Curricular Teaching and Learning in the Secondary School ... English brings together ongoing debates about personalised learning, creativity and ICT in education to establish a clear theoretical framework for cross-curricular teaching and learning in English and literacy. Presenting an appropriate pedagogy for cross-curricular teaching that draws on this framework, it promotes radical new approaches to English teaching as part of a widened curriculum through practical examples and theoretical discussions blended with engaging stories of current practice.

With links to other curriculum subjects and current education policy, features include:

- theoretical examination of key issues;
- assessment of the strengths and weaknesses of different curricular models;
- clear principles for effective assessment;
- a wide range of case studies;
- summaries of key research linked to suggestions for further reading;
- professional development activities to promote cross-curricular dialogue.

Part of the *Cross-Curricular Teaching and Learning in the Secondary School* series, this timely interdisciplinary textbook is essential reading for all students on Initial Teacher Training courses and practising teachers looking to holistically introduce cross-curricular themes and practices in secondary English teaching.

David Stevens is a subject tutor for the secondary English course at the University of Durham, UK.

Cross-Curricular Teaching and Learning in . . .

Series Editor: Jonathan Savage (Manchester Metropolitan University, UK)

The *Cross-Curricular* series, published by Routledge, argues for a cross-curricular approach to teaching and learning in secondary schools. It provides a justification for cross-curricularity across the Key Stages, exploring a range of theoretical and practical issues through case studies drawn from innovative practices across a range of schools. The books demonstrate the powerful nature of change that can result when teachers allow a cross-curricular 'disposition' to inspire their pedagogy. Working from a premise that there is no curriculum development without teacher development, the series argues for a serious re-engagement with cross-curricularity within the work of the individual subject teacher, before moving on to consider collaborative approaches for curriculum design and implementation through external curriculum links.

Cross-curricular approaches to teaching and learning can result in a powerful, new model of subject-based teaching and learning in the high school. This series places the teacher and their pedagogy at the centre of this innovation. The responses that schools, departments or teachers make to government initiatives in this area may be sustainable only over the short term. For longer-term change to occur, models of cross-curricular teaching and learning need to become embedded within the pedagogies of individual teachers and, from there, to inform and perhaps redefine the subject cultures within which they work. These books explore how this type of change can be initiated and sustained by teachers willing to raise their heads above their 'subject' parapet and develop a broader perspective and vision for education in the twenty-first century.

Forthcoming titles in the series:

Cross-Curricular Teaching and Learning in the Secondary School . . . The Arts
Martin Fautley and Jonathan Savage

Cross-Curricular Teaching and Learning in the Secondary School . . . English
David Stevens

Cross-Curricular Teaching and Learning in the Secondary School . . . Foreign Languages
Gee Macrory, Cathy Brady and Sheila Anthony

Cross-Curricular Teaching and Learning in the Secondary School . . . Humanities
Richard Harris and Simon Harrison

Cross-Curricular Teaching and Learning in the Secondary School . . . Using ICT
Maurice Nyangon

Cross-Curricular Teaching and Learning in the Secondary School . . . Mathematics
Robert Ward-Penny

CROSS-CURRICULAR TEACHING AND LEARNING IN THE SECONDARY SCHOOL

· ·

ENGLISH

The centrality of language in learning

David Stevens

Routledge
Taylor & Francis Group

LONDON AND NEW YORK

This first edition published 2011
by Routledge
2 Park Square, Milton Park, Abingdon, Oxon, OX14 4RN

Simultaneously published in the USA and Canada
by Routledge
270 Madison Avenue, New York, NY 10016

Routledge is an imprint of the Taylor & Francis Group, an informa business

Typeset in Bembo by
Saxon Graphics Ltd, Derby
Printed and bound in Great Britain by
TJ International Ltd, Padstow, Cornwall

British Library Cataloguing in Publication Data
A catalogue record for this book is available from the British Library

Library of Congress Cataloging-in-Publication Data
Stevens, David.
   Cross-curricular teaching and learning in the secondary school : the centrality of language in learning / by David Stevens. — 1st ed.
       p. cm.
   Includes bibliographical references and index.
   1. Education, Secondary. 2. Multicultural education. 3. Interdisciplinary approach in education. I. Title.
   LC1099.S79 2011
   428.0071'241—dc22   2010015920

ISBN13: 978-0-415-56503-5 (hbk)
ISBN13: 978-0-415-56504-2 (pbk)
ISBN13: 978-0-203-84134-1 (ebk)

*To Mike McPartland, invaluable friend and colleague
at Durham University School of Education, who died in 2009.*

Contents

Acknowledgements

Some sections of this book have been developed and adapted from my contributions to *English Teaching in the Secondary School* (2004) and *The Art of Teaching Secondary English* (2004).

With thanks to pupils of Gillbrook Technology College (Redcar and Cleveland) and Caedmon School (Whitby) for the 'Martian' poems cited in Chapter 3 and to Dr Meic Stephens, as the copyright holder, for his permission to use an extract from *The Ballad of Billy Rose* in Chapter 8.

Don Salter, of Durham University School of Education, read an early draft of the book and made helpful suggestions.

Every effort has been made to contact and acknowledge copyright owners. If any material has been included without permission, the publishers offer their apologies and would be pleased to have any errors or omissions brought to their attention so that corrections may be published at a later printing.

Abbreviations

A level	Advanced level
AS level	Advanced subsidiary level
BECTA	British Educational Communications and Technology Association
c.	circa
CL	Critical literacy
CP	Critical pedagogy
DARTS	Directed Activities Related to Texts
DES	Department for Education and Science
DfEE	Department for Education and Employment
EAL	English as an additional language
EXEL	Extending Literacy
EXIT	Extending Interactions with Texts
HMI	Her Majesty's Inspectorate
HMSO	Her Majesty's Stationery Office
ICT	Information and communications technology
INSET	In-service training
IWB	Interactive white board
KS	Key stage
LEA	Local Education Authority
LINC	Language in the National Curriculum
MFL	Modern foreign languages
NACCCE	National Advisory Committee on Creative and Cultural Education
NATE	National Association for the Teaching of English
NCC	National Curriculum Council
NFER	National Foundation for Education Research
NLS	National Literacy Strategy
Ofsted	Office for Standards in Education
OS	Ordnance Survey
PGCE	Post Graduate Certificate in Education
QCA	Qualifications and Curriculum Authority

QCDA	Qualifications and Curriculum Development Agency (successor to QCA, from 2009)
QTS	Qualified teacher status
RE	Religious education
SATs	Standard Assessment Tests
SEN	Special educational needs
UKLA	United Kingdom Literacy Association
VLE	Virtual learning environment

Introduction

The particular nature of English in a cross-curricular context

This book is intended to stimulate interest in the cross-curricular potential of English teaching in secondary schooling, primarily for English teachers and those concerned with that branch of the teaching profession: student teachers, teacher educators and curriculum managers. As such, I am concerned in effect to develop the nature of English lessons as timetabled and clearly defined in the vast majority of secondary schools – and more or less determined by the subject-based nature of the National Curriculum – by alerting English teachers and others to the vast potential within the subject for making creative and practical use of cross-curricular ways of working and conceiving of the world in the context of English pedagogical traditions and *within English lessons.* However, I am also keenly aware that this book is one of a series considering cross-curricular teaching and learning from the perspectives of all the other secondary school subjects, and that, consequently, there will be almost inevitable overlap between some areas across the series. I view this as constructive rather than unfortunate, in that the very essence of interdisciplinary initiatives demands a broader outlook than that implied by subject boundaries. Making such connections is at the heart of this series and of this particular volume, and I would feel encouraged if, as a result of adopting cross-curricular approaches *within* English, its teachers felt inspired to seek more and more connections with colleagues from other subject disciplines in both practical and theoretical pedagogical contexts.

The combination of practice and theory is, for me, critical, in all senses of the word: the one informs the other in what I hope is a genuinely creative enterprise as outlined in this book and series. As the educational philosopher Wilfred Carr has pointed out, there has been a tendency over the past couple of decades to neglect any philosophical debate centring on the nature of education and schooling – 'education now insulates itself from philosophy …' as he puts it (Carr 2004: 35) – and I should like to think that in its small way, this book may contribute a little to reinvigorating the debate. For debate it has to be, especially as this entire series seeks to endorse a radical curricular turn for secondary schooling, and to ignore the issues is in effect simply to accept the status quo. Those searching simply for teaching tips on how to meet new curricular demands will be disappointed – although I invite them to read on anyway in the spirit of enquiry as to how philosophy and practice may work together in the way Griffiths has shown us: a

> practical philosophy … [that] is interested in the empirical world as a way of grounding its conclusions in interaction between thinking and action … Theory is brought into question by the experience it questions, and is then used to inform practical actions.
>
> (Griffiths 2003: 21)

With this in mind, I shall be drawing upon a number of relevant (I hope) commentators – some familiar from mainstream educational thought, others perhaps less so – as guides for our enterprise.

My own professional record as teacher of English in several comprehensive schools, in two as Head of English, and over the past fourteen years as a teacher educator in English, within the Durham University Post Graduate Certificate in Education (PGCE) course, has led me increasingly to question any rigid adherence to subject delineation. Every year, the PGCE English group at Durham comprises excellent beginning teachers from a wide range of subject specialisms alongside English itself (whatever that term now means, given its own healthy diversity), including, at various times, sociology, media studies, communications, law, modern languages and drama. My own first degree was in Humanities, involving arts, philosophy and humanities modules alongside English itself, and subsequent study has explored further interdisciplinary connections, within the arts field particularly. I am also interested in intercultural connections in the teaching and learning of English, drawing on both the Romantic tradition central to that subject's history, and on perspectives of critical pedagogy through the work of Freire, Giroux and others; I hope the possible syntheses between diverse approaches to teaching and learning will inform and illuminate the interdisciplinary project at the heart of the series. In schools I was particularly keen to foster links with arts, humanities and languages colleagues, and I have attempted to continue and develop this collaborative breadth of approach across these subjects (especially art, music and drama) at teacher education level. For example I, and a few willing colleagues, frequently begin the PGCE course by asking our students, across up to four subject areas, to work in cross-curricular small groups scouring the local area for resourceful teaching and learning connections based on a sense of the place. In part of course this is simply to get people to work together – but then this is important too. I have also been positively alerted to the possibilities of adopting and adapting scientific and mathematical pedagogical approaches for English – a challenge, certainly, but often an illuminating one.

The nature of the curricular subject English, particularly as it appears in the secondary school curriculum, is one characterised by paradox. Something about the subject has ensured that it has been, and remains, at the sharp edge of curricular battles – with both defeats and victories recorded – over the years since its invention as a core subject (some would say, *the* core subject) around the turn of the nineteenth into twentieth century. As Peel maintains in his helpful discussion on the nature of the subject English (Peel *et al.* 2000: 22), its 'most universal quality is diversity'. In the context of the present exploration, focusing on the cross-curricular, interdisciplinary nature and potential of secondary school subjects, English again, predictably enough, has an especially vital role to play, and one almost defined by paradox. On the one hand, the distinctive nature of the subject is fiercely contested, with particular positions regarding its nature defended vociferously; on the other hand, the sometimes startling, often bewildering breadth, and the arguably amorphous quality of English, lead many to conceive of it as the cross-curricular subject par excellence. Effectively, in this book I attempt to argue for a new kind of English teacher: an interdisciplinary English teacher, aware of the breadth of the subject and the interconnectivities involved (the *inter* of 'interdisciplinary', which is why I prefer the term to 'cross-curricular'), but also especially conscious of *language*, in all its textual diversity, as the sharp focus. Certainly few throughout the world of education would disagree that a secure grasp of language and its qualities lies at the heart of effective teaching and learning – and this is the very stuff, the defining characteristic, of English in the curriculum.

1

The contexts for cross-curricular teaching and learning in English

Historical contexts

In recent years, perhaps because of the paradoxical and contested nature of their subject, English teachers in secondary schools have become increasingly used to living with externally imposed strictures on the content and even the delivery of English. The National Curriculum, ushered in by the 1988 Education Act and, for English, substantially revised several times since, could be seen as the instigator of much of this development. The National Curriculum, and much of what has followed in its wake (particularly the methods used to assess and record pupils' and schools' achievements, and the various National Strategies) could be seen as a reaction to the rather piecemeal nature of the secondary school curriculum before 1988, in the sense that what was taught, especially in a subject like English whose practitioners defended, and frequently defined themselves by, their right to safeguard individuality in teaching and learning, depended on the particular qualities of the teachers concerned. Some of these teachers were excellent: creative, thorough and highly effective; others less so (I remember distinctly noticing this division during my early English teaching experience in the 1980s). Much about English teaching prior to1988 was, however, positive: new examination syllabuses at sixteen and eighteen, based largely on coursework, opened up exciting opportunities for effective and innovative teaching of both language and literature, increasingly integrated at all levels. At the same time, pioneering work was going on in English departments in a range of other areas: speaking and listening; integration with drama; media education; active approaches to literature, including Shakespeare; awareness and knowledge of the workings of language; and (especially apposite here) collaboration with other curricular subjects.

English teachers, with commendable skill but not a little embattlement, have by and large managed to convert threats into opportunities: not only to live with the official curricula, but actually to make them work positively. The most recent revisions of the National Curriculum, for English as for the other school subjects, are now firmly embedded in classroom practice, largely uncontroversially despite what D'Arcy (2000: 30) has described as 'the increasingly formalistic emphasis' and a rather more terse, instructional tone than that used previously. The latest manifestation of the National Curriculum, instrumental for Year 7 from 2008–9 and for subsequent secondary year groups over the respective following four years, has included much of the National Strategy (initially the National Literacy Strategy) within itself, although the 'Renewed Framework' for secondary English also sits alongside (at least until 2011), reinforcing key areas, including, notably, cross-curricular concerns. This new curriculum is itself rather more fluid than its previous manifestations, a characteristic underlined by its availability only online, where any revisions or amendments are also publicised. Significantly in the context of the present exploration, the new curriculum seeks actively to promote cross-curricular teaching and learning, especially through its 'creativity' and 'cross-curricular' strands, thus resurrecting the facet of the curriculum that many felt had attracted merely lip service in 1988.

Curriculum initiatives, even when unwelcome, have served to focus attention on the nature of English teaching: why the subject has such a prominent place within the curriculum, and what to do with it once it is there. This is not some esoteric debate undertaken solely by those professionally involved in the teaching of English: for better or for worse, education has been opened up to an unprecedented degree to the wider public – New Labour's battle cry during the 1997 General Election, 'Education! Education! Education!', for example, clearly struck a chord with the electorate; subsequent developments have borne this out, even when (or perhaps especially when) governmental policies have been contentious. With good reason, most people feel that they have something to contribute to the education debate, based either on their own remembered education or on their children's continuing schooling, in a way unlikely to apply, say, to the processes and professions of law or medicine. The position of English is perhaps even more relevant here, in that the English language is almost universally shared (to some extent at least) by the citizens of the UK and virtually everyone feels a degree of expertise. In a sense, of course, there is validity in this feeling – after all, language is by its very nature owned by those who use it, and the learning of spoken English is achieved without any formal teaching – but these same people would perhaps be less likely to pronounce upon the nature of art, geography or mathematics in education. The special position of English teachers in this context presents an opportunity both to influence opinion and to draw on existing views, and the subject's very breadth makes it all the more apposite for an interdisciplinary turn; but it is an elusive opportunity, all too easily missed.

There is not the space here to describe or analyse in detail the history of cross-curricular initiatives in the secondary school curriculum for England, or the particular place of the subject English in these previous attempts. Nevertheless, it could be helpful to look briefly at what has been tried during relatively recent years, what sort of successes have been recorded, and what may be the pitfalls – if only so that we may learn something concerning which mistakes could be avoided in any new developments. Essentially, we need to look at cross-curricular policies and practical initiatives in general, and focus particularly on the role of the subject English in fostering language across the curriculum initiatives.

The Bullock Report

The official report *A Language for Life* (DES 1975), generally known as 'the Bullock Report', is a helpful place to start, signalling as it did the first rigorous attempt to explore and define the nature of language in education, across all phases, and to make specific recommendations as to how schools and others concerned with education should implement the findings. The report, the culmination of exhaustive research and deliberations of the government-established committee chaired by Alan Bullock, carried considerable weight both at the time and for several years after. When I studied for my PGCE in English in 1978–9, our lecturer enthusiastically held up a copy of the report and pronounced that it encapsulated the future of English teaching and its positive impact across the curriculum: I distinctly remember him dramatically encouraging us novice teachers to worship the golden Bullock – and he was only half joking. We were impressed, and not just by the theatrics. And yet when I started teaching English in a comprehensive school a few months later, of Bullock there was no mention, and of cross-curricular initiatives, language-inspired or otherwise, there was precious little either. The crucial question about Bullock and all language-focused whole-school initiatives, then as now, as James Britton presciently realised in 1977 (in Praedl 1982: 190), was and is 'Amid all the talk of "literacy" and "evaluation", both very narrowly conceived, can it survive to keep before us a more enlightened view of language and learning?'

What had Bullock recommended that was so welcomed? And why was his impact so limited? As far as the secondary phase was concerned, the recommendations were indeed radical and potentially far reaching; pertinent in the present context, they included, under the heading 'Principal Recommendations':

- Every school should devise a systematic policy for the development of reading competence in pupils of all ages and ability levels.

- Each school should have an organised policy for language across the curriculum, establishing every teacher's involvement in language and reading development throughout the years of schooling.

- Every school should have a suitably qualified teacher with responsibility for advising and supporting his colleagues in language and the teaching of reading.

- There should be close consultation between schools, and the transmission of effective records, to ensure continuity in the teaching of reading and in the language development of every pupil.

- English in the secondary school should have improved resources in terms of staffing, accommodation and ancillary help.

- Every LEA should appoint a specialist English adviser and should establish an advisory team with the specific responsibility of supporting schools in all aspects of language in education.

- A substantial course on language in education (including reading) should be part of every primary and secondary school teacher's initial training, whatever the teacher's subject or the age of the children with whom he or she will be working.

- There should be an expansion in in-service education opportunities in reading and the various other aspects of the teaching of English, and these should include courses at diploma and higher degree level. Teachers in every LEA should have access to a language/reading centre.

- There should be a national centre for language in education, concerned with the teaching of English in all its aspects, from language and reading in the early years to advanced studies with sixth forms.

- Children should be helped to as wide as possible a range of language uses so that they can speak appropriately in different situations and use standard forms when they are needed.

- Competence in language comes above all through its purposeful use, not through the working of exercises divorced from context.

- In the secondary school, all subject teachers need to be aware of: (i) the linguistic processes by which their pupils acquire information and understanding, and the implications for the teacher's own use of language; (ii) the reading demands of their own subjects, and ways in which the pupils can be helped to meet them.

- To bring about this understanding every secondary school should develop a policy for language across the curriculum. The responsibility for this policy should be embodied in the organisational structure of the school.

- Every authority should have an advisory team with the specific responsibility of supporting schools in all aspects of language in education. This would encompass English from language and reading in the early years to advanced reading and English studies at the highest level of the secondary school.

The ambitious nature of the Bullock recommendations, even from this limited selection, is I hope readily apparent. Perhaps this very ambitiousness was a factor in its (at best) patchy implementation, along with lack of political will, adequate funding, or appropriate education of beginning and experienced teachers. Bullock is, however, now rightly seen as a major landmark in English teaching's development, especially in a cross-curricular context, and remains powerfully appropriate to current initiatives in this direction (which is why it is worth quoting at some length). At the time, it embodied a great deal of the theory and practice relating to the role of language not just in communication but in thinking and in making sense of the world. For example, the development of DARTS (Directed Activities Related to Texts), initiated by Lunzer and Gardner in 1984, for English and some other curriculum areas, revolutionised ways of exploring texts (including diagrams, tables, pictures, musical notation, classroom talk – anything, in fact) imaginatively across the curriculum, and remain positively helpful as we seek to extend the English repertoire:

- text completion (cloze, predictions, diagrammatic completion etc);

- unscrambling/labelling deliberately disordered/segmented texts;

- predictive activities – sequels/prequels/sequencing/re-ordering;

- close reading – specific searching/labelling/annotation/underlining/ICT;

- recording/re-ordering – e.g. written text >diagram, one genre >another;

- summarising of key points – reporting/interpretation for a new audience or purpose.

Writers such as Britton and Barnes in England had emphasised the importance of the relationship between language and *all* learning – a fundamental tenet of the report, and of this book – and the central idea that language develops through its active use in meaningful contexts (both within the subject English and beyond) rather than simply by narrow instruction in skills.

> **Reflective Activity:**
>
> Consider in some detail the nature of the Bullock Report findings and recommendations.
>
> How do these relate to what you know of the current context of secondary English teaching and learning?
>
> From your own practical experience, is there still the potential for development along the lines of Bullock?
>
> What might be the opportunities and dangers of such developments?

The introduction of the National Curriculum

The next significant official report, that of the Kingman Committee exploring the nature of knowledge about language in teaching and learning, came over a decade later (DES 1988). The Kingman position, fundamentally, was to accept that the way we acquire and develop language is essentially through its constructive use, but further stated that, in addition, pupils should be taught specific knowledge about language, in terms of forms (including accents, dialects and the thorny issue of Standard English), social and cultural contexts, and historical developments. In a sense Kingman could be seen as an opportunity to kick-start language across the curriculum possibilities that had by then faded after the first enthusiasm for Bullock, but that would be to ignore the political climate of the time. For despite the positive recommendations of Kingman and the subsequent establishment of the Language in the National Curriculum (LINC) working party, the introduction of the National Curriculum in 1988 in fact militated against such adventurousness: it cemented a rigid subject-based school curriculum (despite the lip service it paid to cross-curricular themes and dimensions), and a similarly rigid assessment and reporting system.

The implementation of the new curriculum was far from consultative, further alienating the teachers who were required to teach it, and the eventual report of the LINC working party was disgracefully undermined by the Thatcher government (thus, incidentally, wasting £4 million) for failing to be prescriptive enough about language education (in other words, it tended to build on Bullock and Kingman rather than insist on a system of didactic drilling in language skills). There were some official comments from the National Curriculum Council (the body then responsible for the development and implementation of the National Curriculum) regarding the possibility of curricular design away from strict subject-based delineation, such as this:

> In due course it is likely that schools will throw all the Attainment Targets in a heap on the floor and reassemble them in a way which provides for them the very basis of the whole curriculum.
>
> (Tate 1994: 34)

However, observations such as these now seem disingenuous at best, given the contradictory weight of pressure to conform to both letter and spirit of a law that was tightly policed by inspections and league tables. Subsequent attempts to reinvigorate the National Curriculum for English (and by implication its cross-curricular role) by Brian Cox and his committee (well documented by Cox himself in his account *Cox on the Battle for the English Curriculum* 1995), in fact came to little. There were language across the curriculum initiatives throughout the 1980s and 1990s, but their effect was limited to individual schools, and occasionally local education authorities. Nevertheless, some signs were distinctly positive.

Writing in the mid-1990s, Alison Tate gave a helpful and thorough appraisal of the state of cross-curricular initiatives in English schools (Tate 1994). Tate's summary of the opportunities and threats concerning cross-curricular developments in schools is particularly relevant to the present study. In terms of the positive values of such developments she noted several features (noted below with my comments in brackets):

- Enhancement of student-centred learning (surely all the more relevant today in view of the 'personalised learning' agenda).

- Encouragement of personal growth (as we have already seen, especially relevant to English) and active learning pedagogical models.

- 'A corrective to an overly content-dominated curriculum' (op.cit.: 59) – (again especially apt for the subject English and its cross-curricular mission).

- The provision of 'a cementing or binding role' (op.cit.: 59) through contextual location (once more, it seems to me, appropriate to the focus on language as the common denominator of learning processes).

Other contemporary commentators recorded similarly positive aspirations; Verma and Pumfrey, for example, welcomed the new emphasis on cultural diversity through inter-subject connections and collaboration:

> The boundaries between the subjects in a curriculum are often artificial and arbitrary. The importance of integrative cross-curricular dimensions, skills and themes ... is widely accepted for all pupils.
>
> (1993: 10)

However, despite Tate's discovery of localised instances of the above curricular developments, she noted, too, several obstacles:

- The traditional departmental structure of secondary schools, implying that cross-curricular initiatives, left unguided, 'have no established power base' (Tate 1994: 60).

- Teachers' subject loyalties, often jealously guarded and embedded in institutional structures of schools, and in the National Curriculum itself.

- The prevalence of didactic, transmission-based models of teaching and learning, especially in some subject areas.

- The size and organisational complexity of secondary schools, as exemplified in timetabling arrangements.

- The focus on competitive assessment and testing, whereas cross-curricular activity as such generally remains unassessed in any recorded or formal sense.
- Initiative fatigue among teachers and school managers.

All six of these problematic issues remain, in varying degrees, fifteen years later, and all demand serious consideration if the interdisciplinary venture espoused and promoted by this series is to succeed. Tate's rather bleak conclusion – 'The overall impression is of isolated local initiatives and of barely any national or co-ordinated drive' (op.cit.: 61) – need not be ours, however. The obstacles remain, but schools are vastly different places now, for better or for worse, than they were in 1994, with distinctive movement towards the dismantling of many of the barriers noted above in favour of the positive value of cross-curricular connections and activity. In part at least, this has been because of the advent of the National Strategy, now embedded in the latest version of the National Curriculum. Because of its instrumental role in this respect, the Strategy deserves detailed attention.

The impact of the National Strategy

The various National Strategies in many ways exemplify both positive and negative aspects of the education system over the past decade or so: on the one hand, all of them in some way or other encouraged teachers to think and act beyond subject boundaries; on the other, they (or at least some of their manifestations) could be seen as inordinately reductive of curricula and pedagogically controlling. The tension between these interpretations perhaps has a bearing on any attempt at interdisciplinary curriculum innovation, and it is well worth exploring in a little detail the contextual background.

The National Strategy as it stands is to be phased out from 2011, but its impact has been enormous and will remain so. Many of the major changes to the secondary English curriculum in recent times have occurred at Key Stage 3, on the foundations established by the Primary phase National Literacy Strategy and its (then) centrally embedded Literacy Hour. The National Strategy: English Strand, as the National Literacy Strategy insofar as it affects English became, now profoundly influences the entire English curriculum, as already noted, through its integration into the current National Curriculum. Perhaps 'influences' is too weak a word in this context, however: certainly all English departments are influenced, but in some schools and some local authorities the English curriculum as it had hitherto developed was (and indeed still is) in danger of being subsumed by the Strategy and its emphasis on a narrowly conceived 'literacy'. It could be argued that because the demands of literacy education are so fundamental to all teaching and learning, any attempt to promote literacy across the curriculum is to be welcomed – especially by English teachers. To a point, there is validity in this argument, but three important questions need to be posed and explored: first, the nature of the literacy at the centre of the debate; second, the nature of the curriculum in place ostensibly at least to service the need; and, third, the perhaps inevitable tension between the basic 'ability' to use language effectively and the more celebratory and/or critical aspects of language use. The third of these areas is especially pertinent to reading, the main focus of literacy initiatives: a basic ability to read, in the sense of inferring some sort of meaning from text, and the desire to read for pleasure, and thus become a more critical and sophisticated reader, are quite different and perhaps demand quite different pedagogical approaches. Because these issues are so fundamental to the teaching of English in secondary schools, especially in an interdisciplinary context, it is worth exploring the matter in some depth.

The rich variety of the English curriculum as a whole, ever-shifting entity could not – certainly should not – be reduced to any one strategy, or Strategy, however laudable. Indeed the fluidity of the subject English should be one of its most enduring qualities, in the sense that David Holbrook meant, writing over thirty years ago but all the more valid today:

> The fallacy of our inherited traditions of thought has been the exclusion of the subjective, and its failure to recognise the element of personal participation, the essential participation of the knower in the known. There is no 'objective' body of knowledge, known once and for all … all knowledge is contingent.
>
> (Holbrook 1979: 81)

This all perhaps suggests a certain tension with which English teachers have to grapple, especially as we seek to extend the nature of the subject precisely through the kind of participation Holbrook alludes to. If indeed the knowledge at the core of any curriculum – knowledge very broadly defined, perhaps better termed 'understanding' – is contingent, we need to discover and develop precisely what it is contingent upon. The context, in this instance, the context of the whole curriculum and the culture it represents, thus becomes all-important. For example, relating to the work of the Strategy in the point made above, what indeed is the point of educating children to read ever more proficiently if the love of reading itself has not been successfully fostered? This kind of question is fundamental to the interdisciplinary venture rooted in linguistic exploration: engagement and enthusiasm (both for teachers and their pupils) should be at the base of the activities and learning we seek to foster, or the entire project will inevitably founder.

In perhaps its most favourable light, however, the Strategy may be seen as something of a fulfilment of the far-sighted Bullock Report. As such the Strategy sought to influence the entire school curriculum, as did Bullock, in ways which focus consciously and rigorously on language as a tool for learning across all disciplines but with particular reference to English. But whereas adherence to Bullock's recommendations depended largely on the leanings of particular schools or LEAs, in the rather more laissez-faire climate of the times, the Strategy in effect became the cornerstone of official education policy. Certainly its impact is now felt across the curriculum, but, perhaps inevitably, it is English departments who are most closely involved with its literacy dimensions. In the late 1990s HMI conducted exhaustive investigations into the literacy models then used in secondary education, including the pilot secondary literacy projects of 1998–9. The resulting 'agenda' provides an interesting list of eighteen literacy issues to consider – pertinent now as then to all teachers, and especially to English teachers concerned to foster broad literacy across the curriculum. They include (Lewis and Wray 2000: 6):

- What is meant by a literate secondary age pupil?
- What strategies and structures are necessary to sustain literary development beyond Year 7?

- Is literacy development for all? What are the particular needs of boys, EAL pupils and higher attainers?
- What is the relationship of literacy developments to English and to existing SEN work?
- What kind of guidance do schools need?
- To what extent can/does literacy development entail a 'dumbing down' of English?
- What level of knowledge about language do teachers need?

All these questions require debate and resolution, and all are distinctly pertinent to the work of English teachers in a cross-curricular context. Indeed, it may well be that the general direction of the Strategy, following HMI's lead among others, has been in furthering the cross-curricular and adult needs approaches to the subject English (two of the five models for English suggested by Cox (DES 1989; see page 20), virtually eschewing other more arts-based and personal-growth focused conceptions of English. The introductory words of the resulting *Framework for Teaching English: Years 7, 8 and 9* (DfEE 2001: 1), in fact, managed to avoid the subject (in both senses of this word) of English altogether, stating that:

> The Key Stage 3 National Strategy is part of the government's commitment to raise standards in schools. Effective literacy is the key to raising standards across all subjects, and equipping pupils with the skills and knowledge they need for life beyond school.

This terse and uncompromising tone is typical of the official pronouncements we have become used to, and contrasts markedly to the language of Bullock, for example, or the language of persuasion English teachers habitually and effectively use in their teaching. However, putting this reservation aside, there does seem to be enough in Hertridge's original list of issues to enable English teachers to focus questioningly, realistically and creatively on the nature of their subject knowledge and pedagogy as the keys to cross-curricular teaching and learning focused on language and literacy.

Essentially the Strategy, in terms of its recommended pedagogy, was based around what Harrison, in his officially sponsored appraisal (*The National Strategy for English at Key Stage 3: Roots and Research*) has approvingly called 'the five elements of the [then] proposed teaching sequence' (Harrison 2002: 3):

- Identification of prior knowledge
- Teacher demonstration of process
- Shared exploration through activity
- Scaffolded pupil application of new learning
- Consolidation through discussion/activity.

Essentially, these observations are pedagogically uncontroversial; indeed much of the thrust of this book's recommendations is along these lines. Effective English teaching acknowledges pupils' immense linguistic experience and knowledge as its starting point, building collaboratively with appropriate leadership, modelling and scaffolding towards deep learning (and, in today's curious terminology, 'teacher fade'). If there is a devil at work at all here – and many would maintain there is, as we shall see – it must be in the interpretation of these five points for classroom activity. The main danger, it seems to me, is in too narrow or restrictive an interpretation of these laudable aims. If, for example, 'identification of prior knowledge' comes to mean simply 'ascertaining what's been previously taught', or, worse, 'what officially assessed level has been attained', or if 'teacher demonstration of process' implies merely the teacher showing – instructing, in effect – just one way of conducting an activity according to the conventions of a particular genre, then a real opportunity imaginatively to strengthen English pedagogy – in terms of both breadth and depth – will have been missed. Similarly, 'consolidation' could mean simply a mechanistic reinforcement of what the teacher thinks has been learned, as opposed to anything of a genuinely consultative or exploratory nature. Secondary English teachers have learned a great deal, in my experience, from the more negative aspects of the often painful implementation of the Strategy during the latter half of the 1990s and beyond. The principle lesson has been that sensitive and critically reflective flexibility has to be at the centre of pedagogy – especially as we seek to develop the nature of English teaching in an interdisciplinary direction.

Practical implications of the Strategy

We need now to understand more profoundly the implications of the Strategy for secondary English teachers, especially with any cross-curricular ambitions in mind. The model of literacy teaching and learning upon which the Strategy is based, and other possible models, require some critical exploration. A helpful starting point here is that offered by Pat D'Arcy (2000), who characterised the teaching and assessment of writing (but extending into all forms of literacy) in terms of 'two contrasting paradigms'. The first possibility D'Arcy presents as

> a paradigm which focuses on writing largely as a matter of construction and correctness – at word level, sentence level and text level. This kind of linguistic analysis is mechanistic because it pays little or no attention to the meaning of any specific piece of writing. Instead it restricts itself to generalisations about aspects of composition such as structure, organisation, spelling and punctuation.
>
> (D'Arcy 2000: 3)

On the other hand, the 'contrasting paradigm' is

> centred on a meaning-related approach both to how a text is constructed through the thoughts and feelings of the writer and also how a text is interpreted through the thoughts and feelings it evokes in the mind of a reader.
>
> (op. cit.: 3)

Appropriately enough, this fundamental distinction between approaches brings us back to the tension between technical proficiency and enthusiastic willingness in reading, and in language activity more generally, that I alluded to earlier. As D'Arcy elaborates, 'these paradigms are not mutually exclusive' and any difference is 'crucially a matter of focus'. However, although this particular paper was written before the Strategy's implementation at secondary level, the author already feared that 'this second paradigm ... has vanished without trace beneath the weight of a steady and relentless spate of official publications' (op.cit.: 3). Certainly there is a strong sense, in my reading at least, that the Strategy's theoretical base leaned – perhaps alarmingly – towards the former conception of literacy: a model essentially based on analysis of generic form as the key to understanding any given text, rather than emphasising more subtle senses of meaning and value.

Essentially, then, the Strategy's conception of literacy based itself on textual analysis to answer questions of intended audience and purpose as the twin keys to understanding genre. Resulting insights into generic characteristics and conventions were intended then to lead into fully literate understanding, at word, sentence and text levels. Such understanding should then give pupils the tools needed for textual replication or adaptation. This conception of literacy – essentially a cross-curricular conception – is based (perhaps insensitively, even erroneously) on the 'functional grammar' position as developed in the 1980s and 1990s by such linguists as Kress and Littlefair. Although in many ways persuasive, there are clearly lacking in this model any proper consideration of key elements in developing fully critical literacy: elements of value and values, for example, and the importance of the subjective voice (and ear). I have elsewhere considered more fully these and other elements (Stevens and McGuinn 2004), however, concluding reasonably positively that although these qualities may not be readily evident in the Strategy's theoretical or practical bases, neither are they actually excluded. Given the will, indeed, classroom practice is already demonstrating that secondary English teaching often creatively includes precisely these positive facets of literacy, integrating them constructively with more generic and cross-curricular considerations. This fuller sense of literacy is much closer to that offered, for example, by Margaret Meek (1991: 238):

> To be literate we have to be confident that the world of signs and print, in all the different mixtures of mode and meaning that surround us, is a world we can cope with, be at home in, contribute to and play with. If it is simply mysterious, threatening, unreliable or hostile, then we feel at a disadvantage, victimized and inadequate. There is no guarantee that literacy makes the world a more benign place, but it helps everyone to consider how it may be different.

There is evident here a humane quality perhaps understandably lacking in the more hard-nosed official pronouncements of the Strategy or subsequent documents – and yet nothing in these communications actually precludes such an approach. Harrison, indeed, in the officially sanctioned 'Roots and Research' investigation into the Strategy's implementation, acknowledged that 'there may not be simple answers to complex questions' in this context, going on to quote approvingly Linda Flower:

> A literate act ... is an attempt to create meaning, and in doing so, reflects – is itself shaped by – literate, social and cultural practices ... At the same time, literacy is also a personal, intentional action, an attempt to understand, express, explore, communicate, or influence.

(in Harrison 2002: 7)

In the cross-curricular context at issue here, the Strategy's approach to literacy, at least in terms of its preoccupation with non-literary texts, can be seen to have been founded on the 'Extending Interactions with Texts' (EXIT) model. Developed by Lewis and Wray in the late 1990s through the Nuffield Extending Literacy (EXEL) Project, this model involves ten elements, expounded in persuasive detail by Lewis and Wray (2000). The authors acknowledge the 'difficulty of representing a complex and essentially recursive set of processes in the two-dimensional space defined by print on paper' – a familiar issue for any writer – and explain that 'we do not intend the model to be read as a linear description of what happens when we interact with information texts' (Lewis and Wray 2000: 17). Although 'information texts' are specified here, there is a sense that, whatever the text, this conception of whole-school literacy tends to view it as potentially informative rather than, say, primarily affective – a point well worth bearing in mind as English teachers simultaneously concerned with an interdisciplinary approach *and* creative, affective aspects of the subject. The ten points of the EXIT model are (op. cit.: 17):

- Elicitation of previous knowledge
- Establishing purposes
- Locating information
- Adopting an appropriate strategy
- Interacting with text
- Monitoring understanding
- Making a record
- Evaluating information
- Assisting memory
- Communicating information.

My reservations notwithstanding, there is something positive at stake here: all of the approaches may be interpreted in imaginative ways, as adventurously as the English teacher sees fit, and all could imply a cross-curricular dimension. It is vital also to be acutely sensitive to the particular characteristics and needs both of the audience in question – the nature of the class being taught, normally – and of the kind of text being studied. Selectivity and imaginative interpretation are the watchwords here, but, as long as this is understood, English teachers – along with colleagues from other disciplines, which is one of the main points – can benefit from critically and reflectively adapting the EXIT model.

However, issues of linearity and hierarchy in models of learning, perhaps implied in the EXIT model and similar approaches, are problematic for English, which is essentially recursive by nature: an issue we shall revisit in Chapter 4 with the focus on assessment. Implicit (or explicit) in a great deal of what passes for literacy teaching is the assumption that the learner has to master 'basic' skills as a precondition of developing towards higher order understanding. This model, for instance, is embedded in the organisation of the Framework document, as it is in the National Curriculum with its progressively presented levels of attainment across the various subjects of the curriculum. Although there is clearly some validity in this view – not all ways of reading would be apt for all readers at all stages of development, or indeed for all texts – too rigid an adherence to it would be severely limiting and would risk demotivation for both learners and teachers. 'Basic' readers would be treated as this term suggests: in a basic, unimaginative way – at least until some point of take-off towards greater sophistication. Thus pupils in this category may miss out on creative – and critical – aspects of literacy. Again the English teacher needs to maintain a delicate balance between making literacy accessible to those pupils finding parts of it difficult, and creating exciting learning opportunities at *all* levels of textual engagement. Harrison (2002: 17) characterises the 'basic skills for basic readers' approach as essentially cognitive, maintaining that

> To take only a cognitive perspective, and to focus on teaching basic skills, therefore, and to ignore the wider rhetorical and social purposes of text, is to deny to the novice models of how to behave like an expert.

Literacy, in other words, needs to be involving, fascinating, critical and challenging at all levels and ages, and in relation to all texts. Perhaps if it were, and it is after all in the hands of real teachers in real classrooms, the disjunction between reading capability (whatever that means and however it is measured – serious issues in themselves) and the desire to read for pleasure would wither away. I have seen plenty of experience of precisely this occurring in my own and others' English classrooms: find the key to a pupil's interest, and the necessary literacy follows (as portrayed so vividly in Ken Loach's film *Kes* all those years ago). In effect, this means a literacy that is at its heart both actively critical and positively celebratory, rather than merely passively received. As Comber (in Hunt 2002: 133) makes clear, we need

> to question any suggestion that critical literacy is a developmental attainment rather than social practice which may be excluded or deliberately included in early literacy curriculum … in the early years of schooling, students learn what it means to read and write successfully in terms of school practices. They need opportunities to take on this text analysis role from the start, as part of how culture defines literacy, not as a special curriculum in the later years of schooling or in media studies.

Towards a Strategic synthesis: linking theory and practice

Three prominent critics of the curricular direction English appeared to be taking under the influence of the Strategy – Philip Pullman, Pat D'Arcy and Richard Hoggart – also offered interesting possibilities for resolving the disjunction between apparently opposing conceptions of literacy in education. Their observations remain valuable now as we attempt to develop radically from that position. As ever, so much depends on viewpoint. Pullman (2002: 22), for example, maintains that 'Education ought to be concerned with the basics. We just disagree about what the basics are.' He goes on to explain his idea of what is basic: 'the joy of discovery, wonder, excitement, pleasure … the whole attitude we express in our work, the attitude we express by working … that truly is basic. So I'm all for basics.'

Pullman ended his paper (it was originally a speech given to English teachers at the NATE Conference of 2002): 'The one thing that sustains my hope about education is actually talking to teachers. … Do what you know is right, ignore what you know is wrong, but carry on teaching' (op. cit.: 23). Cue tumultuous applause – but in effect this is precisely what I recommend too – provided the principles of critical reflection are genuinely applied. Taking the point a little further, D'Arcy (2000: 38) quotes approvingly from David Moffet:

> The process of writing cannot be realistically perceived and taught so long as we try to work from the outside in. The most fundamental and effective way to improve compositional 'decisions' about word choice, phrasing, sentence structure, and overall organisation is to clarify, enrich and harmonise the thinking that predetermines the student's initial choices of these.

The position outlined here sets itself against the genre-orientated approach, but of course the two aspects of literacy (essentially, in old-fashioned terms, form and content) cannot exist in isolation from each other, but rather in a dialectical relationship – albeit one based on a fundamental sense of engagement and commitment to the process and product. Richard Hoggart (1998: 68), further, reminds us that

> All serious writing is about discrepancies, discordances and their possible resolution between the world outside as we would wish to see it and as we encounter it; between what others have made of it and what we are now making of it; between the world of relationships we inhabit and the world inside our selves.

Such observations as those cited above imply a thorough, humane and critical approach to literacy, strongly implying interdisciplinary connections (it would be hard to conceive of this kind of literacy otherwise). As English teachers, we may need to shift our perspective significantly towards an interdisciplinary conception of literacy, however, in order to play a real part in the transformation of literacy teaching centred on what actually happens (or could happen) in the classroom. Harrison, again in the officially sponsored Roots and Research appraisal of Key Stage 3 literacy teaching, reinforces the point, arguing that professional development is crucial, and must 'recognise teachers as professionals and not as technicians' (Harrison 2002: 11). Harrison's research (op. cit.: 13) highlighted literacy teachers who

> regarded theory as emancipating and professionally empowering – it was what enabled them to make confident and professionally informed decisions about their literacy teaching. It was what enabled them to move beyond the role of technician or educational paramedic and into the role of professional, to become teachers who could use the Strategy as a toolkit, not a script, and apply it with flexibility and confidence, rather than obedience.

Ultimately, as Harrison concluded, 'If we want to create skilled, confident, independent and adaptable pupils, they need to be taught by skilled, confident, independent and adaptable teachers' (op. cit.: 34). As ever there is a need both for critical clarity and breadth in our conception of literacy; as Goodwyn and Findlay (2002: 22) remind us, teachers need to be sensitive to the literacy practices and events pupils experience outside school and the relationship between home and school literacies. ... beyond a simplistic ... model of literacy to recognize that some literacies are more powerful than others and all are inherently ideological. ... The ideological effects of literacy are transparent but nowhere are they more powerful than in educational settings.

Again the *Roots and Research* document is helpful, focusing as it does on the conditions of successful literacy teaching:

- There must be a central emphasis on language, particularly that related to understanding and managing the activity;

- Teaching should be grounded in culturally meaningful experiences that help pupils to be able to transfer learning to new contexts;

- Effective teaching and learning occur in collaborative activities, with active learning in contexts in which individual differences are respected;

- The basic form of teaching is dialogue that leads to an integrated approach to listening, speaking, reading and writing, with an emphasis on pupils increasingly directing their own learning.

(Harrison 2002: 18)

It is probably now true, after much struggle and lack of clarity, that the National Curriculum and the National Strategies (in the form of the 'Renewed Framework' as now available at www.nationalstrategies.standards.dcsf.gov.uk/secondary/english/framework) support and reinforce each other in terms of what they say about cross-curricular aspects of English. For example the vocabulary that appears in all of the different subject programmes of study implies a cross-curricular approach to reading, writing, speaking and listening, and language study. The Strategy, in its various forms, has always promoted literacy across the curriculum (predictably enough, given its inception as the National Literacy Strategy), starting in 2001 with its subject-specific advice giving guidance on effective pedagogical approaches and then renaming it in 2004 as Language and Learning. This second set of materials attempted to encourage different subject areas to focus on specific 'English' objectives, but this approach had only limited success, as we have seen. More useful to cross-curricular developments now, perhaps, are the progression indicators that underpin Functional Skills English – Independence, Familiarity, Complexity and Technical Demand – because these have the potential to send us back to pedagogy. Functional Skills have been driven by the Strategy and are essentially cross-curricular in nature: based on the idea that you cannot claim competence in a skill unless you can apply it in different contexts, so you cannot teach Functional English without linking to other subjects, and, by the same token, ideally other subject areas should also take responsibility for teaching aspects of Functional English. The links to this in the National Curriculum for English are very clear, especially in the Key Processes and the Curriculum Opportunities sections. The 'compelling learning experiences' that the Strategy suggests that all children have a right to experience are there, with the emphasis on real life, real contexts and real purposes, and also in intervention packages such as Study Plus and Literacy Plus. These have all been written with explicit cross-curricular links very much in mind.

Reflective Activity:

Consider further the nature of Functional Skills in both English and cross-curricular contexts, and the documentation available:

How do you think that this initiative will influence and change the nature of English as taught in secondary schools, drawing on your own professional experience?

Choose one other curricular subject and reflect on how English may relate to its teaching and learning in the context of Functional Skills.

Diversity and models of English

English teachers at secondary level have become accustomed to acknowledging and responding to a huge diversity of opinions and expectations as expressed by pupils, their parents, governing bodies, colleagues and many others, and it is part of the English teacher's function to integrate, discuss, adapt, confirm and debate the viewpoints as appropriate. In this context of perpetual flux, the English curriculum is best seen as a broad spectrum of approaches and expectations. In its official forms, of course, the curriculum may appear – indeed it seeks to appear – as completely authoritative; in truth it offers a series of touchstones, and the real nature of the subject has to be discovered and invented ever anew by those most intensely involved. This observation is perhaps especially relevant in the present context as many involved in English teaching seek to broaden its appeal on the basis of interdisciplinary connections and explorations.

This process requires a certain subjective immersion in the subject, and at the same time an objective ability to see both wood and trees in formulating overarching aims and values. An appreciation and practical awareness of the combination of subjectivity and objectivity is fundamental to the thesis of this book, and will be explored in various contexts; certainly, it is crucial to any conceptualisation of English as a focus for interdisciplinary pedagogy, fostering ways of thinking, teaching and learning that consciously draw upon the breadth of outlooks involved, from the subjectivity traditionally seen as the basis of the arts to the more objectively orientated frameworks represented by the humanities and sciences. The combination is also at the heart of the radical pedagogy that any truly interdisciplinary venture involves, in my view: again, a recurring theme of this book as I seek to represent both the 'language of critique' with the 'language of possibility' (developing, as we shall see, the ideas promulgated by such major pedagogical figures as Paulo Freire, among others).

As many teachers readily acknowledge, however, it is all too easy to be drawn into thinking that mechanistic teaching of the official curricula is an end in itself, spawning its own self-justification. Following Rex Gibson (1986), we could term this position 'instrumental rationality': the dichotomous separation of fact from feeling, demanding an absence of thought about the consequences and context of one's actions in any profound sense. The process thus becomes its own legitimisation with its own particular – sometimes impenetrable – rationality. What is missing here, of course, are questions of value and purpose in the entire project of education – and these questions require perpetual revisiting as the curriculum and its contexts change, including the interdisciplinary venture endorsed here. In a sense, this is nothing new. The poet Thomas Traherne (1960 [c.1660]: 48), for example, having initially paid tribute to the breadth of learning possible during his own Oxford education in the seventeenth century, went on to regret that,

> Nevertheless some things were defective too. There was never a tutor that did expressly teach Felicity, though that be the mistress of all other sciences. Nor did any of us study those things but as aliena, which we ought to have studied as our enjoyments. We studied to inform our knowledge, but knew not for what end we so studied. And for lack of aiming at a certain end we erred in the manner.

For Traherne, the notion of felicity, the full and visionary enjoyment of life's possibilities, ought to be the central tenet, the 'mistress', of the entire curriculum. The Oxford education of the mid-seventeenth century seems perhaps rather distant from our own concerns, but it may be that what was missing then is still perhaps avoided by the curriculum legislators of today. It is important to develop and keep a keen sense of what may be the broad purposes of education as an entire enterprise, and each individual curricular subject – especially perhaps English – has to be seen in this broader perspective. In effect, this perception is the true premise of this book and series.

To sharpen the focus once more on English itself, we can see that in the version of the National Curriculum for English based on the Report of the Cox Committee (DES 1989), it was suggested that there were essentially five models of English teaching, and that most English teachers combined in their teaching several if not all of these. The types of English teaching posited by Cox were as follows:

- a *personal growth* view, which tends to emphasise the pupil as a creative and imaginative individual developing, in terms of the teaching and learning of English, primarily through an intensive engagement with literature and personal creative writing;
- a *cross-curricular* approach, stressing the distinctive nature of English as the language of learning for virtually all curriculum areas and implying a definition of service to these areas and to education in a generic sense;
- an *adult needs* emphasis, as essentially a preparation for the demands of life beyond school in terms of effective understanding of and communication through the English language in its many forms, including those vocationally based;
- a *cultural heritage* model, with the teaching based heavily on 'great' works of literature, generally drawn from the past;
- a *cultural analysis* view, leading pupils to a critical understanding of the social and cultural context of English, particularly the value systems which are inevitably embedded in the ways language is used.

An amalgamation of these English teaching characteristics underlies all the subsequent versions of the National Curriculum – but we need to consider whether they suffice as a statement of principle. Do the five 'versions' of English sit as comfortably together as

Cox implied in his accompanying explanation: 'they are not sharply distinguishable, and they are certainly not mutually exclusive'. Is there not rather something of a struggle for ascendancy between some, if not all, of these views? Certainly, the subject English has been something of a battleground for years – since its comparatively recent inception, in fact – and it is all the more important to take a principled position with regard to its teaching, eschewing the temptations of a superficial compromise. Interestingly, in the context of the present exploration, many in the field of English teaching took particular exception to the second of Cox's models – that emphasising the cross-curricular potential: as Goodwyn (1997: 39) put it,

> English teachers do not … recognise the cross-curricular model as a model of English … They are quite clear that this model belongs to the whole school and should not be identified with English … The other four models are acknowledged as a normal part of English, but they do not have a comfortable or neutral relationship with each other; neither are they politically or historically innocent, they are not simply 'there'.

There is, in my view, validity in this critique. However, what we need to do here, with a degree of urgency, is seek to reintegrate models of English – not in any superficial way, but recognising differences and diversity of approaches as the essence of whatever the subject is about. The cross-curricular model in reality, and certainly in my experience of English teaching both in schools and as a teacher educator at university, was all too often conceived of negatively: either as a convenient stick for beating English teachers from other subject perspectives (failing to provide the rudiments of grammar, for example, required for foreign language learning, or to teach appropriate note-taking techniques for the humanities or sciences), or as the basis for some sort of language across the curriculum policy frequently doomed to reductivist practice. This is precisely why we need here to start with the English classroom with its practices and theoretical frameworks, if we really are to reinvigorate English as a truly interdisciplinary subject, rather than proceeding from the outside in and inviting superficiality at best. And this is the emphasis of the entire book, in a range of contexts.

If we consider carefully the nature of the five models, the potential for such an interdisciplinary reinvigoration is, I hope, clear. Leaving aside for the moment the second model, with its obvious, if contentious, relevance here, each of the other four positions offers a great deal as a basis for subject development. The personal growth view, long close to the hearts of many English teachers (frequently cited, for instance, by applicants for English PGCE courses during interview as the essence of the appeal of the subject), suggests clear links to the subjectivity and emotional engagement of the arts, and the encouragement of historical, geographical and religious empathy fostered through the humanities. The adult needs model has, it seems to me, increasing credibility as we move towards a firmer and more principled connection between vocational and academic aspects of education – a connection necessarily parallel to the connection between subjects, with language always at the heart of learning. The danger here is in moving towards a reductivist curriculum steered by employment or economic needs; the opportunity, though, is for an enterprising curriculum centred on interdisciplinary problem resolution, and the vocational courses being developed now, by definition, draw upon diverse conceptual positions. As ever, so much depends on what are defined as adult needs and by whom: it is indeed possible to take a view of adult needs based on critical literacy for adulthood as radical as that proposed, for instance, by Lewison *et al.* (in Glazier 2007: 377), although I doubt this was in the minds of the original framers of the curriculum: 'Critical literacy involves four dimensions: 1) disrupting the commonplace; 2) interrogating multiple viewpoints; 3) focusing on socio-political issues; and 4) taking action and promoting social justice'. The point here is that by reading critically, against the text where need be, English teachers have the potential to transform 'official' conceptions of literacy and its teaching: we need to practise what we preach.

The arts and humanities, again, have a clear appropriateness to the cultural heritage model, in that literature may be imaginatively linked to the development of other art forms and to the historical, geographical or spiritual contexts for its own fuller appreciation. Less obvious, and certainly less explored in school practice, is the potential here for linking literature to the development of scientific and mathematical ideas and practices in ways that would certainly not have been alien to many of the writers themselves (the metaphysical poets, for example, or the young Mary Shelley in her writing of *Frankenstein*). Finally, the cultural analysis view of English (with strong connections to versions of critical literacy as outlined above) strongly implies an interdisciplinary context, and the broader the pedagogical appreciation of cultural context (again, very much including scientific and mathematical paradigms), the more valid the critical cultural analysis.

Tensions in the nature of English

With such interdisciplinary possibilities in mind, it may also be illuminating to consider further the name and nature of the subject English. Clearly, as it stands, the term 'English' carries many connotations beyond its definition as one subject in the curriculum: some, perhaps, of nationality and exclusivity which may not be entirely desirable. A consideration of alternative possible names may serve to focus on what precisely the subject is all about, how it relates to other curricular areas, and where the thrust of its teaching should be situated. Some possibilities could be:

- the language arts (favoured by Abbs (1976) among others);
- rhetorical studies (implied by Eagleton (1983));
- literacy studies (certainly in line with recent concerns);
- cultural studies;
- communications;
- discourse awareness; and
- language and literature studies.

Examining English and the connotations of its name from the perspectives of different people in society – parents, diverse professionals, curriculum legislators, other subject teachers, or manual workers, for example – may serve to illustrate a wide diversity of thinking. In part, this kind of examination is itself an interdisciplinary model of good practice, demonstrating the aptitude of any linguistic study whatever the subject (including of course the subject English itself). A principled position is necessary but it is of course practicable to remain reasonably eclectic in approach, keeping an open mind not only to different philosophies – which assuredly will develop and change with time – but to the different needs and ideas as discerned in and expressed by the pupils themselves. It is perfectly feasible, for example, to cover all five of the Cox models, even highlighting their possible contradictions and rivalries, within one English lesson; indeed, this may be a very effective way of ensuring breadth of entitlement. What we need to do as practitioners, above all, is to reflect on our own preferences and predilections, compensating when appropriate for any personal shortcomings through a conscious effort to adapt to new ways and areas of English teaching, especially in the context of interdisciplinary innovation. The subject provides an extremely fertile field for exploration and experimentation, for differing relationships between theory and practice.

It may be instructive here to examine some of the tensions involved in this complex interrelationship, and I should like to use Stead's theories of poetic creativity to draw some illuminating parallels with the subject English and its contextual relationships. Stead (1964: 11) wrote of poetry and its contexts:

> A poem may be said to exist in a triangle, the points of which are, first the poet, second, the audience, and, third, the areas of experience which we call variously 'Reality', 'Truth', or 'Nature'. Between these points run lines of tension, and depending on the time, the place, the poet, and the audience, these lines will lengthen or shorten … There are infinite variations, but … the finest poems are likely to be those which exist in an equilateral triangle, each point pulling equally in a moment of perfect tension.

The geometrical tensions alluded to by Stead seem to me directly relevant to the teaching of English and its possible cross-curricular extensions, largely depending on what goes into the triangle, and what exactly is represented by each of the three points. If we take the triangle to enclose and express the whole business of English teaching, which, like Stead's poem, is an artefact consciously created, then it may follow that one point represents the English teacher; another, the audience of pupils (although this may not be the only possible audience); and the final point symbolises the context – the outer world, perhaps, including the world of other curricular subjects and experiences, which exerts so many often contradictory pressures on the processes of teaching. If we pursue the parallel further, we can see that effective teaching depends on the maintenance of a certain tension along the lines joining the points: if the points become too close to, or too distant from, either each other or the central project of teaching itself, there may well be a danger that the creative art of teaching could be damaged. The educational philosopher John Dewey elaborated further, relating the contrasting aspects to Classical and Romantic models, representing

> tendencies that mark every authentic work of art. What is called 'classic' stands for objective order and relations embodied in a work; what is called 'romantic' stands for the freshness and spontaneity that come from individuality … if there is a definite overbalance on one side or the other the work fails; the classic becomes dead, monotonous and artificial; the romantic, fantastic and eccentric'

(Dewey 1934: 382)

This is in the end an argument for a dynamic combination of reflective distance *and* imaginative involvement – qualities which may seem like opposites, but potentially at least operate in a mutually beneficial dialectical relationship. As William Blake had it, significantly in his *Marriage of Heaven and Hell,* 'without contraries is no progression'.

To aim for such a dynamic combination of involvement and critical distance is to inform the totality of the experience of teaching English, not only in relation to the considerations outlined above but, perhaps more importantly and certainly more immediately, as affecting classroom practice. The principle of reflective distance combining with imaginative involvement must be a principle encouraged in pupils' attitudes towards their own experience of the subject as well as being embedded as a pedagogical cornerstone. Indeed, in terms of any cross-curricular venture such as those endorsed by this book, the dynamic tension is all-important: clearly, the thrust is positive, but by the same token, if we allow English to be submerged within, say, an arts or humanities faculty (as has been threatened in my own schoolteaching experience) there are dangers of the subject being reduced to a service role – the perceived threat of Cox's second model, in fact. We need, again paradoxically, to be rigorous in creating the objective circumstances to allow our pupils' own subjectivities to take root. In addition to ensuring appropriate coverage of curriculum requirements, the interdisciplinary English teacher must also be prepared to give space, to keep a distance, to allow for genuine and autonomous development among colleagues and indeed pupils. I am reminded of the Zen *koan* that the way to control a flock of sheep is to give them a wide pasture to wander in. Harrison (1994: 7), pursuing the apt metaphor of education as theatre, asks pertinently:

> Could the theatre of education … be trying too hard to 'deliver the goods' to its clients, the learners, and leaving no space for them to create their own vision? Are we providing enough space for learners to bring their own minds and cultures into taking part in learning? Have we lost sight of essential qualities such as play, curiosity and friendship in learning? Whose 'production' is it, anyway?

Whose indeed? The question demands an affirmative answer: ours, both as English teachers and as teachers keenly aware of the artificial and all too often debilitating nature of disciplinary division. It is not simply a matter of standing back, of showing more tolerance – although these are often underrated virtues – but of being able at times to live with a Keatsian negative capability, 'that is when man is capable of being in uncertainties, Mysteries, doubts without any irritable reaching after fact and reason'.

Practical and phase-related considerations

The interdisciplinary teaching and learning of English requires a sense of adventurousness, in that it is a departure from the norm, not least in terms of most teachers' own schooling histories. As such, it has to be accompanied by a positive effort to create the right conditions and provide the appropriate boundaries to ensure a sense of security for those involved: the shepherd of the Zen *koan* (and it is interesting how often the pastoral metaphor finds its way into education) would be less than wise if the ultimate boundary of the wide pasture was a cliff edge. One of the implications for practice is the need to create an appropriate environment for learning, if possible as part of whole-school cross-curricular practice. To achieve this, teachers need to pay conscious attention to such features of the interdisciplinary learning environment as:

- the layout of the classroom to facilitate genuinely exploratory learning;
- excellence and relevance of displays, including those linking subjects and ways of looking at the world;
- provision of designated areas for reading, audio-visual work and other activities – essentially a workshop approach rather than a traditional classroom;
- class libraries with a healthy representation of texts from all subject areas;
- facilities for ICT and self-directed studies.

In this cross-curricular context, secondary English teachers need to learn, as indeed many have learned already, from the best of primary school practice: it has often struck me that by Year 6 many youngsters have become significantly autonomous learners ready and willing to take responsibility for their own learning and make innovative connections across subject boundaries, only to take a step or two backwards on arrival in secondary school. The generally positive impact of the National Strategy has been considerable here, however, and has altered the relationship between primary and secondary school phases. Since 2001, when the Strategy was first implemented at Key Stage 3, secondary English teachers have needed to acknowledge more readily the work of primary colleagues in fostering literacy-based learning in their incoming Year 7 pupils. Indeed this aim was made explicit in the original NLS Framework of 1997, applicable then only to the primary phase:

> Because it is vitally important to ensure that there is continuity between primary and secondary schools in the efforts to improve literacy, we recommend that in their strategy for literacy, local education authorities give deliberate attention to creating and maintaining co-operation between secondary schools and their feeder primary schools.
>
> (DfEE 1998: para 119)

In fact the shift in the balance of power and influence between primary and secondary schools has gone a great deal further than this 1997 pronouncement has suggested, so that it is now somewhat inappropriate to speak, perhaps patronisingly, of 'feeder' primary schools. In this context, Goodwyn and Findlay have coined the term 'phase-related role reversal', maintaining that curriculum changes and developments have 'broken the implicit belief that primary and secondary schools are actually different planets in an age when interplanetary travel for teachers themselves is just possible but not really very desirable'. Nowadays, increasingly, secondary English teachers

> find the young aliens alarmingly knowledgeable and their teachers challengingly expert; as a result secondary teachers are discovering how to travel and are returning mightily impressed and not a little daunted at the task they face.
>
> (Goodwyn and Findlay 2002: 50–1)

For the most part this has been a positive change, bringing the two phases closer in a mutually beneficial spirit of collaboration – including collaboration across subjects as well as phases. During both primary and secondary phases, enhanced awareness of colleagues' work and concerns has suggested that we need all the more determinedly to safeguard principles of independence and creative English teaching against the onslaught of insistence from some quarters for more and more didactic teaching as narrow preparation for equally narrow SATs or similar tests – essentially the policing mechanism for adherence to official policy. Although the KS3 SATs have now been abandoned (but not those at Key Stage 2, as yet anyway) – due in no small measure to the sustained opposition of the English teaching community – this policing is still very much in place through the inspection regime, stringent target setting and similar pressures. We have too to realise that the separation of subjects from each other in the traditional secondary curriculum did not just happen, of course, and is not without its benefits – its essential *raison d'être* has to do with the need for increased disciplinary specialisation. The interdisciplinary challenge here is to ensure that the positive qualities of particular subjects, including of course English, may thrive and actually develop from cross-fertilisation with other disciplines and pedagogical paradigms: a challenge again fundamental to the present book and series.

A collaborative spirit: subject knowledge and understanding

Perhaps there is a need here for a word of warning. Although the emphasis is very much on what is possible in the English classroom as managed by an English teacher, as I hope I have made clear in this introductory chapter, interdisciplinary innovation and development in the secondary school would be unlikely to really take root without a spirit of working collaboration with other teachers and educators. Indeed it would be surprising if this were not the case, given the nature of the particular curricular innovation in question. David Carr makes the point that

> despite powerful arguments to the effect that a subject-centred curriculum affords a rather more systematic and focused approach to the study of specific scientific or artistic disciplines – especially at secondary stages of schooling – there is certainly also a real case for linking areas of the curriculum in the interests of greater educational intelligibility.
>
> (Carr 2003: 142)

Part of the positive spirit of the interdisciplinary turn we are commending in this series is to ask secondary-phase subject teachers to examine their own disciplines more closely and with greater explicitness – not in order that such subject knowledge and understanding may be 'watered down' (as some practitioners may fear) through mingling with other disciplines, but rather so that good practice may be shared in a spirit of open-mindedness and mutual understanding. There is necessarily something of a break here with established curricular subject-orientated tradition, as Sefton-Green perceives:

> At the school level … there has been a remarkable continuity over the last hundred years in terms of the structure of the curriculum, the use of a timetable and the notion

that what is to be taught can best be managed in terms of traditional subjects: the building blocks of knowledge itself.

(Sefton-Green 2000: 1)

Sefton-Green goes on to point out that subjects do not merely signal bodies of knowledge: a helpful perception in the context of interdisciplinary curricular development:

Subjects, especially in schools, however, cannot be defined in terms of types of knowledge, or even understood in terms of the history of education – how certain kinds of knowledge came to be viewed as belonging to specific subject disciplines. Subjects also include particular practices, activities and experiences as well as their own models of development and progression. ... subjects tend to settle and define themselves as a series of conventional activities and discourses, which often mask the rationales for the activities or progression in the first place.

(ibid: 1–2)

Clearly, the implication here is that what is required is a new-found spirit of reflective openness in curricular development, both with colleagues within and beyond particular subject disciplines, and, crucially, with pupils.

The fundamental issue at stake here is whether the opportunity offered through the new National Curriculum and its attendant policy developments may be imaginatively, and cooperatively, grasped. Certainly there is the chance, for the taking, and English teachers, resilient and resourceful as ever, are not slow on the uptake. Characteristics of positive collaboration across both subjects and phases, in practical terms, may include:

- shared schemes of work, collaboratively formed across and within subject (and phase) boundaries;
- sharing of, and shared making of, apt resources with the emphasis on cross-curricular teaching and learning;
- regular meetings, again with and across subject departments, to share pedagogical ideas and practices;
- mutual observation of lessons and team teaching as a foundation for examination of cross-curricular potential;
- involvement in wider subject-based and broader contexts such as subject associations (for English, NATE, UKLA, or the English Association) or initial teacher education partnerships;
- collaborative mentoring and professional development of beginning and student teachers;
- involvement of pupils in formulating and responding to cross-curricular practice; and
- informal involvement in extra-curricular and social activities (the traditional school play, for example, frequently makes positive use of expertise from many disciplines with a creative end in mind).

Clearly, collaboration without individual flair or constructively critical engagement can be sterile, as Fullan and Hargreaves (1992: 14) note:

> People can find themselves collaborating for the sake of collaboration ... and, contrary to popular opinion, it can reduce innovation and imaginative solutions to individual situations, as susceptibility to the latest chosen innovation and 'groupthink' carry the day.

English teachers seem to me particularly well equipped to avoid pitfalls like these, but it is a position that has been hard won and that will need to be defended with a watchful eye by those entering the profession.

As I stated in the Introduction, I am in effect arguing here for a new kind of English teacher – on an interdisciplinary model. I am of course aware that for some, certainly on first reading, this may seem like a potentially disastrous watering down of the subject and its pedagogy; a return to the threat Abbs, among others, was acutely aware of two decades ago, whereby

> the English teacher becomes responsible for all kinds of language and all kinds of learning. He becomes a general adviser rather than an initiator into a specific kind of knowing through a specific kind of procedure and through a specific kind of language. The English teacher thus becomes like a man carrying a bag of tools but with only other people's jobs to do.
>
> (Abbs 1982: 9)

I am certainly not arguing for this sort of 'jack of all trades, master of none' model; rather, I am suggesting that it is conscious study and critical exploration of language in all its forms and texts that crucially defines the English teacher – and I know of no other subject discipline where this is the prime focus. Our natural inclination – certainly my own – may be towards Abbs' conception of 'English within the arts', but we have now also to acknowledge that language operates more broadly, and that if we as interdisciplinary English teachers fail to give it our critical attention, the likelihood is that nobody else will. This is what I mean by the necessity of taking the interdisciplinary turn, and of course it involves too an acknowledgement (even an endorsement) that the subject English is now (and probably always was) far too broad for even the ablest practitioner to profess expertise in all or even most areas. This is certainly apparent in my professional work as a teacher educator in the field of secondary English, as has been borne out by recent research into subject knowledge backgrounds and developments in student teachers across several PGCE courses. Through this research (Stevens *et al.* 2006), we explored, among other aspects of initial professional development, the nature of subject *pedagogical* understanding:

> Interestingly, teacher educators notice often a wide range of early attitudes towards subject knowledge, from self-confidence (sometimes verging on the complacent) borne of attaining good first degrees in English, to anxieties often centring on the quality of the first degree, or its lack of traditional English focus, or the sense that most of its content has been forgotten anyway.

As the PGCE course progresses, various transformations occur – and some of these may seem quite paradoxical. … With regard to their [student teachers of English] own awareness of subject knowledge, initial self-confidence may dwindle as it is realised that the requirements for teaching English are quite different from (and sometimes contradict) the content of traditional degree courses, whilst for those embarrassed at their lack of a straightforward English degree the opposite transformation may take place as the variety of school English becomes apparent.

(Stevens *et al*. 2006: 100)

As we turn to look in more detail at the areas of experience involved in the interdisciplinary teaching of English, whether stemming from the official curriculum or bursting its boundaries, it is as well to keep this in mind. To conclude this chapter we could do worse than finish with the words of William Blake, himself of course a highly innovative and resourceful interdisciplinary artist, who asserted through his character Los in Jerusalem,

I must create a system or be enslaved by another man's.
I will not reason or compare: my business is to create.

Language, principles and purposes for cross-curricular teaching and learning in English

The current situation

In the previous chapter I attempted to summarise some important aspects of the recent historical contexts for cross-curricular teaching and learning of English, in the hope that we may better understand some of the present possibilities and potential stumbling blocks. We have arrived now at the newest version of the National Curriculum, already referred to several times, which incorporates many of the educational initiatives of the previous few years – including, with special significance for English teachers, much that has previously manifested itself through the various literacy strategies culminating with the National Strategy, English Strand. The QCDA 'Big Picture' diagram (QCDA 2010) clearly represents the various curricular strands and dimensions now applicable, and is well worth studying. The curriculum now comprises seven 'whole curriculum dimensions': identity and cultural diversity; healthy lifestyles; community participation; enterprise; the global dimension and sustainable development; technology and the media; and creativity and critical thinking. The summary goes on to state that, 'Although dimensions are not a statutory part of the national curriculum … they can provide a focus for work within and between subjects, in personal, learning and thinking skills (PLTS), and across the curriculum as a whole'. The National Curriculum is, further, informed by six 'statutory expectations': communication, language and literacy; creative development; knowledge and understanding of the world; personal, social and emotional development; physical development; and problem solving, reasoning and numeracy. Overarching all of this are the 'curriculum aims' – the development of successful learners, confident individuals, and responsible citizens, the 'Every Child Matters' agenda (be healthy, stay safe, enjoy and achieve, make a positive contribution, and achieve economic well-being), and three 'focuses for learning' (attitudes and attributes, skills, and knowledge and understanding).

At first glance, this may seem an intimidating assembly of components to represent in any curriculum, especially when combined with a welter of other priorities in teaching and learning. However, teaching has always been something of a balancing act; the challenge lies in creatively and flexibly adapting to curricular needs and initiatives as they help to revitalise pedagogy and foster imaginative, purposeful engagement, rather than simply ticking an ever-expanding series of boxes. This is all the more important as we seek to explore beyond the traditional subject boundaries of secondary schools in a spirit of interdisciplinarity. However my premise here is that we start, as English teachers, with the English classroom and its possibilities. Official curriculum guidance in the English context, as embedded in the National Curriculum which itself has drawn heavily on the Strategy's approaches, in practical terms focuses on the '4 Cs': competence; creativity; cultural understanding; and critical understanding. In all four, clearly, there is significant scope for cross-curricular ventures, but we need first to clarify in a little more detail what they may mean.

Competence tends to coincide with the 'adult needs' view of teaching English that

focuses on communication outside the school: it emphasises the responsibility of English teachers to prepare children for the language demands of adult life, including the workplace, in a fast-changing world. Children need to learn to deal with the day-to-day demands of spoken language and of print; they also need to be able to write clearly, appropriately and effectively

(Cox 1991: 21)

In official terms, it is further defined as:

- Being clear, coherent and accurate in spoken and written communication. Reading and understanding a range of texts, and responding appropriately.

- Demonstrating a secure understanding of the conventions of written language, including grammar, spelling and punctuation. Being adaptable in a widening range of familiar and unfamiliar contexts within the classroom and beyond.

- Making informed choices about effective ways to communicate formally and informally (QCDA 2007).

Creativity is outlined as:

- Making fresh connections between ideas, experiences, texts and words, drawing on a rich experience of language and literature.Using inventive approaches to making meaning, taking risks, playing with language and using it to create new effects.

- Using imagination to convey themes, ideas and arguments, solve problems, and create settings, moods and characters.

- Using creative approaches to answering questions, solving problems and developing ideas (QCDA 2007).

The key concept of *cultural understanding* is intended to enable pupils to:

- Gain a sense of the English literary heritage and engaging with its important texts.

- Explore how ideas, experiences and values are portrayed differently in texts from a range of cultures and traditions.

- Understand how English varies locally and globally, and how these variations relate to identity and cultural diversity (QCDA 2007).

Finally, the orders define *critical understanding* as:

- Engaging with ideas and texts, understanding and responding to the main issues.
- Assessing the validity and significance of information and ideas from different sources.
- Exploring others' ideas and developing their own.
- Analysing and evaluating spoken and written language to appreciate how meaning is shaped (QCDA 2007).

Expressed like this, perhaps inevitably, these curricular stipulations appear bald, if largely uncontroversial. The 2009 Ofsted report *English at the Crossroads* indicates the kind of opportunity now available for English teachers:

> The National Strategies have recently revised the frameworks and guidance that teachers use for planning. There have been changes to the National Curriculum in Key Stage 3, including an end to national tests at fourteen, and GCSE courses are being rewritten to include a new element of functional skills. New A-level courses began in 2008. At the same time, schools are being encouraged to personalise the curriculum, in order to meet pupils' needs more effectively. The best schools visited during the last year of the survey were revising their programmes in the light of national recommendations and this was leading to positive developments. Where the curriculum was least effective, the teachers had found it difficult to respond creatively to the new opportunities. They were implementing national policy changes unthinkingly, often because they had no deeply held views about the nature of English as a subject and how it might be taught.

We need now to explore the implications in terms of the language, principles and purposes of cross-curricular teaching and learning in English.

Reflective Activity:

Consider the implications, drawing on your own and colleagues' professional experiences, of the curricular initiatives as outlined above. One way of doing this is through a 'SWOT' analysis, with characteristics noted under the four headings 'Strengths', Weaknesses', 'Opportunities' and 'Threats', diagrammatically presented. The object, ultimately, is to find ways of transforming the latter half of each pair into the former, through being imaginatively creative.

Language and principles

If we return for a moment to the seventeenth century poet Thomas Traherne, who, as we have seen, pleaded for an overarching sense of meaning and purpose for education (the notion of felicity, in his terms), we may find a key for making sense of the current curriculum – especially, perhaps, as its very breadth (signified above all by the interdisciplinary sense of connectedness) gives ever greater urgency for the discovery of and adherence to a guiding principle. That a sense of wonder at the nature of existence may be combined with a strongly critical and reflective standpoint, and that both these distanced positions may complement active, engaged immersion in teaching and learning, are key ideas of this book. An important tension here is that between engaged involvement on the one hand, and critical, reflective distance on the other: already hinted at with reference to Stead's poetic triangle. In many ways this tension is at the heart of any creative activity – emphatically including teaching. If we unpick the notion a little, we can see that, ideally at least, the sense of involvement represents the powerful motivating force in teaching and learning, and the sense of critical distance implies and can develop towards greater understanding. Both are essential if effective teaching and learning is to flourish. The purpose is critically to challenge prejudice – even when it is effectively prejudice couched in the everyday language of 'common sense' – seeking to deconstruct and question commonly held views about the nature of education in its individual and social contexts. In this sense, the subject English is especially significant, beyond the generic concerns of teaching and learning which affect all disciplines, in its sharp and defining focus on language – how it both expresses and conceals meaning, often simultaneously. For as Wittgenstein (in Kenny 1994: 24) reminded us, 'the limits of my language mean the limits of my world'. But that word 'limits' is itself a slippery one, contentious and open to various interpretations. In an important sense – certainly important for the intentions of the interdisciplinary English classroom – for 'limits' we could read 'infinite possibilities of meaning', for that is precisely how language operates.

Broad notions – of awe and wonder on the one hand, and of critical, evaluative distance on the other – were taken up a century or so after Traherne's time by many of the Romantics, although it is the former position that has come popularly to characterise Romanticism. As Abbs has noted (1976: 5), the very roots of English as a subject are embedded in 'the tougher side of Romanticism' – the celebratory and the critical complementing each other – and it seems timely now to re-establish, and develop, this foundation from an interdisciplinary perspective. The important principle here is in the discovery *and* in the making of meaning. In this context, subjectivity (the intensely personal) and objectivity (the social and cultural context which enables meanings to be explored and found) should be held to be mutually beneficial rather than mutually exclusive as is often, and damagingly, supposed. An important principle in the interdisciplinary English classroom is that of 'informed subjectivity' (a notion I shall return to in the context of assessment): an acknowledgement – a celebration, indeed – that we are dealing with complex relationships between subjectivities, but that this has to be carefully balanced by rigorously gathered and sensitively applied information concerning broader contexts – what might be commonly understood as 'objective' reality. Kress (1995: 90) shows a subtle awareness of the creative possibilities here:

> In a view of English as central in the making of a culture of innovation the production of subjectivity is at the centre, between social and cultural possibilities and forces on the one hand – available resources, structures of power – and the individual's action in the making of signs on the other … [the child's] interest in the making of signs may range from dispositions called 'conformity' to those called 'resistance' … Whether in solidarity

or subversion, the child's own production of her representational resources is intimately connected, in a relation of reciprocity, with her production of her subjectivity.

This kind of formulation does indeed amount to a tough side of Romanticism, especially if we enlarge the illuminating focus to include the English teacher as well as the English taught. The author John Fowles has suggested something similar, furthering the connection between teaching and any artistic project:

> All artefacts please and teach the artist first, and other people later. The pleasing and teaching come from the explanation of self by the expression of self; by seeing the self, and all the selves in the whole self, in the mirror of what the self created.
>
> (Fowles 1981: 146)

Unless the processes of teaching and learning may be seen in this sort of perspective, there is the distinct and very real danger that teachers, and by implication learners too, may become merely functionaries, alienated from the essential nature of their activity – however laudable the curriculum aims, such as those noted in the previous chapter, may appear to be.

I believe this to be an important perception, especially with reference to curricular innovation (such as the interdisciplinary turn the present series endorses). The late Rex Gibson has characterised the debilitating sense of impotent initiative fatigue so widespread in schools as essentially 'a structure of feeling', although it clearly has its foundation in the realities of politically motivated educational legislation – an important factor in the failure of many of the interdisciplinary ventures hitherto undertaken. If it is indeed a structure of feeling - like Blake's 'mind forg'd manacles' in his similarly radical critique of contemporary society, the poem *London* – it is all the more insidious and, therefore, dangerous. Structures of feeling tend to become deeply embedded, and take a great deal of shifting. In this instance, there is a tendency for such anxieties to signify

> a preoccupation with 'How to do it?' questions rather than with questions of 'Why do it?' or 'Where are we going?'. It is thus concerned with means rather than ends, with efficiency more than with consideration of purposes. In schools one manifestation is a stress on management and organisation at the expense of consideration of 'What is education for?'.
>
> (Gibson 1986: 83)

All this amounts to a damaging, alienating and certainly unhelpful separation of means and ends, of activity and purpose. Maybe all this sounds only too familiar for those professionally engaged in education, and the realisation can itself be rather debilitating. However, precisely through a principled and critical consciousness of this potentially precarious situation, there could be something far more positive at stake here: an awakened appreciation of the possibility of a new synthesis between the functional aspects of the subject English and its creative facets, based on a radical and interdisciplinary re-interpretation of the Romantic foundations of English teaching (and clearly endorsed by the new curriculum as outlined above, particularly in terms of the connections between its various elements and subject strands). Any such synthesis, however, has to be rigorously grounded in good practice and speculatively reflective thought.

I am certainly not suggesting here that all we need to do to avoid the trap of instrumental rationality is to reconsider and clarify our original aims in the teaching of English. The relationship between means and ends is at once more complex, more subtle, and more potentially exciting than this position would imply. In practice, aims and activities inform and constantly modify each other, sometimes harmoniously, but perhaps rather more often in terms of struggle for coherent meaning-in-practice. The process is best seen as a dialectical one, with the meanings of teaching and learning constantly renewing themselves through praxis. Unavoidable in this context, as it determines the real and transformative possibilities of teaching and learning, is the culture of the classroom. In my professional experience, it is often claimed by English teachers that the culture of the English classroom (the microcosmic notion of culture, in effect) is unlike that of any other subject classroom, and that English is fundamentally concerned with the transmission or mediation of particular models of culture in its macrocosmic sense, ranging from notions of 'high culture' to multicultural ideas (indeed, as we have seen, this was one of Cox's models of English teaching, broadly defined). As Eagleton has pointed out in his important consideration of the nature of culture (Eagleton 2000), the term is often considered in opposition to an equally complex, slippery term – 'nature' – which from a sometimes rather narrowly conceived 'cultural heritage' viewpoint may be metaphorically likened to the pupils themselves. However, as I hope to show, the reality is at once more complex than this, and much more exciting in terms of teaching and learning.

To summarise this rather simplistic (but implicitly prevalent) culture/nature model of education: according to this formulation, underlying much of what is generally understood as education (especially in the particular context of schooling), is a kind of binary opposition, where the raw material of the classroom – pupils in their untaught state, in effect – correspond to 'nature', to be modified – taught – by those representing, in some form or other, 'culture'. Eagleton, though, cuts into this all too familiar notion of culture, noting that

> Within this single term, questions of freedom and determinism, agency and endurance, change and identity, the given and the created, come dimly into focus. If culture means the active tending of natural growth, then it suggests a dialectic between the artificial and the natural, what we do to the world and what the world does to us. ... So it is less a matter of deconstructing the opposition between culture and nature than of recognising that the term 'culture' is already such a deconstruction
>
> (Eagleton 2000: 2)

As far as the interdisciplinary English classroom is concerned, the matter is significant, and centres on notions of empowerment. I shall explore more thoroughly throughout this book the whole area of the culture of the classroom; suffice it to say now that perhaps the cardinal rule of effective and adventurous (and interdisciplinary) English teaching is to recognise, critically develop and celebrate what is already there in the classroom, inevitably, as embodied in the linguistic experiences of all present (including, of course, the teacher) – and, by implication, many others not physically there at all but implied through their influences. Conversely, the mistake so often made, not least in official pedagogical statements, is that teaching ought to start from some kind of clean slate. The centrally Romantic notion of the validity of all experience, and not simply that which is officially sanctioned, is powerfully appropriate in this context. Here, teaching is similar to any other creative activity: an especially important realisation as we seek to establish an interdisciplinary foundation for English.

I have made already several mentions of Romanticism as in many ways the cornerstone of the subject English. Of all the Romantics, it is the insights of William Blake which I feel have most to say about the nature of education, and he is one of the guiding figures in this book's discussions. It seems to me that Blake alludes to a tension at the heart of the process of education no less now than in his own time. Blake's letter to his patron, the Reverend Trusler (1798) shows vividly his faith in the imaginative potential of children: 'Neither youth nor childhood is folly or incapacity. Some children are fools and so are some old men. But there is a vast majority on the side of imagination or spiritual sensation.' However, Blake was also acutely aware of the joyless, materialistic and deterministic approaches to teaching and learning he saw all around him, as presented through the eyes and voice of his 'schoolboy':

> But to go to school in a summer morn,
> Oh! It drives all joy away;
> Under a cruel eye outworn,
> The little ones spend the day
> In sighing and dismay.

> (from *The Schoolboy* in *Songs of Innocence and of Experience*)

For most young people, and indeed for their teachers, the experience of school life, hopefully, has improved enormously since Blake, himself largely unschooled, wrote this bleak description. But there is no room here for complacency: the stifling of the celebratory by means of initiative onslaught, intended or not; the strengthening of institutionalised education as a means of social control; the all-pervading sense of boredom that characterises school hours for many pupils – surely the tension remains powerfully apposite. The value of Blake's insights lies also in his own insistence that 'General knowledge is remote knowledge; it is in particulars that wisdom consists and happiness too' (from *Descriptive Catalogue* for *Vision of the Last Judgement*): a timely reminder that the focus needs to be what is actually possible in the classroom rather than on vague, general ideas. The point here is to notice, evaluate and either contest or develop the significance of the subtle nuances of the classroom and its culture. As Tripp (1993: 24–5) reminds us:

> The vast majority of critical incidents, however, are not at all dramatic or obvious: they are mostly straightforward accounts of very commonplace events that occur in routine professional practice which are critical in the … sense that they are indicative of underlying trends, motives and structures.

To balance and provide meaning for such 'critical incidents', however, Blake's insistence on a clear, all-encompassing sense of direction is important too: such a sense informed his entire life's work. I believe this to be hugely important for us too, as English teachers and indeed as citizens: it is all too beguiling in today's troubled world to seek refuge today in local contexts – whether these be personal, familial or professional – without seeking and seeing broader meaning and possible impact. To return briefly to our initial concerns, formulated here as questions: what are our overarching intentions in the classroom and beyond? What kind of education are we offering tomorrow's adult citizens? Questions like these address fundamental hopes and anxieties about our future, and in that sense any answers – even tentative ones – are essentially prophetic. Here again Blake is helpful: 'Every honest man,' he declared,

> is a prophet; he utters his opinion both of private and public matters. Thus: if you go on so, the result is so. He never says, such a thing shall happen let you do what you will. A prophet is a seer, not an arbitrary dictator.
>
> (Marginalia to Watson's *Apology*)

I shall return in the final chapter to the theme of future possibilities, concerning empowerment and the perennially urgent question to do with what sort of life we want to live. And English teaching plays its part here, at a time when many people, teachers and pupils alike, see the future as somehow ordained by others – not even people sometimes but faceless organisations. This is precisely what cross-curricular notions of citizenship and responsibility, especially as addressed in the English classroom, should address. In the same context, Blake's dictum that 'One law for the lion and the ox is oppression', appropriately included in his deliberately provocative *Proverbs of Hell*, addresses pertinently the issues of difference, of respect for subjectivity, and of the thorny problem of whether a mass education necessarily 'levels down' and too readily generalises. Part of the philosophy of the interdisciplinary venture is in allowing pupils, and their teacher, to make fertile connections across boundaries, away from limiting generalisations and an attendant insistence on uniformity. As Gale and Densmore note:

> The proposal that adopting uniform standards for teaching and learning will automatically result in academic success is challenged by an inclusive discourse of difference that views formal education as perpetuating pedagogical practices and which impede academic growth of certain groups of students in ways that most people do not seem to recognise.
>
> (Gale and Densmore 2000: 123)

Precisely in order to achieve this elusive recognition, interdisciplinary English may play a decisive role. Diverse textual readings and the creation of wide-ranging artefacts, fostering simultaneous breadth and depth in meaning-making, are fundamental to successful and adventurous English teaching. Few would disagree with this statement, but the implications are in fact huge. I intend to explore in this book some of these possibilities in practical and theoretical terms, especially in their relationship to the current structure of the English curriculum and its potential for fostering cross-curricular teaching and learning. There is indeed good cause to celebrate the expanding diversity of texts available for study and creation in the English classroom, whether as separate entities or in intertextual combinations: media, ICT, political and intercultural contexts all invite exciting, if simultaneously complex and demanding (and almost by definition interdisciplinary), pedagogy.

The place of literature

The teaching of literature should, I think, not be seen in opposition, or as hierarchically superior, to other dimensions of English teaching, but rather in dynamic relationship with them. As such, its role in English teaching and learning has the potential for enhancement through the interdisciplinary turn, as I hope to show especially in the later chapters of this book. John Dewey lucidly stated what many English teachers still strongly feel, that

> Art breaks through barriers that divide human beings, which are impermeable in ordinary association. This force of art, common to all the arts, is most fully manifested in literature. Its medium is already formed by communication …
>
> (Dewey 1934: 244)

A great deal of writing about English literature teaching has concentrated on its empathetic possibilities – how it *feels* to be of another culture in terms of time, place or class, for instance, or even to be working within a contrasting discipline. I endorse this aspect of literature's place in the English curriculum, but I intend here also to explore ways in which literature may be taught as a liberating force in terms of a rediscovery of innocence in the Romantic idiom: a sense of wonder, *and* of strangeness. Bruner's telling formulation 'violation of expectancy' springs to mind here, and there is pedagogical as well as literary validity in the breaking of habitual patterns of thought and feeling, whether this be in literature or lessons (or of course both). Literature in this context may be seen to carry fundamentally aesthetic as well as social connotations, and for this reason, in interdisciplinary terms, its study is as much an arts-based as a humanities-based subject, insofar as this distinction is helpful. The uses of literature in teaching are at once profoundly intense and enormously wide-ranging, and, like all arts, literature in its broad sense has humane impact: as the novelist Aidan Chambers maintains,

> I would go as far as to say that it is this particular use of language – the literary use that some have called 'storying' – that defines humanity and makes us human. … this particular form of language and our skill in using it empower us in being what we are, and make it possible for us to conceive of being more than we are.
>
> (Chambers 1985: 2–3)

Another author much read by children and young people, Anne Fine, echoed this perception in her (unpublished) speech to the National Association for the Teaching of English (NATE) (North East) Conference in June 2002, defending the empathic relevance of imaginative fiction: 'People who can't understand how others tick are impoverished'. The possibilities for intertextual, social and aesthetic combinations of experience and insight are exciting – indeed they characterise much of the best English teaching in practice. C.S. Lewis, whose magical-realist writing certainly awakened many children's and adults' eyes to the possibilities of wonder, has reminded us, 'through literature I become a thousand people and yet remain myself' (in Chambers 1985: 5).

As we go on to explore the practical implications of cross-curricular learning and teaching in English, several of the presented examples are literature-based, or at least have literary allusions. Literature teaching – especially, perhaps, when involving poetry – has this vast, magical potential; and it is not merely a matter of extending empathy, important though this is, but of awakening to the wonder of any experience, even when culturally denoted as trivial. This is important, for in our celebrity obsessed world it is all too easy to be gulled into thinking that real life exists somewhere else. There is an implication here too for media education in the cross-curricular English classroom: the sense that with ever increasing media sophistication in the creation of virtual realities on the one hand, and a tendency to dehumanise language into sound bites on the other, it is all the more important critically to deconstruct the resulting texts and their means of transmission. Through both literary and media study (and their combination in the conscious use of crafted intertextual and interdisciplinary language, as I hope to illustrate) there may be a means of creating meaning (critical, questioning) *and* celebration (magical, convivial) out of everyday experience. Neil Astley, in the introduction to his vibrant poetry anthology 'Staying Alive' maintains that

> sensitivity to language is what distinguishes us as civilised people, both as human beings and as individuals, registering our intelligence as well as our alertness and attention to the lives of others. A poem lives in its language, which is body to its soul. Joseph Brodsky believed that our purpose in life as human beings was 'to create civilisation', and that 'poetry is essentially the soul's search for its release in language.
>
> (Astley 2002: 21)

If my years of teaching English in a wide range of schools, and of visiting many more English classrooms in the context of teacher education, have taught me anything, it is that this wealth of experience and insight is always there. In this respect the teaching of English is a thoroughly creative endeavour, in the sense that Raymond Williams suggested:

> To communicate through the arts is to convey an experience to others in such a form that the experience is actively recreated, actively lived through by those to whom it is offered
>
> (in NACCCE 1999: 70)

The culture of the classroom

As we have seen, a great part of the skill of teaching English lies in fostering the appropriate culture of the classroom to give credibility to pupils' insights and experiences, and in making creative connections with and between them – including, significantly, interdisciplinary connections. This is not to suggest that the purpose of teaching English is simply to enable, in a passive sense: we are back to the 'tougher side of the Romantic movement' here. The skill of the English teacher lies in stimulating the recollection of such experience – in tranquillity or otherwise – and in listening intently to the voices of the classroom in order that genuine meaning-making may occur. Whatever the content of the lesson itself, whether it be prescribed or not, whether it be obviously 'creative' or not, effective English teaching starts from what is there. The teacher's repertoire has then to include the ability to take this further, making interdisciplinary, intertextual and intercultural connections in a critical context as appropriate, either towards planned and pre-stated learning objectives or, if necessary, being guided by the tone of the lesson towards uncharted territory.

The themes touched on in this chapter will be returned to in greater practical detail subsequently. Two areas, however, deserve special attention at this stage. The first is concerned with notions of culture and its various relationships to interdisciplinary English teaching and learning, and to creativity in general: an exploration of the nature of the interdisciplinary and intercultural classroom as the model that best meets the needs of English teaching for the twenty-first century. The second area, closely related, focuses on critical literacy and the relationship between empathetic engagement and distanced evaluation, or immersion and distance. As Barbara Comber writes, 'we need as a profession to re-invent school literacies' (in Bearne and Marsh 2007: 116), and with a radical agenda in mind. For now, however, it is time to explore in rather greater depth and detail the 'minute particulars' Blake referred to as preferable to 'remote knowledge'; in other words, the vivid reality of English as it may be taught.

Reflective Activity:

'Culture of the classroom' is a problematic term; try to summarise the culture of your own (or a colleague's) English classroom over one or more lessons, including as many aspects of classroom life and environment as possible. Pupils' views would be interesting in this context.

How important is the 'culture of the classroom' in fostering effective teaching and learning?

Does the notion of 'culture of the classroom' relate to the subject English in any particular ways – with regard to the teaching of literature, for instance?

For the following illustrative sequences of English classroom practice, a certain structural pattern has been adopted in order to facilitate the kind of culture of creative learning endorsed in this book. Broadly, and rather more descriptively than prescriptively, the pattern involves three stages: first, an exploratory stage, during which reactions to a given stimulus or theme are tentatively elicited and offered; then, second, a phase involving rather more carefully negotiated meaning, focused on various possibilities for understanding, interpretation and broader contextual exploration; and finally, the making, sharing and critical evaluation of artefacts as appropriate. Stated, and if possible negotiated, objectives would need to correspond to this shape and would require continuing pointed reference throughout the teaching and learning processes. The teacher's role is varied – at first stimulating a broad range of responses, opening up to learners' experiences and perceptions, and providing the necessary texts and contexts to encourage their expression; then the development of a phase of 'intensification' of meaning through rigorous questioning and negotiation, and if appropriate the judicious introduction of further resources to stimulate deeper thought. I have found it helpful here to compare such a process to the musical development of a symphony (or, conceivably, another art form): tentative exploration of thematic possibilities through trial and error following a captivating opening, subsequently giving way to intensification of a particular theme or motif. There is also an interesting parallel with the Blakean sense of progression through stages of innocence, experience, and possible synthesis of the two on a higher level. Critical evaluation, pertinent reflection and celebratory creativity all have a part to play throughout the sequence of activities – which may span one or more lessons, depending on the nature of the teaching and learning taking place. However, some kind of combination of the three has a particular role as the culmination of the period of study.

To illustrate this kind of lesson planning and teaching, involving an interdisciplinary base, I turn now to a concrete example developed through my own teaching experience: a scheme of work comprising a four lesson sequence focusing on three contrasting texts' portrayals of advice to the young – a subject eminently suitable for the English curriculum, and with added relevance to citizenship education – taught to a mixed-ability group of Year 10 pupils (aged fourteen to fifteen) in a comprehensive school. By way of introduction, in the light of the comments made above concerning the nature of lesson openings, we read and discussed – briefly – Heaney's poem *Digging*. This was very much an introductory activity with three publicly stated purposes: first, raising the class's awareness of the potent possibilities of poetic language; second, introducing orally the theme of the expectations adults have of the young and how the latter respond; and, third, playing with the central metaphor of 'digging', with some discussion of the semantic field of this word, including the 1960s 'hip' connotation of enjoyment and/or understanding (a meaning most of the group were surprisingly familiar with). To extend connotation further we looked also at Van Gogh's early (1885) painting *Peasant Woman Digging* and discussed how studying this subtly evocative representation modified or expanded our appreciation of the poem.

From this opening, the class went on to consider three contrasting but thematically linked texts: Bob Dylan's 1965 classic *Subterranean Homesick Blues*, an extract from *Hamlet* in which Polonius gives fatherly advice to his departing son Laertes (see below), and an extract from a contemporary website offering guidance to the young (this particular website is at www.crab.rutgers.edu/~chmarkey/adviceforadolescents.html, but a swift search of the web should reveal several similar). The lyrics to the Dylan song may be found in his compilation *Lyrics 1962-1965* (1985) and the song itself is on the 1965 album *Bringing It All Back Home* and on the DVD of the 1965 Pennebaker film *Don't Look Back*.

From *Hamlet*: Act 1, Scene 3, l. 58–80: Polonius (to his son Laertes, about to leave for university in France):

And these few precepts in thy memory
Look thou character. Give thy thoughts no tongue,
Nor any unproportioned thought his act.
Be thou familiar, but by no means vulgar.
Those friends thou hast, and their adoption tried,
Grapple them unto thy soul with hoops of steel,
But do not dull thy palm with entertainment
Of each new-hatched unfledged courage. Beware

Of entrance to a quarrel; but being in,
Bear't that th' opposed may beware of thee.
Give every man thine ear, but few thy voice;
Take each man's censure, but reserve thy judgement.
Costly thy habit as thy purse can buy,
But not expressed in fancy; rich, not gaudy,
For the apparel oft proclaims the man,
And they in France of the best rank and station
Are of a most select and generous chief in that.
Neither a borrower nor a lender be,
For loan oft loses both itself and friend,
And borrowing dulleth edge of husbandry.
This above all, to thine own self be true,
And it must follow as the night the day
Thou canst not then be false to any man.

The ensuing sequence of activities proceeded with a three-stage reading and exploration of *Subterranean Homesick Blues*: first, as a written text only, read aloud with copies for each pupil; second, through listening to the recording; and, finally, through watching the video clip in which Dylan stands nonchalantly leafing through and discarding placards depicting key words and phrases – the opening of the 1965 Pennebaker film *Don't Look Back*. The readings and discussions considered how each layer, or 'framing', of the text altered and modified possible interpretations, with written, sung and visual elements complementing each other, and how the text relates to the theme of adult advice to the young. Particular poetic/playful elements of the text were explored and re-presented by small groups, focusing on given sections. Notable here were points made about 'manhole/man whole', 'success/suck cess', 'dig yourself', 'twenty years of schooling' and 'the day shift', and 'you don't need a weather man to know which way the wind blows'. The general subversion of adult advice disdainfully running through the text, alongside the possibility of a different way of living ('manhole/man whole', 'success/suck cess'), was appreciated – by some in the group, in any case – and various connections made to more contemporary songs dealing with similar issues.

At this point, two lessons into the sequence, the group were introduced to the extract from *Hamlet*, a volunteer reading Laertes while the teacher read the part of Polonius and provided a brief context for the scene. Subsequent discussion perceived both validity and hypocrisy in Polonius' advice, and, having carefully interpreted the words, groups of three experimented with different ways of handling the scene with the emphasis on contrasting attitudes shown by Laertes and the silent Ophelia to their father's advice.

The next activity combined elements of the two texts, with groups preparing and performing the Polonius speech in the manner of the Dylan performance, providing a rhythmic sense of the verse, and discarding placards displaying the chosen key words and phrases. As a pop video there is much to be said for choosing to emulate something which is both straightforward to enact and produce, unlike the slick MTV varieties, and is outside young people's usual repertoire. Some of the results were startlingly effective.

The next stage involved pupils' research into appropriate texts dealing with the theme of adults' advice, from a wide range of sources and relating to notions of citizenship. Each group took two or three examples and presented them to the rest of the class as the basis for further discussion. The website example, provided by the teacher as a further resource, was used and analysed as an example, with the focus on how and if its appearance online rather than in print may alter its tone, reception and form – eliciting various responses from some who felt it made good sense, to others who regarded it as patronising or vacuous or both.

By now, the pupils were at home with the interdisciplinary way of working, having for this exploration used a combination of literary texts, art, music, performance drama (the pop video and their own) and ICT texts. The final activity was based on improvised drama: to create a meaningful expression of dialogue between adults and young people, choosing the medium that suited each group best. Extracts from each of the three texts could be, and were, used, alongside students' own expressions. Poetry, song, mime, and letter-writing were all successfully represented in a celebratory finale.

Of course this bald summary does scant justice to the richness of the experience for all concerned, in terms both of critical understanding of texts and creative modelling. It may, however, serve as some sort of prompt to suggest how interdisciplinary and intertextual connections may be made and remade in a context of vital engagement. One conceivable adaptation could be as a starting point for A/AS level study of *Hamlet*, in that an underlying theme of both these resource materials and the play itself is the distinction between appearance and reality; the perception about who exactly may be trustworthy in a duplicitous world: 'Seems, madam? Nay it is. I know not seems'. One pupil, illustrating on his placard the final words quoted from Polonius' speech to Laertes, chose to highlight just one word: 'False' – uncannily apt in the light of Polonius's subsequent devious, untrusting and manipulative behaviour towards both his son and daughter.

Indeed, perhaps the most fitting testimony to the pupils' ideas and verve is in my own seeing of a familiar text in new ways. Kierkegaard's insistence that, 'to be a teacher in the right sense is to be a learner. I am not a teacher, only a fellow student' might seem a little disingenuous, but at times it rings true – especially in the openness to experience characteristic of a creatively orientated classroom. I refer here to the Dylan song and its performance, which yielded riches that even I, as a long-standing and ardent Dylan admirer, had not expected. For instance, one pupil pointed out that Dylan's reference to the vacuous 'day shift', the reward for 'twenty years schooling', is mirrored and accentuated in his style of delivery in the film version: seemingly bored by the meaningless, repetitive nature of his action in discarding the placards in turn. This sort of perception brings to mind two quotations from quite different sources. The first, from the Strategy (DfEE 2001: 10), behoves teachers to encourage literacy that is 'sensitive to the ways meanings are made', and 'reflective, critical, discriminatory'. The second refers to a comment made by the poet Liz Lochead (NATE North East Conference 21 June 2003) insisting that 'the poem should teach the reader how to read it'. It seems significant that teaching and learning of this kind may satisfy such contrasting sets of criteria: exactly the challenge English teachers need to meet and resolve.

Creativity and the intercultural dimension

Of the 'cross-curricular dimensions' and informing principles of the English curriculum (the 4 Cs) mentioned at the beginning of this chapter, creativity and criticality stand out as significantly characteristic of the subject English – indeed it is this combination that is central to my thesis here. English, relatively unburdened by a huge body of information to transmit to its pupils, may be more free than many other subjects to focus on the nature of understanding and insight as the basis of knowledge; the danger otherwise, in Saul Bellow's pithy phrase, is that 'We are informed about everything, but we know nothing' (in Nobel 1996: 125). Brindley (1994: 11) elaborates on this theme, emphasising the radical, inherently critical role of the subject:

> English has a special power to challenge conventions, institutions, governments, business interests – any established system. This resides in the fact that English is concerned with the uncontrollable power of a shared language that we all speak and the uncontrollable responses to what we read. The work of English teaching involves continual pressing for the expression of alternative ideas, inviting challenge to received opinions, seeking strong personal responses, establishing debate.

Crucial to the argument are issues associated with creativity on the one hand, and those related to the critical and intercultural dimension on the other: both, I maintain, are fundamental to an interdisciplinary conception of English, in the sense that both are based on the idea of making connections, within and beyond the traditional confines of the subject.

The notion of creativity, especially as pertaining to the teaching of English, is notoriously complex. Not least this may be because all English teachers, or certainly all I have encountered, like to feel that their craft is in some way or another creative – even if, or perhaps especially when, there are external constraints on creative practice. In this, I suspect, there is something of an urgent imperative for teachers (and by the same token learners) to fit themselves for the (post-) modern world; Hargreaves makes the point that

> It is plain that if teachers do not acquire and display this capacity to redefine their skills for the task of teaching, and if they do not model in their own conduct the very qualities – flexibility, networking, creativity – that are now key outcomes for students, then the challenge of schooling in the next millennium will not be met

> (1999: 123)

There are, however, difficulties of definition and shared meaning in the field of creativity, perhaps inevitably, possibly stemming from overuse of the term 'creativity' – perhaps I have been guilty of this myself in this book. We need to start from a clear vision, and in this respect, the much neglected and, hitherto at least, officially overlooked report of the National Advisory Committee on Creative and Cultural Education, aptly titled *All Our Futures* (NACCCE 1999: 29–30), is helpful. In this report, creativity is defined and presented as 'imaginative activity fashioned so as to produce outcomes that are both original and of value'. Interestingly, the report also makes it clear that

> The essence of creativity is in making new connections. These possibilities can be frustrated by rigid divisions in subject teaching which the current pressures tend to encourage. Outside schools, some of the most dynamic developments are the result of the interaction of disciplines

> (op. cit.: 72)

and goes on subsequently to recommend that, 'The QCA should disseminate successful models of curriculum organisation and timetabling that promote creative and cultural development within *and between* the main subject areas' (op. cit.: 87; my italics).

In many ways, it seems, curriculum development is only now, ten years on, beginning to catch up and implement these key findings. The interdisciplinary turn is very much part of the development in question.

NACCCE's working definition of creativity is then qualified and elaborated on with reference to four features of creativity: using imagination; pursuing purposes; being original; and judging value. All four features, it seems to me, are vitally important, and the combination provides us with a useful framework for cross-curricular conceptions of teaching and learning through English. Clearly, the use of the imagination for a particular purpose is at the heart of the matter – indeed possibly at the heart of whatever education is all about. Warnock, for example, holds that the imagination is essentially

> a sense … that there is always *more* to experience, and *more in* what we experience than we can predict. Without some such sense, even at the quite human level of there being something which deeply absorbs our interest, human life becomes not actually futile or pointless, but experienced as if it were. It becomes, that is to say, boring. … it is the main purpose of education to give people the opportunity of not ever being, in this sense, bored; of not ever succumbing to a sense of futility, or to the belief that they have come to an end of what is worth having.
>
> (Warnock 1976: 202–3)

In this context, the judgement of value too is an easily neglected but crucially significant element, and it is closely linked to the sense of the imagination evoked by Warnock. I would argue that imagination is the means of finding value, and as such is implicit in all educative processes; its particular significance for English is in the study of the ways in which value and values are embedded in language itself.

The third of the qualities associated with creativity in the *All Our Futures* definition is also relevant: the idea of originality. Again, as we probe more deeply into this concept, however, it becomes problematic. Certainly teachers need to avoid any celebration of originality simply for its own sake, or any inevitably frustrated insistence on total originality – which clearly would be well nigh impossible to achieve except at some cutting edge activity in any given discipline. In one sense, though, everything is original, in that the precise circumstances and conditions are unique to the occurrence; in another respect, nothing is – for we must always work with and from whatever resources, techniques and ideas already exist. The interdisciplinary English teacher has to find and develop ways to acknowledge both these apparently contradictory senses of originality – celebrating the moments of creativity on the one hand, and working within the discipline of study on the other. The emphasis in the context of *All Our Futures* is on individual originality ('a person's work may be original in relation to their own previous work and output') or on relative originality ('original in relation to their peer group; to other young people of the same age, for example'), and it would not be hard to find excellent examples of both in our classrooms and studios – although awareness of what we find and its particular qualities might be rather more of a challenge.

In classroom practice, it is the dynamic relationship between the previously cited four elements (using imagination, pursuing purposes, being original, judging value), and the skills needed to realise them, that give rise to meaningful creativity. And yet the subject English itself is not always seen or constructed primarily as a 'creative' discipline – indeed the current emphasis on functional literacy may be seen as something of an erosion of notions of creativity in the classroom. As Marshall (in Craft *et al*. 1999: 123) points out, the *All Our Futures* report makes scant reference to English, being

> a good example of the way in which English is no longer considered central to the arts debate. In the appendix, which considers the impact of their proposals, English does not appear anywhere within the list of arts subjects. The contribution of English acknowledged in the body of the document is equally marginal.

Part of my intention in this book is to reposition English as a creative subject, with all the interdisciplinary connections that entails and implies, making full use of the insights into creativity in such texts as *All Our Futures*. Literacy itself, if construed in broad terms of meaning, value and an intercultural context, as well as function, need not necessarily be narrow in scope: the more functionally orientated aspects of English, many of which, as we have seen, are central to its cross-curricular role, need to be seen through a creative, imaginative and interdisciplinary lens if teachers and pupils are to be properly engaged. All this rather begs some important questions concerning the meaning and validity of creativity, and why it is especially valuable. If indeed it is valuable, as I and many others maintain, then we need to explore just how, and what kinds of values lie at its heart. It is possible to act creatively, as is commonly understood by the term, for highly questionable ends: exploitative, destructive, damaging. History is littered with ghastly examples of just this, implying that to make radical social meaning in a pedagogical context, creativity needs to be situated in a coherent place of values. Creativity's minute particularities, its celebratory subjectivities, its potential for social meaning-making, its liberating connective power only really come to life when values are emphasised.

But which and whose values are these? As so often, the answer lies in the framing of the question: in the sense that values are culturally specific, and as such are contested – often energetically, sometimes creatively, and sometimes destructively. There are indeed multiple places for creativity, and each relates to the cultural context and the values implied. In a way, this realisation implies multiculturalism, a celebration of diverse cultural values and characteristics, but I am here also interested in the connections *between* different values and their cultural places. How creativity and value relate to each other may then become rather clearer, in practice. With the emphasis on connections – relationships, contrasts, distinctions and compatibilities – it may be more helpful to suggest an intercultural rather than merely a multicultural understanding of creativity and value. The implication of this kind of understanding is that creativity may be placed in multiple sites and have roots in diverse cultural values, and that it is in the relationships between these entities – the 'inter' of the intercultural (and interdisciplinary) project – that deep value-laden meanings may be discovered, recognised and developed. Importantly, this conception is suggestive of both individual and social transformation, as the damaging distinction between the two is eroded. As Alred *et al*. (2003: 4–5) have clarified:

The locus of interaction is not in the centripetal reinforcement of the identity of one group and its members by contrast with others, but rather in the centrifugal action of each which creates a new centre of interaction on the borders and frontiers which join rather than divide them. This centre is experienced not only in relation to others, but also in relation to oneself. … An inevitable consequence of intercultural experience is that it presents a challenge to customary modes of perception, thought and feeling. Hence, when intercultural experience leads to creative, rather than defensive, learning a concomitant is serious self-reflection and examination, bringing with it consequences for self-understanding and self-knowledge. … Frontiers become less barriers and prohibitions and more gateways and invitations.

Powerfully relating to the culture of the classroom, as discussed above, at the centre of concern here is what Brecht aptly called *Lebenskunst*, the creative art of life itself. If interdisciplinary and intercultural variety and vitality are the aims, they must also be the means – and the culture of the classroom is that which both stimulates and emanates from the totality of experience. That familiar unit of school-based time, the lesson, must in some sense or other become a microcosm of broader issues. I have in mind here particularly a transformative model, through which innocence is brought into some sort of relationship – even one based on conflict – with experience. In a fully dialectical process, fostered by careful teaching, the interplay between innocence as thesis and experience as antithesis may lead to a higher, fuller awareness – based on innocence in the Blakean sense of wonder, but acknowledging and encompassing the nature of often harsh experience. This culmination may be conceptualised as a kind of synthesis, which of course will then play its part in further dialectical encounters. In the same way as each individual struggles in his or her life with this fundamental transformative process in a fully social context, so too must human institutions and the various elements that comprise them. School itself is one of the most basic of those institutions, but I am more interested here in smaller, more manageable units within school: the lesson, particularly, and the classroom – for which areas individual teachers still have enormous responsibility and autonomy. Significantly too, the age range of the schools we are dealing with here (roughly eleven to eighteen) precisely includes the time when the clash (or, sometimes, harmony) between innocence and experience is most striking. Any concern for a truly creative classroom culture must start from this realisation; conversely, failure fully to acknowledge the interrelationship leads all too often to endless unresolved conflicts in schools. As Nobel (1996: 37) observes,

It is a matter of seeking out ways of reaching a development of knowledge which looks to *the whole person*, which in itself is a prerequisite for the person himself [sic] being able to see the *whole comprehensive context*.

In the best English classrooms, through literary, linguistic or thematic exploration, serious issues are confronted – and it should be especially so in the interdisciplinary context proposed here.

As W.B. Yeats is popularly supposed to have said, 'education should be not filling a pail but lighting a fire'. Structures, however imaginatively conceived, tend to become ends in themselves – further examples of instrumental rationality, mere buckets to be filled – unless the creative fire is perpetually stimulated. The signs of creativity are indeed varied, often hard to discern, but are there to discover or make nevertheless. Bill Lucas has offered a helpful list of some of the characteristics of what he terms, appropriately enough, learner-centred creativity (Lucas 2001: 40); all are pertinent to the interdisciplinary approach to English, it seems to me. They are:

- Being respectful rather than dismissive.
- Encouraging active not passive learning.
- Supporting individual interests rather than standardised curricula.
- Engaging many learning styles not one.
- Encouraging and exploring emotional responses.
- Posing questions not statements.
- Offering ambiguities rather than certainties.
- Being open-ended rather than closing down.
- Being surprising rather than predictable.
- Offering many patterns rather than a standardised model.
- Moving the 'classroom' to varied environments.
- Recognising multiple intelligences.
- Including visual representations.
- Including tactile and experience-based activity.
- Stimulating social as well as private learning.

In many ways the recognition of some or all of these qualities helps us as teachers to define something that can sometimes seem very nebulous, as long as definitions are regarded as tentative openings rather than as restrictive impositions. In this sense, it is important that both teachers and learners experience involvement in, and ownership of, the creativity in the classroom through what Gardner has called 'good work'. Anything else would clearly run counter to the very nature of creativity in education. Csikszentmihalyi (1990) has conceptualised creativity as the experience of 'flow' or 'optimal experience', suggestive of engagement, empathy, connection, interplay; such a formulation sits easily with the interdisciplinary model proposed here. Further characteristic symptoms, according to the 'flow' model, would include complete involvement in the activity through both intellect and feeling, immediate feedback through an intrinsic sense of the worth of the activity in and for itself, and an appropriate balance of challenge and capability. In respect of all this, it seems to me essential that the subject English – and by implication its interdisciplinary teaching – is conceived of in terms of a creative endeavour, in the sense that Iris Murdoch meant: 'Art is not a diversion or a side issue. It is the most educational of human activities and a place in which the nature of morality can be seen' (in NACCCE 1999: 67). The interdisciplinary turn may prove to be the necessary catalyst for this kind of transformation.

So, at the risk of appearing to seek an exhaustive definition for something that by its very nature must constantly strive to burst boundaries, it is important that creativity is positively recognised in the classroom. In many ways it is the opposite that is more obvious. As Boden (in Craft *et al*. 2001: 98) points out,

It is easy enough to say what will smother creativity in the classroom: three things above all. First, an unbending insistence on the 'right' answer, and/or on the 'right' way of finding it; second, an unwillingness (or inability) to analyse the 'wrong' answer to see whether it might have some merit, perhaps in somewhat different circumstances …; and third, an expression of impatience, or (worse still) contempt, for the person who came up with the unexpected answer.

Although there is a clear distinction to be made between teaching creatively, which may cover a vast range of pedagogical models, and teaching for creativity, the two frequently complement each other, and both may contribute vividly to the aim that Ross (1985: 60) postulated: 'to refresh the vital spirit'. Ultimately my emphasis here is on teaching *for* creativity, but the role of the teacher as creative practitioner – modelling the qualities sought in the learner – is also fundamental. A critical and celebratory emphasis on language and meaning – literacy in its broadest sense – is crucial here, and is thus central to effective and imaginative English teaching. Characteristics of good teaching practice in this respect – teaching creatively to foster creativity – are characteristically diverse, and may include a range of techniques: the giving of early and meaningful opportunities for all to excel in some aspect of the work covered; the successful communication that risk-taking is acceptable even when unsuccessful; the teaching of the skills necessary in any particular discipline for satisfaction to be realisable; the stimulation of a supportive, critical-friendly classroom culture; and the tolerance of difference.

Safran (2001: 82) appropriately terms teaching for purposes such as those outlined here 'mindful teaching', suggesting further that, consequently, 'mindful learning' should form its complement:

> In defining 'to teach' I draw on its original meaning 'to show'. … Mindful teaching facilitates learning by showing, explaining or passing on a skill or knowledge while being mindful of the subject matter, open to new information, creating new categories and being aware of many perspectives within the subject matter. More importantly, the mindful teacher is also mindful of the learner, that is open to their perspectives, and receptive to information from the learner. The mindful teacher is therefore learner-led. A mindful teacher begins from where the learner is and opens up the unknown, showing new possibilities to the learner at a pace appropriate to them. … The mindful teacher makes critical thought possible for the learner through questioning the learner, showing them areas and avenues the learner may not yet have discovered for themselves.

Teaching for creativity, then, is quite a challenge, requiring the conscious ('mindful') courage of conviction, yet is within the pedagogical potential of the classroom teacher. Essentially, making connections across and within the subject areas defines the creative teacher: an interdisciplinary definition, too. In effect this means that an appropriate balance between challenge and capability should be sought and modelled through teaching, as noted above in the context purely of learning. The Ofsted report *English at the Crossroads* (2009) is again helpful in fostering this aim:

> Where teaching was good, the teachers knew the subject well, were highly enthusiastic and established strong relationships with pupils. Practical or creative activities engaged

pupils' interest; they worked effectively in pairs and groups, which involved them in discussing ideas, and helped them to think for themselves. The teachers provided encouragement and practical guidance on areas for improvement and often gave additional individual support outside lessons. Because good relationships had been established, teachers were confident to take risks in their teaching. Unusual approaches elicited very positive responses, especially from higher attaining pupils.

And further:

Teachers need to decide what English should look like as a subject in the 21st century and how they can improve the motivation and achievement of pupils who traditionally do less well in the subject. To engage them more successfully, schools need to provide a more dynamic and productive curriculum in English that reflects the changing nature of society and pupils' literacy needs.

Tentatively summarising and developing the various suggestions already made, it may be helpful to pause here to recollect and specify some of the characteristics of what could be called a creatively interdisciplinary classroom. Above all there must be concern for the meaningful generation and practical implementation of ideas and feelings, even when unexpected and unplanned, through the making of varied and sometimes unusual connections and contrasts. Planning is thus to be seen as a process rather than a fixed or rigid imposition on the flow (an echo of Csikszentmihalyi here) of a lesson, achieved ultimately through the conscious, critical and reflective refinement and development of the teacher's own (or the group's own) activities. Inevitably any creative act, and certainly any creative lesson, involves the teacher in the release and appropriate channelling of energy. The creative teacher seeks ways of inventing, adapting, extending and completing tasks in new or exciting ways. Completion, in fact, is particularly important in response to the charge, frequently levelled, and with some justification, that anyone can be creative for short snatches without being able necessarily to sustain any real momentum towards fruition. Alertness is vital here, seeking and seeing possibilities for the use of diverse resources, and always remembering that the most fruitful resources, linguistic or otherwise, are the people in the classroom. Ultimately there has to be a sense of value in teaching and learning: it is not too grandiose an ambition to seek to change the world for the better, enhancing the *quality* of life – especially in the active embodiment of aesthetic and celebratory dimensions. The imagination is fundamental in this context for both teacher and learners, in the sense that, as Blake had it, 'what is now proved was once only imagined'. Throughout all this and much more, for even these tentative suggestions can do no real justice to a vividly creative classroom, there has to be a genuinely reflective awareness of the possibilities for continual re-interpretation and re-formulation of materials, 'knowledge' and meaning.

One particular formulation remains absolutely central to creativity; it is, in the words of Herbert Read, that 'art, widely conceived, should be the fundamental basis of education' (1958: 6). However, we have to be careful here, lest the inference is taken that only 'artistic' subjects (according to some definitions excluding even English) can be creative – the very opposite of my intended message. In this context, the word 'art' itself connotes a great deal more than is often, rather narrowly, supposed; Hagerstrand makes the interesting point that in both research and practice it is necessary to revive the original double meaning of the concept 'art' which previously encompassed both practical skill and works of 'fine culture'. It ought to present itself as a fascinating task to so permeate, by means of research and teaching, the personal philosophy of people with a new aesthetic keynote that their philosophy would become strong enough to keep narrow rationality, fanaticism and commercial tricks at bay. ... That thought is an interesting challenge to all those engaged in the business of teaching ...

(in Noble 1996: 25)

It is indeed, and this book is in part an attempt to take up the challenge, as indicated in the title itself, suggestive of both of Hagerstrand's meanings. In this sense teaching is itself an art, and also part of the bigger – and aesthetically stimulating – interdisciplinary landscape.

Reflective Activity:

Drawing on your own professional experience, and your experience as a learner, consider further the nature of creativity and values: are the two inextricably linked?

What elements of creative teaching and learning would you expect to see particularly in an English classroom? How can we develop these ideas further, especially in an interdisciplinary context?

In terms of the 'language, principles and purposes' of cross-curricular teaching and learning in English, the chapter's theme, try to write a brief mission statement for your English department.

3

Intertextuality, generic interplay and ICT for cross-curricular teaching and learning in English

Contexts

The world of information and communications technology (ICT) has changed incredibly fast, and continues to do so. The authors of *English for Tomorrow,* for instance, found it necessary in 1997 to explain in a footnote what 'World Wide Web' meant (Tweddle *et al*. 1997: 2). The speed of change is important, as it can lead to confusion as to what is valuable and what can be discarded; indeed, in the same book the authors make the key point that 'The question for English is how the subject might change in order to accommodate a growing body of knowledge and skills' (op.cit.: 1). That question remains fundamental, especially in the context of any proposed development of the subject in an interdisciplinary direction.

For those English teachers who see themselves working primarily in the 'cultural heritage' and 'personal growth' paradigms – no small number, in my experience – the relationship with information technology can be a fraught one. The insertion of the word 'communication', central in every way to the developing field of ICT, has saved that whole area of pedagogical experience for many English teachers, and in the context of cross-curricular teaching and learning, ensures that English is once more central to the entire curriculum. Nevertheless, even the term ICT has grown to connote technology as something of an end in itself; witness any educational conference where there are likely to be several papers presented extolling the virtues of ICT in this or that context with scant thought as to whether the technology actually improves the learning experience in any significant way (in my view, it often lessens it by getting in the way, but that's another story – or is it?). The technophile discourse is at once beguiling and intimidating – perhaps these are two sides of the same coin – and not least to English teachers. So when I came to look again at the proposed title of this chapter, I decided that 'ICT' by itself failed to convey the true breadth of possibilities, and that the addition of such terms as 'intertextuality' and 'generic interplay' communicated more fully the multi-modal potential of interdisciplinary English and ICT.

There are other potential dangers involving the politics of ICT, as Tweddle warned over a decade ago:

[Information Technology] carries a threat of producing a new generation of haves and have-nots in a society which increasingly values knowledge as the key to wealth and power; in a global economy which depends upon technological literacy; in a multimedia culture for which linear print literacies are inadequate'

(Tweddle 1995: 4)

McGuinn takes up the point lucidly:

What might have seemed like a new, exciting textual space has already been colonised. Familiar words – 'program', 'drive', 'worm', 'spam' – have taken on new meanings with which to confuse (and exclude?) the uninitiated; particular physical and cognitive procedures have to be learned and followed through in order to access software packages and Internet resources; self-access learning materials take individual pupils, working in isolation with a computer rather than a human teacher, through rigidly-programmed exercises which allow scant opportunity for dialogue or interaction. The writing process itself can be subjected to an ostensibly benign 'policing' by cartoon-style icons which offer templates for business letters or memoranda, or by grammar and spell-checking devices which urge the adoption of a particular syntactical form or punctuation convention – and which are thrown into confusion when invited to 'proof-read' an extract from a poem or piece of unconventional prose.

(Stevens and McGuinn 2004: 96)

These are warnings that we, as interdisciplinary English teachers enthusiastic to use ICT as a tool for enhanced learning, would be well advised to heed. However, in an important paper, *Secondary English with ICT: A Pupil's Entitlement to ICT in English*, the combination of BECTA and NATE maintain that

ICT has fundamentally altered the way we communicate with each other and how we think about reading and writing. It has unique potential to extend and enhance pupils' learning in English. Used appropriately and imaginatively, it provides possibilities, insights and efficiencies that are difficult to achieve in other ways.

(2009: 1)

The key here, in my view, is the phrase 'used appropriately and imaginatively', and it is with this stipulation clearly in mind that I'd like to explore the impact of ICT in an interdisciplinary English context. The specifically interdisciplinary dimension and potential of ICT should, I hope, be apparent; as Sinker (2000: 211–2) observes, 'As complex constructions of aesthetic, symbolic and narrative conventions, multimedia technologies cry out for a joint approach to teaching and learning by art and media education, which threads through all the subjects'.

Perhaps a small autobiographical note may add a little flavour here. Although, as I hope I have already established, my philosophical position is one based on Romanticism with a critical edge (and I think this is the most apt stance to take as a basis for developing cross-curricular models of teaching and learning in English), I have always been attracted to the possibilities of new technologies. I enjoy working with gadgets and gizmos, but I also have something of the Romantic hobbit about me; so my history as an English teacher is probably fairly well balanced and pretty typical. A couple of years into my teaching career, in the early 1980s, the comprehensive school I was teaching in attracted some LEA funding for computers; the head teacher, announcing this in a staff meeting, invited bids from technology and science departments. I was probably as astounded as he was when the Head of English asked why other departments, including his, couldn't also bid; his response was to question how an English teacher could possibly improve classroom practice through computers – he intended the question to be rhetorical, but received a detailed and convincing answer. This experience and NATE conference networking around the same time at least set me thinking. My next school was much more progressive in this context, and as second in English I had the chance to dip my toe into the waters of technology: the school, newly built and serving a London overspill clientele, went for a network of Nimbus computers, and the benefits for English lessons were quickly apparent. The high point was in gaining funding for a professional writer to work with pupils, using word-processing to write convincing short stories, internally published. Around this time I bought my first computer, an Amstrad (still in the loft as I write, possibly accruing value!) with a gigantic instruction book and a few uses – I still have usable worksheets printed in the inimitable font of the time (there was no choice).

Leading my own English departments in my next two schools, I probably trod technological water, although the coming of media studies, which we pioneered in one of these schools, introduced new equipment and possibilities, including the much vaunted video camera and lengthy but most enjoyable LEA training sessions on how to use them (those happy days never to return I suspect). Meanwhile the pace of change for ICT accelerated, flashing past me in a blur, and it wasn't until I entered the world of university-based teacher education, in the mid-1990s, that I realised how much I'd been left behind. Email, for instance, was even by then the preferred mode of communication, but I'd never even heard of it. CD-ROMs were the big thing in the school I'd just left, installed for pupils and teachers alike to marvel at in the rapidly diversifying library, but at university the Internet was everything, and of this I was pitifully ignorant. And in teaching or presentational terms the PowerPoint facility was seen as revolutionary and liberating (nobody spoke of death by PowerPoint then); I remember one student teacher asking me if I had a PowerPoint facility to aid his presentation, and I pointed to the electrical mains socket on the wall. My knowledge of such things has improved since then, I hasten to add, but then so has the technology available, as my students frequently remind me, even inadvertently. The issue, of course, lies not in being expert in every available technological advance, or to embrace everything that comes along (e-books, for example, could never replace the incredible technology of the printed page for me), but in being able to see the wood for the trees and use ICT 'appropriately and imaginatively', as suggested above. Given this, I could perhaps agree with Michael Fullan that 'the kind of teacher who is afraid that they are going to be replaced by a computer should be' (2010: 96). I hope in this chapter to illustrate this through a few practical examples of cross-curricular teaching and learning in English, and some exploratory commentary.

Martians and related creatures

I should like to start with poetry, the mainstay of the cultural heritage conception of English: a series of lessons involving intertextual, media and ICT-based dimensions developed and adapted over the years (and of course still further adaptable). The initial teaching centres on Craig Raine's 1979 poem *A Martian Sends a Postcard Home*. If, in the present context, the appeal of poetry is to engender a sense of wonder in our familiar surroundings (very much including the world of technology we tend to take for granted) through the stretching, exploratory use of language, then this poem performs that role admirably. I have been greatly impressed by the responses of Year 9 (age thirteen to fourteen) pupils to a reading of this poem – responses which showed a depth of feeling for the strangeness and wonder of life which I and other adults present in the lessons found quite startling. But first, a little background. Raine's poem belongs to the 'Martian' school, for whom the 'making strange' of the familiar is central. As James Fenton, a fellow 'Martian poet', has observed of Raine: 'He taught us to become strangers in our familiar world, to release the faculty of perception and allow it to gorge at liberty in the field of experience' (Fenton 1978: 521). In this there may be an instructive echo of Brecht, for whom 'alienating an event or a character means first of all stripping the event of its self-evident, familiar, obvious quality and creating a sense of astonishment and curiosity about them' (in Brooker 1994: 191). Brecht's term *Verfremdungs Effect* is once more appropriate here: a potentially liberating, even celebratory, defamiliarisation. Warnock, in her seminal study of the imagination's power, (1976: 197) elaborates usefully on this essentially imaginative process:

> the creative artist, then, constructs an external form which is to be interpreted as signifying something which does not, in the same sense, exist. Both artist and spectator have to detach themselves from the world in order to think of certain objects in the world in a new way, as signifying something else.

From a rather different perspective, all teachers, but particularly those of language, are indebted to Wittgenstein for showing us something of the inherent strangeness of language as habitually used: what may be termed, in a phrase itself curiously apposite to the project of native-language teaching, the poetics of everyday life. It is a major theme of this book that the attendant tension between involved engagement and critical distance must surely be central to the notion of the interdisciplinary classroom. Like so much else of value, too, this notion is essentially Romantic: Shelley in his *Defence of Poetry* (written 1821, in Wu 1994: 954) maintained that poetry, potentially, 'strips the veil of familiarity from the world … [and] … purges from our inward sight the film of familiarity … It compels us to feel that which we perceive, and to imagine that which we know'. This seems as good a starting place as any.

For the teaching of Craig Raine's poem, the activities comprised several stages:

- The teacher reading the poem aloud, with the text projected above.
- Subsequent discussion on the nature of the poem, with an explanation given that the poem deals with eight different everyday objects or experiences seen through the eyes of the 'Martian' visitor to earth, with annotations added by pupils on the IWB.

■ Whole-class guessing as to what precisely these objects/experiences may be. Several are pretty self-explanatory, although couched in unusual terms, such as:

'Mist is when the sky is tired of flight
and rests its soft machine on the ground:

then the world is dim and bookish
like engravings under tissue paper'.

■ Others take more discovery, which is where the fun (and the mystery of technology, even if dated) lies. For example, the telephone:

'In homes, a haunted apparatus sleeps,
that snores when you pick it up.

If the ghost cries, they carry it
To their lips and soothe it to sleep

With sounds. And yet, they wake it up
Deliberately, by tickling with a finger'.

And the penultimate object, the lavatory, can cause much amusement – and not a little bemusement – before successful guessing of the 'answer'.

By Craig Raine, © Craig Raine, 1979

■ Small groups then discuss, note and report back to the whole class on possible subjects drawn from familiar everyday experience, with a view to eventual poetic expression. Using the Internet, pupils were asked to include photographic or artistic representations of 'normal' objects seen from unusual angles, or in a new light (both literally and metaphorically), again with the possibility of awakening from the unseeing contempt so often bred by familiarity: an opportunity to develop a media-based exploration of images. A possible variation would be to ask that this research be conducted over a longer period, including for homework, with the opportunity for digital photography.

■ Pupils then fashion their ideas and observations into 'Martian' poems, using the given convention of the Martian visitor trying to make sense of Earthly objects, customs and ideas. Possibilities include school (including the 'strangeness' of subject divisions!), money, items of furniture, and articles of clothing. Illustrations could be added digitally at this stage. Volunteers go on to read poems aloud and/or present images, again using ICT, with the class guessing the subject matter of each poem.

I include some examples of extracts from poems written by pupils following this scheme of work, to give a fuller flavour of the possibilities:

It lives on the ceiling
It never moves

But when it grows dark
It gets angry and explodes.

Kimberley, age 13

I lie there watching the world
Through a television that's been switched off
I feel so scared
I daren't even cough.

Laura, age 14

It's a giant snake with many mouths
Which travels very fast
Swallowing all its victims whole
But people wave as their friends get eaten.

Paul, age 14

It is important in planning and teaching literature-based work that acknowledgement is made of the likely stages of learning. In case this seems rather deterministic and mechanical, ignoring the subtle nuances of classroom relationships, we need too to keep a realistic sense that what is *taught* does not necessarily correlate in any predictable way to what may be *learned*. This important rider notwithstanding, it is useful to envisage the stages of learning in terms of

- the descriptive – the initial reading/presentation of the poem, for example;
- the reflective – which may include general or specific textual discussion and questioning, opened up through ICT;
- the speculative – the kinds of activity arising from textual study, such as pupils writing their own poems or providing pictorial images, stimulated by, but possibly wandering some way from, the initial reading.

In a different teaching context, with a Year 8 'upper ability' group following a similar scheme of work, interestingly, the pupils' resulting poems sometimes took a more critically political slant. For me, this demonstrates the necessary flexibility for creative (or critical) thinking and writing to emerge. This group's poems included the following extracts:

Time is kept in disk shapes
To be lost and never found.

Pippa

Humans see life through flashing boxes
As if trapped in their private dream worlds.

Luke

They spend time inside large boxes
Watching a smaller box
Some are imprisoned most days
In a special large box
Forced to read and to write.

Rebecca

(A striking comment on school-based literacy, this one!)
And, perhaps most movingly, Hannah's poem:

The poor and needy live in hope.
Suffering silently the pain runs deeper
Than their outer shells reveal.

City life on the opposite side,
Fast, furious, full of bright lights.

How can these two worlds
Ever live together in peace?

In terms of *A Martian Sends a Postcard Home*, teaching the poem suggests that it is possible to find in everyday experience exciting scope for observation, description, reflection, and illumination, not least through empathetic consideration of the 'narrative voice'. Further, there is a sense that everyday language works through metaphor, and an opportunity thus arises for an exploration of the nature of figurative colloquial language in diverse cultural contexts: poetry, as language working hard, can provide a springboard into various aspects of study. ICT for this learning sequence played a pivotal part: for the teacher and pupils presenting text and images; as the basis of exploratory research; and as enabling pupils more easily to share and build on each other's work. In this broad context, the role of ICT is as exploratory facilitator, opening up new fields of research across disciplines, and new, ever more creative, modes of presentation and communication. This very much includes the discovery (by both teachers and pupils) of parallel texts and artefacts: sometimes the forms of the poems themselves derive from different cultural sources, and this too can be helpful. Anglo-Saxon *Kennings*, for example, work by shocking the reader into seeing something through its function, and then there are *Haiku*, tightly formed Japanese poems suggestive of a flash of insight. As well as ICT, of course, there is a distinctly cross-curricular art and design component, in both active and appreciative aspects, in this learning sequence: indeed, in this context, art and poetry are close allies.

'Autogeddon': critical dimensions

One of the objects portrayed from a Martian viewpoint in the poem *A Martian Sends a Postcard Home* is, clearly, a car. The sense of childlike wonder at the endless picture show seen from inside the car is vividly evoked. Seen from another point of view, however, there is rather less to celebrate in the car and all the commercial and industrial baggage that comes with it: in a sense this is the distinction between the vantage points of innocence and of experience. There may be, too, a gender issue here, well worth bringing to the fore in the English classroom, and pertinent not just to cars but to all technology, as Thomas (1997: 27) notes:

> Men like controlling things. They enjoy gizmos like computers and cars and mobile phones because they can operate and control them. Cars are the ultimate in gizmo control, with limitless scope for supplementary gizmodification: turbo, mobile phone, CD HiFi, 4WD and remote control demist on the tinted glass wing mirror. The car, for men, is not simply transport or carriage – it's for driving, a verb which needs no preposition.

Interestingly, Heathcote Williams (1987) in his critical poem *Autogeddon* (the critique signalled by the title) uses the same 'Martian' conceit as does Raine, but with a quite different outcome: highly political and intensely critical of the domination of the car in our society. It is a long, often quite complex poem, but even in the brief excerpt below both the similarity and contrast to *A Martian* … are abundantly plain. A version of the work was also made for the BBC TV programme *Forty Minutes*, presented by the actor Jeremy Irons and using a wide range of audio and visual footage to amplify the poem's message – and very powerfully too. A brief extract gives the flavour of the poem:

> …Were an Alien Visitor
> To hover a few hundred yards above the planet
> It could be forgiven for thinking
> That cars were the dominant life-form,
> And that human beings were a kind of ambulatory fuel cell,
> Injected when the car wished to move off
> And ejected when they were spent …

Again, I have used this poem with remarkable success in the classroom, either independently or as complementary to (and contrasting with) *A Martian* …. The *Forty Minutes* presentation is essentially an intertextual, multimedia, highly persuasive version of the poem, incorporating extracts from TV car ads, archive film footage, music, snatches of soap-type dialogue and still images amongst many other elements. As such, it may be used as an appropriate model for pupils' own experiments with media-based persuasive texts, cutting across disciplines and genres in a vividly exciting way and giving the notion of performance poetry an inventive breadth. Given the availability of ICT tools such as digital cameras (video and still), sound recording techniques, computer-based cutting and pasting across genres, and Internet texts/images, computer-graphics, and animation, interdisciplinary English teaching can lead here to exciting results; or, as *All Our Futures* puts it: 'Teaching for creativity must take account of the new opportunities presented by information technology. Information technologies provide for new forms of creative practice. … They are also making available new ways of working within traditional forms of creative practice' (NACCCE 1999: 94).

Because of this potential, teaching the poem may be said to blend a 'language of critique' with a 'language of possibility', to use Freire's and Giroux's intercultural terms. Guilherme elaborates further on this potentially telling combination:

A language of critique entails a critical understanding of society as it is, with different layers of meaning and with several forces in interaction. … It involves a deconstructive view of reality and a challenge to fixed interpretive frames. … A language of possibility results … from the urge to explore new alternatives, to envision a revitalisation of democratic ideals and to engage in social change. …The combination of a language of critique with a language of possibility turns education into a form of cultural politics …

(2002: 34)

This sort of valuable, value-laden (to echo the debate of Chapter 2) and challenging insight may be given particularly sharp focus in the English classroom through the creative use of texts such as *Autogeddon*, which, in a sense, models through its intertextuality and critical questioning the very qualities recommended as characteristic of the interdisciplinary English classroom.

To extend the activities further, explicitly involving geography and music through the lens of ICT, two additional texts could be woven into the fabric of the interdisciplinary learning sequence. Both use the conceit, noted in *Autogeddon*, of viewing the world from a distance, and both convey strong messages worthy of exploration and discussion. First, a brief extract from the poem *Geography Lesson* by Zulfikar Ghose (n.d.):

When the jet rose six miles high,
it was
clear the earth was round
and that he had the more sea than land.
But it
was difficult to understand
that the men on the earth found
causes to
hate each other, to build
walls across cities and to kill.
From that
height, it was not clear why.

Apart from the political message of the poem, it is worthy of study on the grounds of its formal characteristics, and, alongside photographic images of the planet Earth, can be, in the hands of the imaginatively creative teacher, a powerful catalyst for exploration of relativity of response to worldly events. The same could be said of the lyrics of the song written by Julie Gold (n.d.) *From a Distance*, popularised by Bette Midler (although personally I prefer the version sung by Nanci Griffith).

There is here, clearly, the opportunity to push back the boundaries of interdisciplinary English still further, integrating facets of religious education. For both poem and song, I have worked with pupils on the everyday metaphor of maps (central to the geography curriculum of course), exploring (and subsequently making) maps based on texts intended to highlight certain aspects, whilst by the same token hiding other areas. In a sense, the alienating techniques of the Martian poets are used here to defamiliarise pupils from habitually used learning tools from across the curriculum; certainly, maps are fascinating in this respect, and I shall return to them later.

Reflective Activity:

Consider further the 'Martian conceit' and how it may be used to engender a sense of wonder or critical distance (or, of course, both), particularly through the agency of ICT.

Drawing on your own broadly cultural interests and experiences, are there any further texts – across written, pictorial and musical genres – that you think would be especially apt here?

If so, how would you use them pedagogically, and in what contrasting or complementing combinations?

Further possibilities: writing

As McGuinn again helpfully demonstrates, the defamiliarising potential of ICT extends across diverse aspects of the English curriculum:

> English teachers can exploit ICT to disclose the ways in which 'authoritative' texts of all kinds seek to position the reader. Using the wide variety of marking devices which the technology places at our disposal, for example, we can 'text map' a piece of writing – by colour-coding its various linguistic features, by commenting upon what we read as we read it, by animating the text so that words and letters move across the screen, or by creating hyper-links with other texts. … Techniques such as these can provide young people with a powerful, multi-sensory model of resistant reading – one which not only challenges ideological assertions, but also encourages a fundamental reappraisal of 'common sense' assumptions regarding the linear, chronological nature of the reading act itself …
>
> (Stevens and McGuinn 2004: 116)

The possibilities for adventurous, but also strongly purposeful, teaching and learning are indeed exciting, and again it is the cross-curricular dimension that may be the key to opening up the English classroom to these possibilities. Another example of ICT-guided activity in which I was involved focused sharply on the writing process, and I was keen to work in a mathematical component. The basis, with a Year 8 mixed-ability group, was to compose short stories in which readers would have a choice in (or have dictated by chance) the direction of the narrative. There was quite a vogue for stories such as these a few years ago, and they remain popular especially with younger readers: readers coming to the end of a particular chapter or section, for example, would be presented with narrative choices (in a fairy tale context – 'if you think Cinderella should try on the slipper, turn to page 15; if not, go to page 12') to be either considered like this, or to be determined by the throw of dice. There is a more intellectual tradition involved here too, of course, in what could be seen as a liberating, postmodern enterprise: the alternative endings presented by John Fowles for his novel *The French Lieutenant's Woman*, for instance (and reflected in the film of the same name), made for a fascinating teaching sequence when I taught this book at A Level. The self-consciously postmodern writing of Alain Robbe-Grillet provides an even more startling parallel, concerned as he was to liberate the novel genre from what he saw as the constrictions of plot and character, and to use mathematical models for structural experimentation: geometric, frequently repetitive descriptions of objects provide the basis of Robbe-Grillet's work, requiring that the reader painstakingly assembles the story in which the emotional and interpretive impact manifest themselves through the flow and disruptions of free associations. Timelines and plots are fractured, and the resulting novel resembles the literary equivalent of a cubist painting with its structurally geometric associations. As stated in the *Guardian* obituary,

> The novels of Robbe-Grillet are, in a sense, a game. He invites the reader to take part in a mind-testing exercise. The narrative is in search of its own coherence. The reader must understand why it takes the form that it does.
>
> (Johnson 2008)

The point here is that experimenting with text can be interpreted at vastly different levels, but the element of exploratory play remains fundamental. As Andrews elaborates:

> Different versions of a text can be created, saved and displayed – either on the screen or in hard copy form – for comparison and further composition. Texts can be reviewed at different levels: their spelling, grammar and textual structure can be scanned. … The great value of all this is not so much the technical wizardry, but the opportunity it gives us to play with language shapes, to reframe them according to different needs, to subvert propriety as well as to observe it.
>
> (Andrews 1997: 2)

There is perhaps an echo here also of the Romantic conception of the value of play, as presented by the poet and philosopher Friedrich Schiller, for example: 'Man plays only when he is, in the full meaning of the word, Man, and is only wholly Man when at play' (*On the Aesthetic Education of Man*).

This was precisely the basis of my work with the Year 8 group, who started in small groups playing with narrative sequences (using a 'Writing Consequences' game as a way to get the creative juices flowing and demonstrate that writing may be entertaining and painless). From this basis each group decided, after constructive (but occasionally quite heated) discussion, which plot opening to go with, and, using ICT, each individual then took the same opening as the starting point for his/her plot development as a broad plan. The advantage of ICT here, of course, lies in enabling notes and written synopses to be swiftly shared within groups (and potentially between them, although we didn't do this). Once a selection of plot strands had been completed, embryonically at this stage, groups were ready to negotiate (in itself of course a valuable aspect of this ICT-enabled activity) how the plots would interact on the basis of key choices to be made by readers. This is quite a tall order for any writer, novice or expert, and the teacher's guiding role is fundamental here – if anything, significantly enhanced rather than replaced by ICT usage. To simplify matters, we used mathematical structural models and accompanying mathematical language (about which the pupils knew more than I did – again a key aspect of this kind of learning enterprise) constructed diagrammatically on screen. The eventual results, in terms of the pupils' writing, were impressive, but in many ways it was the processes of learning that were even more so. For all participants – certainly for me – this project involved a steep and sometimes messy learning curve, but this is characteristic of leaving that comfort zone of tried and tested pedagogy: itself a valuable lesson in defamiliarisation.

Media education and ICT

Moving into the perhaps more familiar field of media education, another aspect of ICT in its broadest sense, the cross-curricular opportunities are again striking. It is worth looking back at the Cox (DES 1989) conception of media education: we may uncover rather more useful approaches than those in the substantially less detailed – some would say less satisfactory – account in the current orders. Cox was able to make full use of the expertise of the British Film Institute, then as now pioneering the cause of media education, by quoting from its publication (Bazalgette 1989: 96) of primary phase curriculum policy:

> Media education … seeks to increase children's critical understanding of the media … How they work, how they produce meaning, how they are organised and how audiences make sense of them, are the issues that media education addresses. [It] aims to develop systematically children's critical and creative powers through analysis and production of media artefacts. This also deepens their understanding of the pleasure and enjoyment provided by the media. Media education aims to create more active and critical media users who will demand, and could contribute to, a greater range and diversity of media products.

This provides us still with a useful guiding principle, at once wide-ranging and encouraging depth of study. Indeed, the term 'media education' implies breadth of teaching and learning, and must be distinguished from 'media studies', which has come to mean rather more specialised syllabus-based study, usually at GCSE, AS or A level. It is the former that I shall be mainly concerned with here, exploring the possibilities of creative media-based activity as central to the interdisciplinary English curriculum. In this context there is too a cross-phase element, and a great deal of inspiring media education is taking place at Key Stages 1 and 2 in many primary schools which may be successfully built on in the secondary school. The strong cross-curricular possibilities are certainly evident, and much pioneering work has already been carried out by English, expressive arts and humanities departments in this field.

As we have already noted in the context of other aspects of the English curriculum, there may be a tension between immersion in the subject and the keeping of a critical distance. The position for media education may exaggerate this tension, in that, almost by definition, it is the area of the curriculum likely to be most familiar to young people (and, by the same token, least familiar to many of their teachers). The media frequently train their various spotlights on young people, positively and negatively, and are enjoyed by them without too much concern over keeping a critical distance: indeed it would seem strange if otherwise. Traditionally, this may have led to an adult view of young people as passive victims of cynical media operators; Buckingham and Sefton-Green in Brindley (1994: 102) explore this idea:

> The view of young people as 'dupes' of popular media has a long history, and is regularly espoused by critics of all political persuasions. For many on the Right, the media are often seen as a major cause of moral depravity and violence, while they are routinely condemned by many on the Left for their reinforcement of racism, sexism, consumerism and many other objectionable ideologies. Yet what unites these otherwise very different views is a notion of young people as helpless victims of manipulation, and as extremely vulnerable and impressionable. In this account, the text is seen to be all powerful, while the reader is powerless to step back or resist: 'reading' or making sense of media texts is regarded as an automatic process, in which meanings are simply imprinted on passive minds.

The model of passivity alluded to here, often arising from a rather patronising, dismissive judgement of the very media probably most enjoyed by pupils, needs to be both acknowledged and critically confronted. As with all texts, across all disciplines, it is important to find ways both of being constructively critical towards, and of finding pleasure in, the artefacts being studied.

In my experience of teaching both media studies and media education within English, I have found that a worthwhile way into the nature of the subject, and one especially suited to an English teacher's fascination for words themselves, is to pose the question: what do we in fact mean by the word 'media'? It is a short step from there to explore the idea of the 'medium' in its many other contexts: as in 'the happy medium', or as used in spiritualism, for example. It is worth stimulating focused discussion on the nature of a medium as a means of transmitting a message, and with carefully chosen examples (the more immediately topical the better) I have found it instructive to go from there to an investigation into how the medium affects and is in turn affected by the message, the sender of the message and, of course, the receiver. We are here in the realms of semiotics, but such an exploration need not be over-complex: in effect, the teacher is seeking to establish that the medium is not neutral or transparent but is bound up in an intimate and influential relationship with the three other components and with the overall context and purpose. To enliven such a lesson, across disciplines if possible, there are many media artefacts that a resourceful English teacher could bring to bear from a wide range of media genres: advertising and news-based media are especially fertile sources in this respect. As with other aspects of textual and aesthetic education, in the context of media education there exists inevitably a tension between immersion and critical distance: potentially a healthy tension leading to greater understanding and, ultimately, a deeper enjoyment – as long as we avoid the trap of 'murdering to dissect', as Wordsworth warned. If we consider other fields of human activity – music, say, or sport, or motorcycle maintenance – it is surely true that the more we become interested in a particular area, the more we seek to understand its workings, and the greater the resulting enjoyment. Media education, like other aspects of education, should have greater enjoyment and critical appreciation as its aim.

Davies (1996: 60) provides a useful statement of intent for media study:

Media study should look at how meanings about the world are:
- made
- sustained
- contested

in all forms of human communication. It should study what those meanings and beliefs are, where they come from, who makes them and why.

This kind of English operates on the principles that:
- the more those forms or media influence us (by determining our thinking and actions) the more we should study them;
- the more we benefit from them (by gaining understanding, and means of expression) the more we should learn how to use them positively;
- it is not the job of media study to teach people what the right meanings are, or what the right pleasures are – its particular task is to teach people to examine how meanings are made.

These principles offer helpful guidelines for ICT and media education, and have been taken further in the Becta/NATE report previously cited (2009: 2):

As both a medium and a tool, ICT:
- promotes the integration of speaking and listening, reading and writing required in the National Curriculum Programmes of Study for English
- enhances the interactive teaching and learning styles recommended in the Framework for Secondary English
- extends pupils' ability to exercise choice, work independently and make connections between their work in English and in other subjects.

There are six areas of English where ICT can make a real contribution to the teaching and learning of English:
- Exploring and investigating
- Responding and interpreting
- Reflecting and evaluating
- Composing and transforming
- Presenting and performing
- Communicating and collaborating.

The potential again for cross-curricular teaching and learning in English is striking – as the brief list of activities below indicates:

- Cross-genre adaptations, such as a film version of historical events (possibly as context for literature) normally portrayed in a documentary – the Comic Strip TV film *Strike* is a marvellous example of a tongue-in-cheek Hollywood version of the miners' strike. **(History, and possibly art and music.)**

- Given a list of a day's 'newsworthy' items, creating an evening news broadcast and subsequently comparing it with what real news programmes made of the material.

Alternatively, a similar exercise using newspapers, focusing on the distinction between tabloids and broadsheets, and then contrasting newspaper and television presentation of 'news'. **(Citizenship.)**

- A detailed step-by-step analysis of still pictures, starting with one small portion and then progressing to the 'whole' picture, asking how the inclusion of more detail alters interpretation and understanding (along the lines of the British Film Institute's Reading Pictures material). **(Art and design.)**

- Discursive use of newspaper and documentary presentations of (possibly contentious) aspects of science and technology, analysing positive and negative images as a preliminary to storyboarding and/or shooting a short film focusing on either attractive or unattractive aspects the topic in question. **(Science; technology.)**

- The study of the media promotion of a new pop group (the latest boy band should provide plenty of exemplar material), including the all-important 'image' and the perhaps less important 'music', as preparation for an imaginary promotion campaign. **(Music.)**

- An analysis of the presentational styles of several disc jockeys for different audiences, programmes, types of music and radio stations, and the planning of a short sequence of linked records for a particular programme, possibly using an agreed format such as *Desert Island Discs*. **(Music.)**

- Study of media presentation of developing world issues and images across a wide range of media, suggestive of the humanities' concerns for historical, social and moral aspects of the media, again as a prelude to construction of media presentations on the theme. **(Geography, citizenship, RE.)**

Further explorations of interdisciplinary English through ICT

Throughout these examples, I hope that the powerfully democratising potential of interdisciplinary English teaching, as facilitated by a range of ICT-based resources and techniques, is apparent. As Jurgen Habermas reflected, 'The commitment to consider all individuals as potential participants in discourse presupposes a universalistic commitment to the potential equality, autonomy, and rationality of individuals' (1970: 252). These principles inform the following activities also, drawing as they do on the interdisciplinary, language-focused potential of ICT:

- The use of blogs, wikis, podcasts and other similarly interactive tools through the use of schools' virtual learning environments (VLEs) as a means of inspiring pupils' (and teachers') development of understanding of particular themes or texts studied. Clearly, this kind of activity may transcend the limitations of any particular VLE, and could be the basis of productive links to other people normally less accessible: primary school pupils, for example, or specific interest groups relevant to the theme or text studied, or pupils from schools situated abroad.

- Re-presentation of text through such programs as *Wordle*™: any studied text would be appropriate here, with the emphasis on key words, form and structure through textual manipulation and realignment. Rendering certain words invisible (through use of the 'white' font colour, thus easily made visible by changing colour) also works very well in this context.

- The use of (relatively) inexpensive hand-held video cameras (or the mobile phone equivalent, depending of course on school policy towards them) to record examples of text and image for exploration. Street signs, gravestones, school notices, house names and advertising slogans all provide fertile ground here, especially for cross-fertilisation across genres and image types.

- Re-sorting of PowerPoint slides in new sequences, with the focus on the text or theme being studied – a variation, in effect, on the diamond-nine exercise requiring pupils to prioritise their views on a particular subject using given statements.

- Illustration of texts (poems seem especially suitable here) using images easily accessible through the Internet: encouraging both literal and non-literal explorations of the relationship between image and text, and how the one informs and potentially modifies the other.

- Inventive use of some of the many other programs available through the Internet – a rapidly expanding repertoire – to enhance teaching and learning possibilities based on language. For instance, *Windows Movie Maker*™ program enables creative connections between and integration of text, music and image. Use of sound-clips to bring poetry to life, in terms of both form (for example, rhythmic characteristics) and subject matter can be vividly effective: *Anthem for Doomed Youth*, Wilfred Owen's often taught poem, to the background of rhythmic bells, for example.

- Replacement or omission of words from text – easily done through the 'search' and 'replace' facilities in *Word*™ – can illuminate particular aspects of text: for example, changing the gender of personal pronouns in either romantic novels or macho fiction can yield provocative material for gender-presentation discussions and textual explorations. By the same token, the *Word* facilities could enhance the teaching, through highlighting of key words for instance, of specified aspects of studied texts.

There are of course many more possibilities: it's simply a matter of interdisciplinary English teachers being open to ideas. As Sinker (in Sefton-Green and Sinker 2000: 212–3) pertinently notes (in the context of art education, but the point is valid across the curriculum),

> one thing which computer uses have signalled, particularly in the areas of multimedia and web-distribution, is the need to think laterally rather than lineally. That means realising that creative production can happen outside the art room and that art can exist anywhere. … If multimedia production serves to help the curriculum make the leap to cyberspace than it will have earned its place.

I am acutely aware that these areas change fast: in a few years' time the list above, for example, will seem hopelessly outdated. What really counts, as I hope I have illustrated in this chapter, is the receptiveness of teachers and learners to inventive possibilities.

Reflective Activity:

Try choosing one or two of the above-listed approaches to the teaching and learning of cross-curricular English through ICT and developing it with the resources and teaching techniques you'd find appropriate for a particular teaching group.

Consider especially how ICT may facilitate learning through the approach you've chosen, but remember also to think critically and reflectively: as we have noted, there are times when ICT may be superfluous or even a hindrance.

4

Assessment and evaluation of cross-curricular teaching and learning in English

Assessment generally is a hugely contentious, if not actually fraught, area of education, and this is likely to affect new curricular developments in particular, especially when – as is the case with cross-curricular teaching and learning – they are characterised by variety of pedagogical approach, experimentation, and diverse learning outcomes. The link between interdisciplinary approaches to language teaching and what has come to be termed 'critical literacy' (CL) is a strong and positive one, as I hope I have shown, and Morgan's observation about lack of assessment theorising for CL pertains also to interdisciplinary pedagogy: 'In much CL theorising about pedagogy there is a silence so resounding about matters of assessment that one could almost think it a scandal which must be hushed up. The scandal lies rather in the silence' (Morgan 1997: 141). Drawing extensively on certain key commentators on 'matters of assessment' I hope here to disturb this silence ever so slightly.

Broad principles of assessment in education may be seen by some (usually, but unfortunately not always, working outside the education world) as unproblematic, focused on evaluating pupils' progress in a particular area of learning, and providing feedback to the teacher as to the effectiveness of this or that teaching strategy; however, as we probe further, perhaps ourselves using defamiliarisation methods described as learning tools previously, certain tensions begin to emerge. A central tension, it seems to me, is that between formative, encouraging, sensitively formulated and collaborative models of assessment on the one hand, and judgemental, atomised, grade-orientated, externally tested and largely unchangeable (in terms of judgements made) models on the other. I am conscious that in the very language I use here my preference is clear, and in the context of this book, there is (as I hope will become evident) good reason. Certainly, in considering the nature of assessment, we can note two central tendencies: one placing emphasis on assessment *of* learning (with apparently reliable, objective measurements lead to summative judgements); the other emphasises assessment *for* learning, implying a more formative approach with developmental feedback to improve performance.

In an important sense, clearly, assessment – and not just in educational contexts – is virtually unavoidable: we speak of assessing situations and people's behaviours in all walks of life, and the classroom is but one of these walks. As interdisciplinary teachers of

English, following the principles already outlined in this book, we need to ensure that this particular walk is purposeful, open to the surroundings, enjoyable and reaches some desirable destination (even if, sometimes, this is not the destination originally envisaged). In order for this to happen, or at least for the conditions to be put in place for development towards it, the polarisation of approaches to assessment alluded to above needs to be faced, and some sort of synthesis agreed on. For instance, there are likely to be both formative *and* judgemental aspects of any educational assessment: I am keenly aware of this, incidentally, in my professional work as a teacher educator, where my business is in fostering diverse but effective English teaching through encouragement and advice, but also has to do with the 'gatekeeper' role in ensuring that only those who *are* effective beginning teachers (in official terms, meeting the QTS Standards) are allowed through the hallowed portal. My aim in this chapter is to explore the modes of assessment most appropriate to the interdisciplinary venture, and in this my fundamental principle, developing an earlier mention in this book (p. 33), is that of 'informed subjectivity'. Like a good deal else in this chapter, I am guided by vision of interdisciplinary English as creative in its essential pedagogy, if not always exactly an arts subject, even when (perhaps especially when) seeking to connect with the sciences or mathematics. And as David Carr succinctly reminds us, although

> there may be no 'universally' right answers to artistic questions or problems, … there is clearly *qualitative judgement* in the arts, and such a thing as genuine *informed* expertise and opinion about what counts as better or worse painting, music or poetry
> (Carr 2003: 157)

So by informed subjectivity I mean, essentially, that assessment in the creatively interdisciplinary context (at least) has to recognise both that there is an important dimension of evaluative subjectivity involved in the process, and that, so as to go some way towards tempering this recognition, the more contextual information we can bring to bear on the process the more valid it is likely to be.

Before going on to look at some of the more practically orientated aspects of informed subjectivity, a brief survey of key theoretical frameworks pertinent to its place in pedagogical development may be helpful. Clearly, controversies concerning the nature of assessment are not peculiar to the UK, or to the curricular developments around the subject English. Fleming, interestingly, makes the following point in the context of the Council of Europe's continuing attempts to connect initiatives and principles across its member states:

> Constructive debate around differences of opinion is always helpful, but too often disagreements about assessment become entrenched and unproductive. This happens for a number of reasons, including:
> - a failure to recognise that assessment needs to fulfil a wide range of legitimate purposes;
> - an assumption that a single assessment tool will be able to serve all needs;
> - a lack of awareness that it is the *use* made of assessment, not necessarily the assessment process itself, that will largely determine its impact;

- a tendency to search for universal solutions to assessment issues and neglect the significance of context.

(Fleming 2007: 1)

and, significantly, goes on to state that 'A key challenge is to develop a system of assessment that acknowledges the different functions of assessment and it helps to see these as complementary rather than being in opposition to each other' (op. cit.: 3).

In meeting this challenge, the work of Black and Wiliam is widely recognised, and very helpful. In their hugely influential paper *Inside the Black Box*, they commend the essential principles of effective development of assessment in schools thus, drawing on exhaustive research:

- All such work involves new ways to enhance feedback between those taught and the teacher, ways which require new modes of pedagogy—which will require significant changes in classroom practice.
- Underlying the various approaches are assumptions about what makes for effective learning—in particular that students have to be actively involved.
- For assessment to function formatively, the results have to be used to adjust teaching and learning—so a significant aspect of any programme will be the ways in which teachers do this.
- The ways in which assessment can affect the motivation and self-esteem of pupils, and the benefits of engaging pupils in self-assessment, both deserve careful attention.

(Black and Wiliam 1998: 1)

Black and Wiliam continue their argument by summarising the major obstacles to such progress:

The most important difficulties, which are found in the UK, but also elsewhere, may be briefly summarised in three groups. The first is concerned with effective learning:

- Teachers' tests encourage rote and superficial learning; this is seen even where teachers say they want to develop understanding—and many seem unaware of the inconsistency.
- The questions and other methods used are not discussed with or shared between teachers in the same school, and they are not critically reviewed in relation to what they actually assess.
- For primary teachers particularly, there is a tendency to emphasise quantity and presentation of work and to neglect its quality in relation to learning.

The second group is concerned with negative impact:

- The giving of marks and the grading functions are over-emphasised, while the giving of useful advice and the learning function are under-emphasised.
- Use of approaches in which pupils are compared with one another, the prime purpose of which appears to them to be competition rather than personal improvement.

- In consequence, assessment feedback teaches pupils with low attainments that they lack 'ability', so they are de-motivated, believing that they are not able to learn.

The third group focuses on the managerial role of assessments:
- Teachers' feedback to pupils often seems to serve social and managerial functions, often at the expense of the learning functions.
- Teachers are often able to predict pupils' results on external tests—because their own tests imitate them—but at the same time they know too little about their pupils' learning needs.
- The collection of marks to fill up records is given greater priority than the analysis of pupils' work to discern learning needs; furthermore, some teachers pay no attention to the assessment records of previous teachers of their pupils.
(op. cit: 3).

During the decade since this seminal paper, there have been significant developments in assessment, much of it along the lines recommended by Black and Wiliam; nevertheless, their list of the most important potential difficulties remains apposite, and worth quoting in detail. There is a particular and very direct relevance to interdisciplinary teaching and learning here too: a distinct and unmissable opportunity to model the kind of curriculum innovation through all its facets, including that crucial area of the curriculum in which the initiative has, over the past couple of decades, been wrested from the teaching profession: assessment. Black and Wiliam, indeed, were (and are) well aware of the import of their research here, especially as, since both are mathematicians, their conclusions were both unexpected and all the more welcome at the time. They conclude that:

What is needed is a culture of success, backed by a belief that all can achieve. Formative assessment can be a powerful weapon here if it is communicated in the right way. ... Pupils can accept and work with such messages, provided that they are not clouded by overtones about ability, competition and comparison with others.

(op. cit: 6).

This is indeed the spirit – and indeed the letter – of the current cross-curricular venture. The danger, as with all pedagogical innovation, is that the modes of assessment will be unsuitable – insensitive, unwieldy, demotivating – for the nature of the curriculum development in question, and may even militate against its success.

From a rather different vantage point, the *All Our Futures* report, although sadly neglected at the time, makes equally important observations concerning assessment in the context of creativity and culture within education. The basic position taken by the committee is abundantly clear:

Reliable and systematic assessment is essential in all areas of the curriculum, to improve the quality of teaching and learning and to raise standards of achievement. This is as true of children's creative and cultural education as for all other areas of education. But how assessment is done must take into account what is being assessed. For many people, this is where the problem lies. As they see it, education is increasingly dominated by methods and criteria of assessment which, at best, take little account of creative teaching and learning, and which, at worst, militate directly against them.

The problem for creative and cultural education is not the need for assessment, but the nature of it. In principle, assessment should support children's learning and report on their achievements. In practice, the process of assessment itself can determine the priorities of education in general. Our consultations suggest four general problems: first, a growing emphasis on summative assessment; second, the related emphasis on measurable outcomes; third, the difficulties of assessing creativity; fourth, the growing pressure of national assessment on teachers and schools.

(NACCCE 1999: 107)

On close examination, then, according to detailed research undertaken authoritatively by two separate sources, many of the tensions in creativity in education, the basis of our interdisciplinary turn, may be reduced to a basic concern for the nature of its assessment. English teachers face something of a quandary here, for in today's educational world formal assessment assigns significance to any activity, and without it the activity is seen by many – not least pupils and their parents – as valueless. Even a cursory visit to a secondary school will validate this observation: if it is not given a mark or grade, the activity's value is questioned (and this culture is also very much part of the climate in higher education). But at what cost is this estimation to any real value? Certainly, even if we agree that giving creative, cross-curricular endeavour some sort of accreditation is welcome, this is an aspect of English calling for great sensitivity. Some aspects of this work may demand a detailed and relatively objective set of assessment criteria well known to both pupils and teacher; at other times, such a public awareness of and concern for the minutiae of assessment may actually hinder the free flow of orally expressed ideas by emphasising the how, the means of delivery, at the expense of the what, the content, the ideas struggling for adequate expression but worth expressing even if imperfectly. In this sort of instance it should be enough for the pupil (and teacher) to be only half consciously aware that the activity, in terms of process and product, is in the long term assessed. Discussions of tentative ideas for developing or sustaining an activity, for example, often spontaneous by nature, are generally best assessed in this way. As Fleming elaborates, focusing, appropriately enough, on language education:

A key concept is embodied in the notion of **'transparency'**, the view that those being assessed are aware of the criteria which are being used to make judgements about them and how those judgements are made. Knowledge of criteria can help performance and improve motivation but once again, in the context of language as subject, the issues are more complex than they first seem. A common assumption is that pupils learn best when they know what they are trying to achieve and why. While this view is largely true, there are exceptions. Because the development of language can in some ways be described as a 'natural' process learners do not always need to be fully focused on specific aspects of their performance in order to improve. In fact too much focal awareness on performance can make them too self-conscious: speakers can appear too groomed and artificial; the writer who has been told to strive for effect by using more adjectives may develop a highly artificial and awkward style. These insights do not negate the importance of transparency as a principle but highlight the fact that in pedagogical practice the principle needs to be interpreted and implemented with care.

(Fleming 2007: 6)

Assessment, then, should match the nature of the activity and should, where possible, involve pupils and teacher in partnership – designing assessment criteria, perhaps, to help each other in the enhancement of the quality of the curriculum. The method of assessment used will arise from the nature of the activity and the logistics involved.

All Our Futures goes on to emphasise the potentially dead hand of assessment on experimentation in learning – again central, by implication, to the cross-curricular project where relationships between subjects, genres and learning styles are developmental and contingent on particular local conditions. The point is well made that 'Children need periods where they can experiment, make mistakes and test various approaches without fear of failure. Immediate assessment can overlook aspects of creative development which only become visible in the longer term' (NACCCE 1999: 110).

The focus on formative assessment as the kind best suited to the long-term evaluation of creative work – central to the concept of informed subjectivity, as even the etymology tells us – is clear:

Achieving a greater role for formative assessment, carried out by teachers with proper moderation, would do much to increase curricular and subject flexibility …. It would emphasise the necessity of inquiry, questioning and experimentation in all areas of the curriculum, and enhance the professionalism of teachers.

(ibid: 113)

There is a significant echo here of Black and Wiliam's realisation that

Many of the initiatives that are needed take more class time, particularly when a central purpose is to change the outlook on learning and the working methods of pupils. Thus, teachers have to take risks in the belief that such investment of time will yield rewards in the future, whilst 'delivery' and 'coverage' with poor understanding are pointless and even harmful.

Underlying such problems will be two basic issues. The one is the nature of each teacher's beliefs about learning. If the assumption is that knowledge is to be transmitted and learnt, that understanding will develop later, and that clarity of exposition accompanied by rewards for patient reception are the essentials of good teaching, then formative assessment is hardly necessary. If however, teachers accept the wealth of evidence that this transmission model does not work, even by its own criteria, then the commitment must be to teaching through interaction to develop each pupil's power to incorporate new facts and ideas into his or her understanding. Then formative assessment is an essential component—but one that is built in with other features which are also needed to secure the responsible and thoughtful involvement of all pupils. This is not meant to imply that individualised one-on-one teaching is the only solution, rather that what is needed is a classroom culture of questioning and deep thinking in which pupils will learn from shared discussions with teachers and from one another

(Black and Wiliam 1998: 9)

Arguments such as these return us to the need to change the culture of the classroom, an area I explored in the previous chapter. This in itself is no easy matter, as habits die hard, but the evidence points now to a gradually emerging greater professional flexibility for teachers, coupled with a firmer emphasis on a research-based profession (the growth of master's-level PGCE courses and masters' degrees in education testifies to this), that at least give us some grounds for optimism.

At this point I should like to take us back to language, the stuff of the English curriculum and the basis of its interdisciplinary adventures – and, of course, the central medium of any realistic assessment or evaluation of learning. In an important sense, whatever else is being assessed, language always is. If, following Vygotsky (see Britton 1994), we see thought as a development of 'interior speech', literally spoken aloud during infancy, then we ignore the delicate relationship between thought and language at our peril. This is particularly important during the years of secondary schooling, for this is the time of continuing, often accelerating, experimentation: sometimes pupils will 'think before speaking', sometimes not; sometimes we, as teachers, need to go with the spontaneous flow, sometimes we need to intervene to focus on the need to reflect before – or even without – speech. Carlyle, writing in his highly personal treatise *Sartor Resartus* (1915 [1834]: 57), realised the intimate relationship between thought and language: 'Language is called the garment of thought; however, it should rather be, language is the flesh-garment, the body, of thought'. And of the forms of language most assessed, perhaps inevitably, it is writing that is by far the most prevalent. Cross-curricular ventures based on English, as we have already begun to see, may involve very diverse modes of expression drawing from a range of activities, but writing should remain central – with the important proviso that it is handled sensitively with regard to the *subject* (in all senses of the word). Writers, of course, generally realise the reflective, thought-shaping potential of their craft: 'How can I tell what I think till I see what I say', wrote E.M. Forster, famously, in *Aspects of the Novel* (1962: 99). But much of pupils' writing in schools, across the curriculum but certainly not excepting English, is rather less valuable. The central tension concerning the role of writing in the classroom is inescapable: a means of control inflicted on a more or less unwilling pupil population, as against a liberating and creative means of expression. The reality of school life may serve to disguise this tension, and indeed the actual experience of most pupils most of the time may lie somewhere between the two poles.

Writing as a means of assessment across the curriculum is one of its chief functions, but of course in this context it remains an *instrumental* function rather than an end in itself. However, as we saw in the previous chapter, exploring the nature of the word 'medium' as the key to media education, no medium is entirely transparent. A written task may be set up by, say, a history teacher to establish how much pupils understand of a given historical topic, but this understanding will only be apparent if the appropriate writing form has been mastered in the first place. I am aware as I write this that my thoughts are modified by the process, and no doubt will be modified again in diverse ways by divers readers. So, the process of writing as undertaken by pupils in schools is the focus of a number of important characteristics, which must at least be acknowledged by teachers – especially English teachers – if effective teaching and learning is to take place. These sometimes contradictory insights could be summarised as follows:

- Writing is often the most painfully and formally learned of the three areas of English (misleadingly termed) 'attainment targets' in the National Curriculum.

- At the same time, as E.M. Forster's observation intimates, writing is perhaps the most important and reflective tool of all learning.

- Writing is the most obviously visible aspect of a pupil's learning, which is presumably why it has such central importance in virtually all examinations of attainment.

- Writing is a powerful means of self and social expression, potentially communicating to an increasingly wide audience through formal or informal publication, easy and quick copying, and information and communication technology.

- Writing is an important controlling mechanism, a means of achieving orderly discipline, in many lessons.

- Perhaps because of this, across the curriculum pupils undergo a huge quantity of directed writing for a large proportion of their time in schools.

- Much of this writing has no particular or specified readership in mind, apart from the teacher or the pupil him/herself, and in practice not always even these audiences.

- Compared to the volume of writing completed during school years, most adults write little, and then mostly short, informal pieces.

- Perhaps for a combination of some or all of these reasons, writing is not generally liked by most pupils in secondary schools.

I dwell here on writing in some detail as it remains the most widespread means of assessing and evaluating classroom learning, but not always for positive reasons or with positive outcomes. However I also firmly believe, from my professional experience and research, that writing is also, potentially, the most helpful method of conducting assessment across a wide spectrum of learning activities. This I believe to hold true even (perhaps most of all) when this learning comprises effectively many different activities, some of which involve no writing at all (as we have already encountered). The kind of writing I have in mind here is the reflective journal, running alongside, and in dialectical relationship to, the learning activities and any portfolio collections as records. In effect, this would be a contextual journal – to borrow a term from arts education – comprising not just a reflective account of the work itself, but also notes, brief plans, readings, ICT and media promptings, records of discussions – the list is endless. Some years ago the National Writing Project (1990) proposed an apposite group of categories for formative response to writing, which could in fact easily, and appropriately, be adapted for a range of learning activities or as guidance for portfolio evaluation:

- surface features (e.g. spelling, punctuation, presentation);
- style and structure (appropriateness of language to purpose);

- ideas and content (coherence, reflective qualities);

- writer as writer (comments on the process showing understanding);

- writer as person (response to personal content and interpersonal dialogue derived from the text itself).

I shall return to the portfolio theme a little later in the chapter when looking at how the activities already recounted, in the previous chapter, could be assessed and evaluated.

I am conscious that I have tended to use the terms 'assessment' and 'evaluation' interchangeably, when in fact there are (despite much overlap in practical usage) important distinctions to be made. As Sefton-Green points out,

> It is ... very difficult to make an absolute distinction between the two terms, because in practice evaluation frequently (sometimes only) takes place during assessments and some assessment procedures are fundamentally evaluative in nature. ... The terms are frequently blurred together by teachers and students themselves ...
>
> (Sefton-Green 2000: 4)

Insofar as there is a useful distinction to be made, the kind of assessment I am interested in fostering for interdisciplinary English is essentially evaluative; Sefton-Green again:

> On the whole ... evaluation is the term used to describe informal judgements made by teachers about individual students or pieces of work. Evaluations will often include an extended or discursive response, but can include a grade or mark. Sometimes evaluation is used as a diagnostic term – to make sense of an individual's progress – although this is also called formative assessment. On the other hand assessment is used to refer to formal summative assessments .... The difference between the two concepts is sometimes a matter of degree – a sort of hard and soft kind of distinction ...
>
> (ibid.)

The eminent American arts educator Elliot Eisner is also helpful here. In his seminal volume, aptly titled *The Arts and the Creation of Mind*, he argues for sensitive evaluation of all classroom endeavour, based on his evolving concept of connoisseurship. Eisner distinguishes between assessment and evaluation on the one hand (effectively conflating the two along the lines of the formative assessment model) and measurement on the other:

> Assessment and evaluation are often confounded with measurement .... Measurement has to do with determining magnitude. Measures of magnitude are descriptions of quantity. They are not appraisals of the value of what has been measured. Assessment and evaluation are pre-eminently valuative; they ask about the merits of something.
>
> (Eisner 2002: 180)

A note here concerning the place of values in creative endeavour (again, the semantic field hints at the relevance of the word): this discussion begs some important questions concerning the meaning and validity of creativity, and why it is especially valuable. If indeed it is valuable, then a sense of value lies at its heart. As has been suggested previously, in discussions about instrumental rationality and its implications, it is possible to act creatively, as is commonly understood by the term, for highly questionable ends: exploitative, destructive, damaging. To make radical social meaning in the context of teaching and learning, creativity needs to be situated in a coherent place of values. Creativity's minute particularities, its celebratory subjectivities, its potential for social meaning-making, its liberating connective power only really come to life when values are emphasised. But what and whose values? As so often, the answer lies in the framing of the question: in the sense that values are culturally specific, and as such are contested – often energetically, sometimes creatively, and sometimes destructively. There are indeed multiple places for creativity, and each relates to the cultural context. And this fundamental realisation, often practically neglected in assessment processes, needs careful, culturally sensitive embedding in all evaluative approaches and responses to classroom activity.

To read Eisner is to sense the centrality of value in his concept of education, but he is aware also of how problematic it may be for teachers to work along his recommended lines when so much of the context – particularly the external policing methods – seems antithetical. Teachers themselves need to learn, as part of a truly professional development, to appreciate what is happening, and here the spirit of connoisseurship is apt:

> Connoisseurship is the art of appreciation. Connoisseurs notice in the field of their expertise what others may miss seeing. They have cultivated their ability to know what they are looking at. *Educational connoisseurship* addresses itself to classroom phenomena; just as individuals need to learn to 'read' a football game, so too do people need to learn how to read a classroom or student work.
>
> (op. cit.: 187)

Eisner continues thus:

> We use educational connoisseurship to see the rich and multilayered events unfolding in the classroom. … Educational criticism is intended to avoid the radical reductionism that characterises much quantitative description. It is designed to provide a fine-grained picture of what has occurred or has been accomplished so that practice or policy can be improved and high quality achievement acknowledged.
>
> (op. cit.: 189)

In the end, Eisner's vision of the assessment process, for all its complexities, has a certain humane simplicity at its heart:

> What the teacher needs to focus on is how students needed to think in order to get the results they did and what they learned as a result. In assessment and evaluation we need to penetrate the surface features of activity to get at what lies beneath it. … The student is also a prime resource in the evaluative process. Teachers can

learn a great deal about what students have learned by listening to them talk about their work.

(op. cit.: 193–4)

Assigning responsibility to learners is here absolutely vital, and this recommendation is again in accord with others working to pioneer models of formative assessment; Black and Wiliam, for example, thoroughly endorse self- and peer-assessment approaches, despite their research disclosing institutional obstacles:

> [I]t should first be noted that the main problem that those developing self-assessment encounter is not the problem of reliability and trustworthiness: it is found that pupils are generally honest and reliable in assessing both themselves and one another, and can be too hard on themselves as often as they are too kind. The main problem is different—it is that pupils can only assess themselves when they have a sufficiently clear picture of the targets that their learning is meant to attain. Surprisingly, and sadly, many pupils do not have such a picture, and appear to have become accustomed to receiving classroom teaching as an arbitrary sequence of exercises with no overarching rationale. It requires hard and sustained work to overcome this pattern of passive reception. When pupils do acquire such overview, they then become more committed and more effective as learners: their own assessments become an object of discussion with their teachers and with one another, and this promotes even further that reflection on one's own ideas that is essential to good learning.
>
> What this amounts to is that self-assessment by pupils, far from being a luxury, is in fact an essential component of formative assessment. Where anyone is trying to learn, feedback about their efforts has three elements—the desired goal, the evidence about their present position, and some understanding of a way to close the gap between the two … . All three must to a degree be understood by anyone before they can take action to improve their learning. Such argument is consistent with more general ideas established by research into the way that people learn. New understandings are not simply swallowed and stored in isolation—they have to be assimilated in relation to pre-existing ideas. The new and the old may be inconsistent or even in conflict, and the disparities have to be resolved by thoughtful actions taken by the learner

(Black and Wiliam 1998: 7)

I have drawn heavily on a few key commentators in this appraisal of assessment and evaluation appropriate to cross-curricular teaching and learning in English, in order to attempt to give some framework of theoretical underpinning to the principles of informed subjectivity. We need now to look at the practical implications of such approaches in terms of evaluations of the schemes of work illustrated in the previous chapter: the Martian poetry project for Year 9 pupils, and the Year 8 scheme of work, using ICT as a tool, aimed at the writing of 'reader's choice' narratives.

> ## Reflective Activity:
>
> Consider carefully the meaning and implications of the principle of 'informed subjectivity' as the basis of assessment in the context of your own professional practice.
>
> In particular, where are the potential strengths and limitations of such a formulation in practical terms? Where is there scope for negotiation? What may be the implications for working within the more rigid and summative assessment paradigms so familiar to teachers and pupils (for instance, external examinations)?

Both projects spanned several weeks – four and five respectively – and involved a range of activities, English attainment targets, and modes of learning. These aspects of the schemes of work are important, as they offer pupils the chance to achieve in different contexts, with a corresponding opportunity for the teacher to make informed evaluations of pupils' achievements: the first part of the 'informed subjectivity' formulation. In both schemes of work the assessment opportunities were integral to the development of the work itself, and were based on three modes of assessment:

1. **Reflective commentary:** a contextual journal written by each individual pupil, responding in detail to the various stages of the project to give evidence of achievement and comprising a combination of the pupil's own journal writing, relevant images, and records of group undertakings. The presentation of the journal itself was part of the overall project, and as such its quality is evaluated; however, there was no 'set' format for the journal as it was intended ultimately to represent each pupil's particular way of working and reflecting upon the activity.

2. **Evaluative dissemination:** for both schemes of work, occasions were built in to allow pupils to share their work with each other (across small groups and the whole class as appropriate), with the teacher, and with a wider audience. For the first of these three opportunities, the context included:
    - shared celebratory readings (either aloud, or by sharing texts for individual reading);
    - media-based presentations generally using ICT; and
    - peer-assessment opportunities (usually after the readings or presentations), either through written or oral commentary.

    In terms of sharing with the teacher, this involved:
    - individual and group tutorials (formally built into the sequence of lessons) and informal discussions as appropriate; and
    - the teacher having access to the contextual journal, which otherwise could be kept individually private by each pupil.

    Finally, possibilities for dissemination to a wider audience could mean:
    - display of written work around the school;

- presentations to other groups of pupils (with the potential opportunity here for cross-curricular and cross-phase collaboration);
- dissemination of published work (for example, a representative folder in the school foyer); and
- publication for a wider adult audience (including in this book).

3. **Formal assessment and evaluation:** essentially the teacher's responsibility, but drawing on all the evidence encountered through the summaries above. For each pupil's work the teacher gave a detailed comment, leading with a positive appraisal of the qualities found therein and inviting the pupil to respond in writing to this appraisal (the assessment form used had space for this). The grade was only allocated after this evaluative assessment process had been completed.

As we go on to explore in more detail, in the following chapters, the pedagogy and practice of cross-curricular teaching and learning in English in the context of a range of curricular connections, further examples of assessment and evaluation will emerge. The framework sketched out above should give a flavour of some of the possibilities in this vital area of education: vital not only in the sense of essential (which it clearly is, in some form or another), but – perhaps more significantly here – also signifying vitality as appropriate to the interdisciplinary venture.

Cross-curricular approaches: English and the humanities

Introductory context

Already in this book there have been plentiful allusions to the close connections between the subject English and those curricular subjects under the convenient umbrella of the humanities: citizenship (a relative newcomer to the stable, but an important one), geography, history and religious education. Some of these connections have been practically orientated, some more theoretical at base, but the intimate relationship between the subjects is readily apparent, and potentially fruitful. Indeed, over the past two or three decades there have been experiments in several secondary schools, notably during the 1980s, along the lines of incorporating English into a humanities disciplinary framework – sometimes named a Faculty of Humanities. The danger with many of these experiments, and judging from my own professional experience and observations the reason they have tended to die away during more recent years, is that the identity of English may simply be subsumed into a broadly sociological approach towards language and its texts, literary and otherwise. As we have seen, the subject identity of English is often contested, and invariably (and in my view rightly) guarded by its practitioners, so perhaps such a sociological approach has inevitable failure built in.

Unsurprisingly (I hope), the approach I take here is different. The principle at stake is one of making connections between disciplinary characteristics: acknowledging, adopting and adapting teaching and learning approaches as appropriate from a position of curricular strength, whilst simultaneously embracing diverse and sometimes challenging views and practices concerning that subject identity. This is of course quite a challenge, but is one worth meeting seriously (it is the basis of the present series of books) if we are to forge a curriculum appropriate to the learning needs of the twenty-first century. The philosophical and theoretical debates of the preceding chapters should have prepared the ground for a more practically orientated exploration of what it means to meet this challenge in this and the next few chapters. Davies *et al.* suggest four guiding principles (expressed as 'rules for classroom action', but I wonder if this is a little inflexible) for experiential learning, and these appear to me to be helpful signposts for the exploration:

- Depth of understanding is more important than coverage and superficial exposure.

- Topics and issues need to be connected through some kind of thematic, interdisciplinary or historical structure. Simply studying one issue after another will not be enough.

- The study of issues must be based on challenging and relevant content.

- Students must experience some measure of control, or at least significant involvement, in the teaching process.

(Davies *et al.* 2002: 76)

Further helpful guidance encourages us as interdisciplinary English teachers, with a little adaptability, to connect our project to the development of democratic and, where appropriate, locally-based education (both areas, clearly, that have a great deal to do with humanities education in general). We are back to the issue of particularity, in effect: as Eagleton maintains (2000: 78), 'For socialist thought, universality is inherent in the local, not an alternative to it' – and for 'socialist' we may read 'interdisciplinary ' – or as William Blake rather more colourfully expressed it: 'To see the world in a grain of sand'. Eagleton, in his illuminating study of the nature of culture, goes on to quote Mulhern (2000: 80), emphasising that communities are 'not *places* but *practices* of collective identification whose variable order largely defines the culture of any actual social formation'. For interdisciplinary English teaching, however, both *place* and *practice* are hugely significant. The two are neatly merged in an official Council of Europe statement on global education and democracy in schools – the sense of universality inherent in the local is clear here:

> Democracy is best learned in a democratic setting where participation is encouraged, where views can be expressed openly and discussed, where there is freedom of expression for pupils and teachers, and where there is fairness and justice. An appropriate climate is, therefore, an essential complement to effective learning about human rights.
>
> (Council of Europe 1996: 15)

Such proclamations, of course, are easily made – but, in practice, the implications are profound. Indeed, as Rogers points out, *practical* engagement with democratic processes in schools occurs only rarely: 'While being taught that freedom and responsibility are the glorious features of our democracy, students are experiencing powerlessness and having almost no opportunity to exercise choice or carry responsibility' (Carl Rogers, quoted in Harber 2004: 19).

Issues of citizenship, critical literacy and the cross-curricular perspectives (particular with the humanities), it seems to me, are all crucial here. Interestingly, the 'Martian' conceit we have looked at (in Chapter 3) in terms of defamiliarisation of the mundane through poetry, can also apply in the citizenship context as prose; take, for instance, this observation on global education:

> We, as adults, must acknowledge that we routinely abuse our power over children. A visiting Martian would have great difficulty in accepting that we are committed to children's education, seeing that in one country we are expelling girls from school if they wear a headscarf, while in another we are expelling them from school unless they

wear a headscarf. Sadly, nobody would be able to persuade the visiting Martian that we really care about education.

(Katarina Tomaoevski, Special Rapporteur to the UN Commission on Human Rights, in *The Independent* 10 September 1999, quoted in Harber 2004: 85)

It seems to me that, in my experience, of all places in schools it is the English classroom that has the clearest potential to realise a radically enlightening education along the lines hinted at above. Peim amplifies this point (2003: 31–2):

English teaching both represents and enacts ideas about culture and language. ... English occupies a special place ... in relation to both culture and language. ... [It] retains a central role in the curriculum and is at the core of issues around culture and values,

concluding that 'language and culture are continuous', as indeed they are, and demonstrably so (as I hope to show).

It may indeed be possible, gradually but more clearly, to see what this sort of continuity could mean in practice – and the act of seeing is here a potentially visionary act, in the sense that seeing a way forward, and an ultimate goal, enables the practitioner to walk purposefully, making a real difference to the immediate cultural context. This may be idealistic, in one sense, but it is not unrealistically so: the vision is embedded in everyday pedagogical practice. The alternative is an abstract, ultimately vacuous idealism, the danger of which, in educational terms, has long been pointed out by radical commentators: Chanan and Gilchrist, for example (1974: 123–4), see that, all too often,

Our values are permeated by an abstract idea of change or progress, instead of a progressively refined image of the condition we want to progress to. In the deification of the idea of progress man [*sic*] is distracted from his capacity for fulfilment in this world just as much as he was in the middle ages by the idea of the hereafter. It deflects him ... from the relatively short-term motivations which are the real springs of *chosen* social change.

As so often, this is both an intercultural and interdisciplinary perspective, and yet, as the very term 'intercultural' implies, the global dimension is equally significant. Here, it is, I think, the shared concern for imaginative empathy that powerfully connects English with the humanities; as Searle, from a radical perspective, has it, the role of the imagination is 'central': 'The imagination in teaching is the great motivator, the dimension that stretches the mind, provokes engagement in learning and encourages empathy and human understanding' (Searle 1998: 2).

At a time when global cultural clashes are constantly threatening human peaceful co-existence – perhaps it was ever thus – it is all the more incumbent upon teachers – especially native-language teachers, paradoxically – to develop an intercultural pedagogy. In the aftermath of the war against Iraq of 2003, Said has offered a powerful analysis of the international situation as it affects education – and, hopefully, as education of the right sort may affect it. Said draws a distinction between two opposing views of what learning about other cultures, at all levels from the particulars of the classroom outwards, may look like, asserting that

[T]here is a difference between knowledge of other peoples and other times that is the result of understanding, compassion, careful study and analysis for their own sakes, and on the other hand knowledge that is part of an overall campaign of self-affirmation

(Said 2003: 4)

Critical engagement and felt empathy are fundamental parts of this kind of understanding – an essentially questioning approach. But there is also scope for intuition, for seeing the whole entity through giving the faculty of insight a chance to operate. In this sense, I agree with Wittgenstein that 'People who are constantly asking "why" are like tourists who stand in front of a building reading Baedecker and are so busy reading the history of its construction, etc., that they are prevented from seeing the building' (1940; in Guilherme 2002: 117).

With these guidelines firmly in mind, we can proceed to our exploration of classroom possibilities, appropriately enough using the geographical metaphor of the map hinted at above, or as Bob Dylan more evocatively put it, 'Using ideas as my maps'.

Historical connections: of war and peace

'To teach English is unavoidably to teach cultural history' asserted Roger Knight (Knight 1996: 80), and, from a range of perspectives, few (in my experience) would disagree. More radically, for instance, McLaren poses the crucial question 'how can students engage history as a way of reclaiming power and identity?' (in Searle 1998: 77). Inevitably, however, statements like these tend to conceal a complex reality, and in addressing that complexity, English and history are close – potentially at least. Part of any creative response to the world and word, and indeed part of any proposed resolution of tensions, must centrally involve intuition and what is increasingly acknowledged as 'emotional literacy'. In terms of the arguments presented here, I agree entirely with Guilherme (2002: 37) when she maintains that

Being a critical thinker involves more than being rational and emotion is not viewed as an inferior cognitive stage. Emotion is given a key role in CP [Critical Pedagogy] in that it is considered as a fundamental stimulus for cognitive, interpretive, critical and creative reflection-in-action.

The following examples may serve to illustrate and even illuminate this aspect of teaching and learning.

Intertextual activities on the theme of war and peace

A good deal of the creative enjoyment inherent in English teaching and learning lies in the selection of appropriate texts, and in the making of connections between them. In the particular context of the cross-curricular dimension, especially in an increasingly crowded curriculum, there is now a greater need than ever to exercise this skill, and to ensure that as many as possible learning outcomes – to use the officially favoured term – are covered in the process of their teaching. I have used these texts and extracts based on experiences of war in a range of classroom contexts, across a fourteen to eighteen age range, sometimes individually and at other times in various combinations. They are:

- 'Reading Pictures' – three expanding versions of a photograph of a soldier apparently aiming his rifle out of the window of a derelict house, strewn with debris including a headless doll (published by the British Film Institute).

- The lyrics and recorded version of a Richard Thompson song 'How will I ever be simple again?' from his 1986 Polydor album *Daring Adventures*.

- The Henry Treece (n.d.) poem *Conquerors*, which centres on the accumulating guilt and grief of an invading soldier through the succeeding images of a dead bird in an abandoned cage, a starving homeless dog and, finally, a dead child. The poem includes the memorable lines:

  Not one amongst us would have eaten bread

  Before he'd filled the mouth of the grey child

  That sprawled, stiff as stone, before the shattered door.

- A printed and audio-recorded extract from the opening stages of Fergal Keane's 1996 autobiographical *Letter to Daniel*.

The unifying theme of the texts is to do with the relationship between innocence and experience, thus *modelling* a favourite Romantic preoccupation – the innocence represented by facets of childhood, directly or indirectly; and war providing the backdrop: human experience at its most brutal and destructive. There is an interesting range of possible further poems appropriate to this theme, several of which have been anthologised in the collection *Peace and War*, chosen by Harrison and Stuart-Clark (1989). They include W.H. Auden's *Epitaph on a Tyrant*, Stephen Crane's ironic *War is Kind*, Denise Levertov's reflections on Vietnam *What Were They Like?*, Alun Lewis's *All Day it has Rained*, Dennis McHarrie's *Luck*, Wilfred Owen's *Futility* (among several others), Siegfried Sassoon's *Suicide in the Trenches*, William Soutar's *The Children*, and Dylan Thomas's elegiac *A Refusal to Mourn the Death, by Fire, of a Child in London*. The stark contrast between a sense of wonder on the one hand and Owen's 'pity of war' on the other provides a moving tension at the heart of this learning, and features vividly in many of these poems. Of course there are many other texts which could also be tellingly deployed here: letters, artefacts, photographs, paintings, music, journal entries, graffiti – the list is endless, and many are easily available online.

There is clearly a danger that study of such texts as these could give rise to the idea that war, destruction and violence happen only in far off places or in the distant past, and intercultural teaching must acknowledge this. As so often, the way forward, it seems to me, lies in focusing on the tension between emotional empathy – and it is not hard to imagine this elicited by these texts – and critical distance. In asking questions about responsibility for the consequences of human actions, such texts, through their effective teaching, provide a way back into more immediate social reality. It is important too to introduce variety of textual form, if only to show that it is not just the poet who feels the pity. Here, for instance, there are pictures, autobiographical prose, the human voice speaking and singing, a song, and a poem – and each extends possible areas of intertextual literacy. Teaching like this has also to be sensitive to the possible responses of pupils, especially if at the younger end of the age range, to the harrowing scenes evoked – that is part of the fine judgement English (and humanities) teachers, particularly, have often to make.

The possibilities for imaginative teaching arising from these texts, and others like them, are vast in scope. All of the suggestions below have been effective in stimulating critical and creative learning activity; the main point is, however, that confident teachers can adapt and adopt freely from these and their own chosen resources. Often, if the initial enthusiasm is there, the appropriate learning outcomes will follow; or, as Blake had it in his *Proverbs of Hell*, 'No bird soars too high, if he soars on his own wings'. Some activities:

- learning focused on intertextual empathy, experimenting with characters and viewpoints across the texts and genres;

- narrative exploration – using the 'moment' of the text as narrative starting point, or linking the different texts together in a broader narrative;

- a study of war reportage, and specifically how the language used – its inevitable characteristics and conventions – is dialectically and critically linked to meaning;

- thematic work on 'war and peace', using the texts among others as the basis of descriptive or persuasive presentations, articles, displays or collages; and

- discursive explorations of the nature of innocence and experience – not necessarily just as characteristic of children and adults, but as Blake's 'two contrary states of the human soul'.

Teaching *The Diary of Anne Frank*

A further text broadly concerned with the impact of war, *The Diary of Anne Frank* has long been widely read by secondary school age youngsters – perhaps more often as an individually read text than as a class reader, but nevertheless with a distinctive place in the English curriculum. Despite its painfully harrowing subject matter – or possibly to some extent because of it – the evocative yet matter-of-fact, narrative of the trapped Jewish girl in Nazi-occupied wartime Holland speaks intimately across the divide of time, culture and personal experience. Its potential impact is immense, but (as for all these texts) demands sensitivity in teaching; the inspiring 2006 film *Freedom Writers,* based on the true story of a young teacher (convincingly played by Hilary Swank) confronting a hugely challenging class in Long Beach, California, shows just how great the impact could be in terms of democratic education and, particularly, as a stimulus for meaningful reflective writing. Ian Davies's book, *Teaching the Holocaust* (2000) is illuminating for cross-curricular thematic connections – especially, in the present context, McGuinn's chapter on teaching about the Holocaust within English. There is in fact a growing subgenre of literature portraying the Holocaust: fictional texts such as *Friedrich* (Richter 1987) and *The Devil in Vienna* (Orgel 1991), both of which are appropriate to eleven to sixteen year olds, or *Fugitive Pieces* (Michaels 1996), *Captain Corelli's Mandolin* (de Bernières 1998), *The Reader* (Schlink 1997), and *Time's Arrow* (Amis 1991), all of which are suitable for an adult or A level readership. Ian McEwan's picture book, movingly illustrated by Innocenti, *Rose Blanche* (1985), cuts right across the age range here, and adds a further reading dimension in the combination of words with pictures. Effective teaching could focus creatively on cross-genre fertilisation here, comparing, say, our emotional responses to fiction and non-fiction and going on to tease out the differences between them. Under which category, for instance, does *Schindler's*

Ark (Keneally 1982, the basis of the successful film *Schindler's List*) fall? Certainly, highly positive use could be made of the interdisciplinary dimension of the curriculum, and many pupils study the Holocaust primarily through history and religious education lessons. With these considerations in mind, the possibilities for teaching *The Diary of Anne Frank* include:

- Using the 'jigsaw' technique, asking groups of four to research, discuss and report back on the historical context or a particular specified aspect of the *Diary*. Each of the four pupils in the group would be allotted a different area to research or discuss, and would then combine with the equivalent individuals from the other groups fulfilling the same role. Subsequently, each of the original 'home' groups would then reconvene, to hear the findings, and eventually feed into a general class discussion or presentation. Clearly, good teaching for this activity needs to include appropriate resources for the research, using (for example) the Internet, library services, and the potential of other curriculum areas. This general approach may take place usefully before, during or after the reading of the *Diary*.

- A consideration of the genre of diary or journal writing, thus focusing on the *form* of this text in relation to other pertinent examples, including, if appropriate, pupils' own writing. Instances are many and wide-ranging, from the light-hearted, fictional *The Secret Diary of Adrian Mole* and the more recent sequel *Adrian Mole: The Cappuccino Years* (Townsend 1992 and 1999), through the moving account of a teenager growing up in contemporary war-torn Bosnia, *Zlata's Diary: A Child's Life in Sarajevo* (Filipovic 1994), to more traditionally literary works such as Daniel Defoe's *Journal of the Plague Year* or Dorothy Wordsworth's *Journal*. Activities may highlight the comparison of texts in terms of *purpose* and *audience*, both of which are interestingly problematic in this context and could lead to lively discussion.

- Taking ideas on the form of diary writing a little further, teaching could concentrate on the uses many writers have made of the genre within broader works of fiction. Useful examples include several Gothic-influenced classics, such as Shelley's *Frankenstein* (1818)*, Dracula*, or *Wuthering Heights*, and more contemporary publications like *The Color Purple* (Walker 1983) or, specifically for a youthful readership, *Dear Nobody* (Doherty 1991). The consideration of journals as some kind of 'framing device' for narrative could then creatively inform pupils' own writing, conceivably at any level. And, of course, there is the tried and tested (and perhaps overused, for some texts) approach of asking pupils to write the diary of a character featured in whichever fictional work is being studied.

Geographical perspectives

Of the four main humanities subjects (including citizenship), it is arguably geography that has traditionally had the least firm links with English. However, there are signs that this is changing, and fast. Increasing ecological awareness among teachers and pupils across the curriculum, for instance, is strongly pertinent to the National Curriculum, as we have seen, and has particular implications for crossing the divisions between subjects. As Matthewman (2007: 75) points out,

Interdisciplinarity is clearly a strong feature of the ideal of ecocritical practice. This means that there are opportunities for productive cross-curricular work with, for instance, science, geography or citizenship where it is possible to explore the differences in the approaches to subjects. … In the case of the environment, an interdisciplinary approach is also necessary.

Curricular developments relating to geographical perspectives include:

- The realisation that literary criticism may benefit enormously through focus on the context of place and setting, both for text and for author.

- A burgeoning sense of ecological awareness and 'ecocriticism', both through literary study and through thematic and language-based textual activity.

- Awareness of the language of geography as a discipline – not only within the subdiscipline of human geography, but in metaphorical concepts such as maps.

- Developing world issues, and in particular how these are represented through media and other texts.

- Study of travel literature, both current and from the past – including the language of exploration.

Teaching Brian Friel's *Translations*

One text that succinctly but highly effectively deals with several of these themes (and alludes strongly also to historical context) is Brian Friel's play *Translations*. Set in late nineteenth century Ireland, the play imaginatively explores the relationship between language and power through the device of showing how British imperialist ambitions depended on the (apparently innocent) project of remapping the terrain, and in the process (not quite so innocently) renaming Irish localities and (blatantly not innocently at all) quelling any rebellion. My own enthusiasm for teaching this text, apart from its literary and humane qualities, had much to do with a personal fascination for maps – a fascination which to my delight has been shared by some pupils. In exploring the wide-ranging connotations of mapping I am indebted to Jeremy Black's fascinating *Maps and Politics* (2000). There are apposite linguistic connections to be made too: the word 'ordnance', for example, central to the impressive and much-loved Ordnance Survey maps of the UK, literally refers to artillery, and the original aim of these maps was to facilitate the deployment of weaponry. The scope of the play actually goes well beyond these themes (to include cultural identity, education, social mobility and romance across boundaries), but the subject of mapping and its language(s) is fundamental: hence the title. The possibilities for inventive interdisciplinary teaching and learning here seem endless; a selection might include:

Contextualisation: historical/cultural
- brainstorm ideas on and impressions of Ireland, contrasted to England, Wales, Scotland or wherever;
- directed research activities on aspects of Irish culture;
- cross-curricular possibilities – history, geography, RE, languages, music;

- the Irish dramatic tradition – Yeats, Synge, O'Casey, Behan *et al.*;
- investigation of media presentations of Ireland, past and present.

Language and communication

- investigation of the relationship between languages and imperialism;
- language, dialect and cultural/national identity;
- the nature of translation and interpretation – connotations;
- the associations and characteristics of the featured languages (Greek, Latin, Gaelic, English) and, by extension, other languages;
- the significance of naming in a variety of contexts.

Other possibilities

- active exploration through music and oral culture, making use of the plentiful Irish resources available;
- focus on the nature of education and schooling – the relationship between learning, subversion and control;
- exploration of character and stereotype – challenges to stereotypical expectations;
- learning through drama – performance, role play, tableau, etc.;
- nature of maps and mapping – metaphorical significance and ideas of control;
- writing tasks, both empathetic and textually analytical.

Significant here, on reflection, is just how many of these approaches to this particular text embody ideas central to interdisciplinary English teaching in more general terms; this serves to underline the idiosyncratic and wide-ranging nature of the subject.

A geographical sense of place certainly may have the effect of transforming the learning experience for English study. I remember early in my teaching career, having signally failed to inspire my first A level English literature group (a two-year lower school apprenticeship had to be served first, especially as I did not have a straightforward English literature degree) with study of D.H. Lawrence's *Sons and Lovers*, deciding to drive them in the school minibus to Lawrence's hometown Eastwood, the setting of his largely autobiographical first novel. Although little had been made of the biographical association by the good burghers of Eastwood (compared to, say, Brontë or Hardy countries), I had done my homework and was able to guide them around several key sites, including Lawrence's childhood home, with resplendent lilies in the front garden, and a view of 'Miriam's' home. Study of the novel came to life, and the power of location for teaching English has never left me. As a further example of successful practice, we could consider the scheme of study below; it is based on reading both of text and of landscape – and the practised eye does read landscape – devised through the collaboration of English and geography teachers to introduce the topic of Wordsworth and the Lake District landscape to Key Stage 4 pupils.

Wordsworth and the Lakes: a sense of place

Resources:

- large scale, detailed OS map of the Lake District, with contours and shading;

- pictures and photographs of the Lakes – past and present, industrial and agrarian, 'realistic' and 'romanticised';

- extract from biography of Wordsworth, and a selection of portraits;

- NATE *Poetry Pack* DVD (see Appendix) imaginatively focusing on the poem 'Daffodils' and its wider connotations;

- a selection of A.W. Wainwright's careful line drawings (themselves works of art mingling mapping with landscape) and evocative prose descriptions;

- extracts from Wordsworth's autobiographical poem 'The Prelude';

- extracts from Dorothy Wordsworth's *Journal* to match the subject matter of her brother's poems;

- tourist information literature based on the Lakes, from different periods and representing contrasting presentational styles;

- other written or pictorial records, such as newspaper articles, National Park information, Dove Cottage information, planning information;

- extracts from pertinent children's literature (such as Beatrix Potter's tales and Arthur Ransome's *Swallows and Amazons*).

Activities:

- Whole-class work: general discussion on the nature of the resources used, emphasising the different types of 'reading' involved and the contrasting messages conveyed by the various materials. The stress should be on the purpose and context of a range of readings, and on similarities and differences between readers/readings.

- Pairs examine and briefly report back on a particular (chosen) resource in the light of this discussion, with explicit guidelines provided.

- Small-group activity: pairs expand to groups of four or six, and work towards re-presenting information from the chosen resources in a different form, making connections across the different types of material in so doing (for example, magazine article in *Country Living*, or similar in *The Big* Issue, a local community radio programme, a guidebook for a specific readership).

Language teaching: geographical dimensions.

The continuing development of the English language, globally and in the UK, has a great deal also to do with geography, and is worthy of study in this interdisciplinary context. Exploration of regional accents and dialects of the English language, and of other languages represented in the classroom, forms an appropriate starting point here, and could be fruitfully developed through language autobiography activity. The sort of experiences and issues which may arise from such an enterprise could each provide a useful stimulus for further, directed, language investigation, much of which could have a geographical dimension:

- experience of languages other than English, in a vast range of circumstances;
- use of nursery rhymes, games, sayings, proverbs and other examples of the oral language tradition, often locally based;
- discovery of different accents and dialects: social and geographical mobility;
- trends in language – 'in' words, slang and jargon – again, often distinctly local;
- the influence of the media on language, particularly television, popular music and certain radio stations – the spread of 'estuary English', for example, from London;
- the impact of 'formal' language requirements and Standard English – itself originally a local (East Midlands) dialect;
- diverse, often exclusive, even tribal 'private languages'.

The language autobiography, properly introduced and sustained, should give rise to many valuable starting points and resources: collected and presented with sensitivity, here is a wealth of valuable language resources. The guiding principle in all this enterprise must be one of respect for each other's languages, and this is not always easily achieved. Many people feel quite ashamed of their own accent, dialect or command of Standard English and, predictably enough, this sense of shame may all too easily be projected into disparagement of others' languages. If knowledge about language is to achieve anything significant, there must be a concerted effort to confront such issues; the general suggestions for activities listed below are intended to be used in this context, and can of course be adapted and extended for particular purposes:

- interviews with older/younger people about language issues and experiences – particularly concerned with acquisition and development;
- the British Library website (see Appendix) is especially helpful here, having a huge range of apt and imaginatively presented resources available;
- subsequent writing of transcripts from taped interviews as a way of exploring the distinctions between written and spoken (standard) English;
- activities based on past examples of language, including the literary, to investigate language change through such activities as cloze and adaptation;
- activities on accent and dialect, including Standard English itself, to emphasise the distinction between the two, using local and media examples;
- research into and exploration of the (often geographical) connotations of names, including personal names, nicknames, brand names, logos, school names;
- invention of new names along similar lines, perhaps extending into logos, crests, mottoes, names for new soaps or other media products;
- invention of new language systems, codes, sign languages and creoles;
- extension of the language autobiography to include a linguistic family tree and, possibly, maps to place variants of language geographically.

Important here is the realisation that shared good practice is possible and desirable even within the discrete subject-based curriculum underlined by the structure of the National Curriculum, not simply because it gets people working together in a common cause, but also because it concentrates teaching on the range of reading styles to be experienced and developed – taught, in fact – as fundamental to the whole business of learning.

Further English activities relating to geographical perspectives could include:

- Construction of a video clip or photo/text montage of the local area presented either positively or negatively: maybe through a specified choice of genres such as the *Crap Towns* series, contrasted to a glossy tourist brochure aimed at attracting visitors.

- Selection and presentation of a particular artefact that somehow encapsulates and represents a particular area and its geographical context, perhaps relating to literature studied, to give an enhanced sense of place: for example, Frank Meadow Sutcliffe Victorian photographs of Whitby alongside Teresa Tomlinson's novel *Flitherpickers*, set in that area and featuring the photographer as a character in the narrative.

- Ecological perspectives, exploring explicit or implicit environmental points of view based on a range of texts, such as the desert landscape of Louis Sachar's *Holes*, or the blighted urban landscape of Robert Swindells' *Stone Cold*. Another strong possibility along these lines is to explore the representation of animals in a range of poetry – an exploration vividly presented by Sasha Matthewman in her paper 'But what about the fish? Teaching Ted Hughes' *Pike* with environmental bite' (2007).

Religious, spiritual and moral education and English

Clearly, as we have already begun to see, there is much overlap between the humanities subjects, and between them all and a subject like English. English teachers (and for that matter student teachers) are usually enthusiastic and inventively resourceful in finding spiritual, moral, and even religious, aspects in their subject, whether the activities in mind are literature or language based (or, as often occurs, a combination of the two). Many of the practical suggestions so far outlined in this book fall into this category: consider, for example, learning about *The Diary of Anne Frank*, or the Martian's postcard home, or the theme of warfare and its impact. I should like now to look at two further texts that could stimulate study of spiritual, moral and religious aspects of English: the opening of Margaret Mahy's novel *Barnaby's Dead*, and Edgar Allen Poe's short story *The Black Cat*.

Teaching Margaret Mahy's *The Haunting*

From *The Haunting* (Margaret Mahy): Chapter 1: 'Barnaby's Dead'

When, suddenly, on an ordinary Wednesday, it seemed to Barney that the world tilted and ran downhill in all directions, he knew he was about to be haunted again. It had happened when he was younger but he had thought that being haunted was a babyish thing that you grew out of, like crying when you fell over, or not having a bike.

'Remember Barney's imaginary friends, Mantis, Bigbuzz and Ghost?' Claire – his stepmother – sometimes said. 'The garden seems empty now that they've gone. I quite miss them.'

But she was really pleased perhaps because, being so very real to Barney, they had become too real for her to laugh over. Barney had been sorry to lose them, but he wanted Claire to feel comfortable living with him. He could not remember his own mother and Claire had come as a

wonderful surprise, giving him a hug when he came home from school, asking him about his day, telling him about hers, arranging picnics and unexpected parties and helping him with hard homework. It seemed worth losing Mantis, Bigbuzz and Ghost and the other kind phantoms that had been his friends for so many days before Claire came.
Yet here it was beginning again …

This is the opening lesson from a scheme of work based on class reading of the novel in question, and one of the prime purposes was simply to whet pupils' appetites to read on. In this context, fostering the desire to read texts-as-literature may be successfully married to an issues-based approach. These need not be contradictory or mutually exclusive – especially if the spiritual and moral dimension is handled in ways sensitive to the nature of the text itself. My other aim was to introduce pupils to aspects of language used by Mahy in this extract, through guided close reading, especially as they pertain to the themes of spiritual uncertainties and explorations that run through the novel. So, the twin objectives as displayed to the class were:

- To introduce the novel and explore some possible themes;
- To examine closely some aspects of the language used.

The first stage was to split the class into five 'home' groups, as established previously on more or less mixed-ability lines. The 'warm-up' for the first few minutes was simply to look at the book's cover and title and then report back briefly with any ideas or predictions; this worked well enough to open up tentative interpretive possibilities, reinforcing the notion that meaning is fluid and open to suggestion. I myself then read the passage aloud to the group, but did not follow up with any whole-class discussion, despite some enthusiasm for this; I preferred rather to funnel this readiness to talk about the book into the ensuing group work. Thus the next stage was to move into 'jigsaw' mode, a way of learning with which the class was already familiar, resulting in five new groups each comprising one pupil from each of the 'home' groups. Each 'new' group was then given a particular aspect of the text to examine:

- Look at sentence structure, use of tenses, and active/passive voice to see how the author creates a particular effect of bewildered uncertainty.
- Think about who is speaking and what we learn of the speaker – What clues are there? Are there other voices too?
- What is the overall tone of the passage? Think about choice of words, differences in spoken/written English, names.
- Consider how you think this story might continue – what possibilities does the author have so early in the narrative? Are there any clues?
- What do we learn about the characters either present or mentioned? Do we get enough information to really picture any of them at this stage?

Interestingly, with some explanation, all pupils in this mixed-ability class were able to engage fruitfully with the questions posed, and the English teachers present (there were two of us) were able to participate in each group's activity – a form of sensitively guided reading. Either at group discussion or whole-class plenary stages, the sort of points emerging, in the context of the spiritual state of Barnaby, included:

- The possible ambiguity of the title 'Barnaby's Dead', hinging on the two plausible uses of the apostrophe (and incidentally raising questions of authorial intent/'reading meanings into text');

- The relationship between main and subordinate clauses in the first sentence, and how the structure of this sentence reflects and amplifies meaning;

- The dramatic effect of the interrupting (remembered) speech – and the use of speech punctuation and attendant conventions;

- The nature of the 'voice' of the passage: third person narrative, yet first person familiarity and sympathy;

- Variations in use of past tenses and relationship to the imagined 'present';

- The informal, familiar, even perhaps confidential, tone of the passage;

- Textual pointers to future narrative directions, including use of punctuation (…) and key words like 'again';

- Opening of sentences/paragraphs with words like 'But' and 'Yet', flouting traditional grammatical conventions, again suggestive of a certain tone;

- The use of commas for parenthesising words, distinguishing between clauses within sentences, and separating listed items.

As ever, a list like this does scant justice to the quality of discussions and analysis, but it may serve to suggest just how stimulating a lesson can be, focused as it was on a close reading of a literary extract dealing with the spiritual experiences of a young boy. Subsequent lessons were able to open out from this close reading towards more general, often anecdotally based, discussions on apparently supernatural or strangely disturbing spiritual experiences as a prelude to reading the entire novel. There are of course many other novels and short stories, often written explicitly for young people, with spiritual dimensions, often controversial in their content and well worth exploring. The Michael Morpurgo short story *The Giant's Necklace* (in his collection *From Hereabout Hill*, 2007) I find particularly apt here, dealing as it does with death and the possibility of ghosts in a very readable and compelling manner.

Teaching Edgar Allan Poe's *The Black Cat*

This somewhat luridly gothic short story demands careful and sensitive introduction by the teacher, but, given this, it is a fertile text for approaching spiritual, moral and – in the broad sense – religious themes. At only seven pages long, the story probably benefits from a thoroughly prepared 'performance' reading from the teacher, especially as, despite its several advantages, the story poses significant difficulties for pupils in terms of accessibility of language. There are many good reasons for making plans for textual study explicit and clear to pupils from the start. The teacher (and pupils, for that matter) may wish to deviate from the plan, and there should always be scope for improvisation in the English curriculum; if necessary, this sense of flexibility may itself need careful stating, and may involve a degree of negotiation with pupils. A scheme of work for *The Black Cat* for a Year 10 mixed-ability group may look something like this, although the pre-reading activities, for obvious reasons, may be better addressed separately from the main body of the worksheet. Clearly, the English teacher will need to organise the activities appropriately to the needs of a particular group in terms of balance of activity and different ways of learning, and in the context of the overall English curriculum.

Pre-reading activities:

- Pairs/small groups: consider the associations and connotations of the words 'cat' and 'black' in that order, using large sheets of paper to jot down any ideas. Then take the two words together: how do they modify and change each other's meaning? What sort of story might you expect under this title?

- Whole class: report back/display resulting ideas and impressions, focusing through guided discussion on the connotations of key words – especially controversial senses of the word 'black'.

Reading of the story and first impressions:

- Listen carefully to the reading of the story, following closely in your own copy. Did anything surprise you in the plot? How exactly does Poe achieve a sense of suspense and horror, if indeed he does?

- Pairs/small groups: go over the text again, considering the questions above. Note down words and phrases which are difficult to understand, thinking of modern English equivalents for some of these. Would you prefer a 'modern version' by, say, Stephen King?

Further activities:

(Individual, pair, or small-group-based.)

- Develop the last activity further to come up with a series of comprehension questions on the story, which should focus on the areas of language, plot, character or style of writing. These can then be collated and discussed for the whole class, or exchanged with another pair or group for consideration and 'answering'.

- Research and collect into an anthology other texts which relate in some way to *The Black Cat*, including poems and other stories (including, possibly, others by Poe), audio and video materials, and pictures. Be prepared to present your collection to the rest of the group, pointing out how it affects your understanding of the original story.

- Explore the question of point of view in the story, focusing on the narrative voice, its placing in the third person, and the possibility of other viewpoints which remain silent in the story itself. The narrator's wife, for example, may have an interesting story to tell, perhaps in the form of a hidden diary up to the point of her death.

- Other 'empathetic' explorations are possible; for example: the final police report, detailing the investigation and arrest; the narrator's own final statement and confession; the report of the American equivalent of the Cats' Protection League.

- Rewrite the story in the form of a ballad, for which it is very suitable: it has the macabre and supernatural elements, sense of tragic decline and disintegration of love, and an atmosphere of dark sensationalism. In terms of the apparently motiveless taking of life leading to a train of self-destruction, the story may relate to *The Rime of the Ancient Mariner* (see pages 105–7).

- The story also lends itself to other kinds of adaptation, and there are opportunities in the following to choose from: a short film, storyboarded and scripted; an artistic design, possibly for the cover of a new edition, or to advertise this film; a dramatic interpretation, perhaps using mime and music to create the right sort of atmosphere.

- Consider what may have occurred before the start of the story and write a 'prequel', concentrating on the psychology of the central character.

The spiritual contexts of Romanticism

Over the past decade or so, the teaching and learning of English literature has benefited from a much greater emphasis (including in English literature examination specifications) on the contexts: historical, social, critical and spiritual (the focus here) in particular. The problem with these approaches is that there is a tendency towards superficiality, perhaps unsurprisingly given the overcrowded nature of the GCSE and A Level courses. To properly address the contextualisation of literary study, English teachers need, in effect, to adopt an interdisciplinary approach; if, for instance, the texts studied were of the Romantic era or idiom (as they frequently are), the contextual teaching and explorations could be conducted along the lines below, with small groups given the brief of researching the four areas (including the information, exemplified below, given and briefly explained by the teacher) with the aim of presenting their findings to the rest of the class (or compiling a handbook for future students).

- *Definitions:* In a famous and telling phrase the philosopher T.E. Hulme (1883–1917) described Romanticism as 'spilt religion'(cited in Stevens 2004: 28). He intended this in a disparaging sense, and had his own agenda in reacting against what he saw as the excesses of late Romanticism. However, it may well be worth exploring the metaphor of 'spilt religion' a little further, in the hope that it might yield something more positive. Something spilt implies something messy, something not quite in the right place, the result perhaps of some accidental, unjudged movement. Or possibly the result of some new entity displacing – spilling – the original contents. If religion is taken to be one of the positive characteristics of being human, a 'pure' entity, its spillage is something to be avoided. And yet … All these points could be turned on their head, even celebrated, by a Romantic outlook. After all, why should something as (presumably) powerful as the religious impulse be safely contained in some kind of receptacle? At least if one spills something it implies that the substance might actually be used rather than simply kept safely intact. And the spillage itself – might that not also form an attractive pattern? Perhaps there are some helpful pointers here towards a fuller understanding of the spiritual nature and contexts of Romanticism.

- *Historical (spiritual) context:* the period was characterised by intense spiritual confusion and seeking. There was in many ways a mounting challenge to the privileged position of the 'official' Christianity of the Church of England. The growth of rationalism and empiricism – basing all ideas on tangible evidence – during the Enlightenment had doubtless led to a devaluation of religious experience in any immediate sense. The vast majority of educated people in the mid-eighteenth century broadly accepted Christian beliefs and morality but saw little reason to go beyond this. Romanticism challenged this conventional stability through its restoration of spiritual experience to the centre of human concerns. Literature assumed a special place in this process and it tended to fill the vacuum left by the decline of orthodox belief, and simultaneously to appropriate some of the language and symbolic systems of religion. Romantic literature, as with other art forms, was frequently intimately confessional, in a strongly autobiographical sense, emphasising the uniqueness of individual experience through the use of the imagination. In this respect, art itself, in the broadest sense, became the means to an end of spiritual fulfilment in a way that was totally unprecedented.

- *Imagination:* the key word here. Writers such as Blake and Coleridge saw the imagination as the visionary faculty, enabling spiritual insight into ultimate truth – and creative art was the imagination truly at work (and play). Blake referred to 'the true vine of eternity, the human imagination' (in Blake 1995). In this conception, the images and symbols are provided by nature, and are often steeped in implied religious meaning accrued over the ages, but are transformed by the imagination. Blake acknowledged that 'it is impossible to think without images of somewhat on earth' (in Blake 1995), but these images become powerfully and meaningfully human only when they enter consciousness. Coleridge echoed these sentiments in his *Biographia Literaria* (1817), speaking of 'the primary IMAGINATION' as 'the living Power and prime Agent of all human Perception ... a repetition in the finite mind of the eternal act of creation in the infinite I AM' (Watson 1975). The religious connotations could scarcely be clearer.

- *Different Romantic approaches:* although there was a great deal of common ground in the spirituality of the Romantics, there were too many important differences. Blake and Coleridge illustrate these differences for all their similar ideas on the nature of the imagination. Blake remained a Christian throughout his life, but a highly unorthodox one, seeing Christ as an embodiment of the imagination rebelling against any imposed external authority. In his very unorthodoxy Blake was very much part of the dissenting tradition in British Christianity, emphasising the authority of personal vision as opposed to the social structures of any established church. Coleridge, on the other hand, left his radical version of Christianity behind as he grew older. There is a sense in which his life and work reflected an inner struggle between radical spirituality and orthodox Christian belief – and in this he typified many others of his day. In 'The Eeolian Harp' of 1795, for example, he characterises his wife, Sara, as reproving him for wandering – wondering, even – too far from conventional codes of belief:

      But thy more serious eye a mild reproof
      Darts, O beloved Woman! nor such thoughts
      Dim and unhallow'd dost thou not reject
      And biddest me walk humbly with my God.
      Meek Daughter in the family of Christ!

- By 1817, in his second 'Lay Sermon' Coleridge was espousing a much more conservative view of the role of religion, as a bulwark of the state through the established Church of England: 'To the feudal system we owe the *forms*, to the Church the *substance* of our liberty' (in Coleridge 1977). Wordsworth and others took similar paths towards conservatism, whilst others still – particularly the next generation of Romantics, Shelley, Keats and Byron among them – explored ever more radical spiritual paths including outright atheism and paganism.

As I hope I have demonstrated throughout this chapter, there are close and (mutually) beneficial connections to be made between English and the humanities in a cross-curricular contest. Much of the emphasis here has been on literature and the various themes and issues that stem from different readings. We must, however, at the same time be aware of the dangers in swamping the enjoyment of a good read of an entertaining book through overkill of approaches, however imaginatively creative. The poet U.A. Fanthorpe, herself at one time an English teacher, issues us a timely warning here. In her poem *Dear Mr Lee* (Fanthorpe n.d.)she speaks with the voice of young pupil studying Laurie Lee's *Cider with Rosie*, a standard inclusion in any secondary school English department stock cupboard:

So Dear Laurie, I want to say sorry.
I didn't want to write a character sketch
of your mother under headings, it seemed
wrong somehow when you'd made her so lovely …
… I'd just like to be like you, not mind about being poor,
See everything bright and strange …

Cross-curricular approaches: English and the arts

Contextual background

John Dewey, a seminally important educational thinker, gives us a sense of artistic endeavour as a state of alertness to present reality, in a way that makes a neat contrast to the humanities' (justifiable) concerns with past and future, and points to yet another facet of interdisciplinary English:

> Only when the past ceases to trouble and anticipations of the future are not perturbing is a being wholly united with his environment and therefore fully alive. Art celebrates with particular intensity the moments in which the past reinforces the present and in which the future is a quickening of what now is.
>
> (Dewey 1934: 18)

We have already seen (especially in Chapter 2) just how important the arts context has been, and continues to be, for the development of the subject English. Throughout my own professional experience I have always considered English to be, fundamentally, an arts-based subject, and I feel this all the more strongly in the context of the interdisciplinary turn we are commending here. Peter Abbs's book *English within the Arts: A radical alternative for English and the arts in the curriculum* (1982), whose title proclaims its mission clearly, was one of the first books about English teaching to make a real impact on my vision of the subject and on my professional practice. As Abbs announces from the start of this book,

> [M]y main intention will be to argue for a concept of English as a literary expressive discipline, a discipline whose deepest affinities lie … with the arts or what I prefer to call, at least in the context of the curriculum, the expressive disciplines. One of the most important claims I will make is that English should now form strong philosophical, practical and political alliances with the undervalued disciplines of art, dance, drama, music and film.
>
> (Abbs 1982: 7)

Abbs goes on to bemoan the condition of the arts in the secondary curriculum:

> Although one could document many fine exceptions, the expressive disciplines in our schools are in a state of confusion, neglect, poverty, demoralisation and absurd fragmentation. The expressive disciplines lie on the very periphery of the curriculum ...
>
> (ibid.)

He argues that the alliances he recommends would have a mutually beneficial effect on both English and the arts: philosophically and practically enlivening the former, and giving the latter curricular enhanced credibility. In many ways matters have improved over the two decades since Abbs wrote these words, but (in my view) this improvement has been patchy, and in some schools the situation is very much as described here. Abbs was himself building on the work of Dewey, for whom the arts were central to any human experience and as such profoundly educational:

> We are carried out beyond ourselves to find ourselves ... the work of art serves to deepen and to raise to great clarity that sense of an enveloping undefined whole that accompanies every normal experience. This whole is then felt as an expansion of ourselves.
>
> (Dewey 1934: 195)

This is all grist to the mill of cross-curricular pedagogical development, of course, although (as has been signalled elsewhere in this book) it is important that any conception of English as an arts subject, with which I still broadly agree, must be inclusive of other disciplinary approaches and not fundamentally exclusive. There are also complex and sometimes thorny issues involved in any arts education – many to do with areas I have already touched on, such as notions of culture and ownership. Sometimes the needs of artistic endeavour have a problematic relationship with humanitarian ideals – 'was the Parthenon worth the sufferings of a single slave? Is it possible to write poetry after Auschwitz?' asked Herbert Marcuse (1969: 50) – and these too require careful consideration in an interdisciplinary spirit.

My own schoolteaching years were punctuated with attempted links with art, music and drama colleagues – some, it must be said, more successful than others – and attempts to ensure English teaching and learning are focused on premises of artistic validity and creative principles. One of my first acts as a newly in post Head of English was to spend some of the precious capitation fund I was suddenly responsible for on a set of musical keyboards to facilitate creative classroom activity – to the consternation of some of my erstwhile colleagues, who were only ever partially converted to the arts cause. As I hope to show in this chapter, I have used music, art and drama in a variety of English teaching contexts, and have continued to develop this aspect of my professional work since entering the world of teacher education. Like many colleagues, I have an intense interest in and enthusiasm for music, art and drama (including film of course), and these personal predilections have certainly informed my teaching of that most personal of subjects, English; in this I am helped further by my family, including my art-teaching daughter, my son, an accomplished musician, and my wife, who is a practising abstract artist: I am indebted to all three for some of the ideas that I hope will emerge in the chapter.

Musical matters

Music, it seems to me, has a huge advantage over just about every other curriculum subject: everyone appears to like music in some form or another (or at least I have yet to meet the person who would be an exception to this observation). Insofar as good teaching is about making creative, potentially fruitful connections with learners, this is a huge advantage – and I could not say the same for other art forms, poetry, for example, or landscape painting, or ballet. As Mickey Hart of the Grateful Dead observed (1999), music is

> a reflection of our dreams, our lives, and it represents every fibre of our being. It's an aural landscape, a language of our deepest emotions; it's what we sound like as 'people'.

Language itself is the bedrock of the English curriculum, and has many links with music. For example, it has been convincingly theorised that a predisposition among humans to use language, at least in its spoken form, could be called an instinct, a natural process; Pinker, for example (1994: 18) (after Chomsky) has argued thus:

> Language is not a cultural artefact that we learn the way we learn to tell time or how the federal government works. Instead it is a distinct piece of the biological makeup of our brains. Language is a complex, specialised skill, which develops in the child spontaneously, without conscious effort or formal instruction, is deployed without awareness of its underlying logic, is qualitatively the same in every individual, and is distinct from more general abilities to process information or behave intelligently.

And for music, the instinct may be even more basic: recent research suggests that even in the womb infants are attracted to rhythm and melody, with the possible corollary that language follows on at a later stage. Clearly there are many rhythmic and sound-based similarities between music and language, and some of the activities and approaches I mention below seek to exploit this connection resourcefully. However, by the same token as everybody appears to like some music in some circumstances – which we could take as a humanely unifying principle – taste in music may also divide people (especially during adolescence, when musical taste tends to be synonymous with personal and group identities) and needs sensitive handling in the classroom. I offer below some of the ways into interdisciplinary English and music activity that I have been involved in.

Music in the English classroom: some examples:

- Use of musical instruments to illustrate/emphasise punctuation and rhythmic structure in language (especially poetry).
- *Desert Island Discs* format for characters in fictional texts, or as a free-standing speaking and listening activity.
- Setting the mood for narrative – either reading or writing (for example, setting the opening of a class novel to music, or asking pupils to do the same for key passages).
- Cultural evocation (especially other cultures and periods) through music.
- Further ways into literature; for instance, Braithwaite's poem *Limbo* with percussion; Shakespeare mimed to music through a silent film format.

- Theme music for each character in a studied text – perhaps reminiscent of *Peter and the Wolf*.

- Sound effects leading to characterisation – for example, *War of the Worlds* soundtrack.

- Links between chanting and poetry – in *Romeo and Juliet* the Montagues vs Capulets; the power of chant as in football matches, political/religious gatherings, or as presented disturbingly in Golding's *Lord of the Flies*.

- Further links between poetry and music – internalising a poem through setting to music (for instance, Blake's poems interpreted through Tavener's music, or the CD compilation of W.B. Yeats poems set to music by various musicians.

- Media work – analysis of pop videos, for example (including Dylan's *Subterranean Homesick Blues*).

- Linking the arts – maybe Tennyson's poem *Mariana* alongside Millais' pre-Raphaelite painting, and Barber's *Adagio*.

The Power of the ballad

In many ways the ballad form illustrates powerfully that primordial fusion of words and music so basic to human experience. The earliest ballads predated mass literacy, and later examples – particularly the 'broadside ballads' appealed to a semi-literate population eager to hear sensational news or fictional tales. Many fuse timeless human emotions and experiences – love, jealousy, injury, death, pleasures – with supernatural dimensions, and with skilful teaching can be very effective in the contemporary classroom. Will Hodgkinson, in his illuminating and entertaining survey of music-making in modern Britain, entitled, appropriately enough, *The Ballad of Britain*, claims that there has been in the last few years something of a renaissance of music-making, reclaiming traditional ground (although often in most untraditional forms) after a twentieth century dearth. Thus Hodgkinson's subtitle, *How music captured the soul of a nation,* hints as much at a narrative as at a journalistic report:

> A hundred years ago, Britain was alive with song. … As much as language itself, music was an inevitable form of communication and expression. … Then something happened. With the growth of the music industry in the 20th century, a myth built up that music was something best left to the professionals. … the average Briton accepted they were rubbish at singing, as they were at most things in life, and simply stopped doing it. … This had to change. Roughly since the dawn of the new millennium, British culture has been heading towards a more organic, anarchic, localised state. … Now it is happening with music. Once more, landscape and folklore are shaping the songs that we sing.
>
> (Hodgkinson 2009: 1)

It is possible, I think, for creative teaching to harness this spirit. Another great advantage of the ballad as a teaching resource is its huge potential to generate imaginative and appropriate learning activities. When the first version of the National Curriculum arrived in the late 1980s, English departments were charged with adapting and (inevitably) changing their curricula to fit the meticulously detailed requirements. In most cases this was a huge departure from the flexible ways of working we had been used to (and of course later versions of the National Curriculum for English were far less detailed). As a newly appointed Head of English in Essex, I and colleagues gathered in a hastily convened conference to share ideas as to how we could adapt our schemes of work (when we had any, that is) creatively, and I remember presenting a series of teaching ideas clustered around the traditional ballad *Little Musgrave*, attempting to show how with a little ingenuity many of the newly formed attainment targets could be met on the basis of limited resources. In the twenty years since then I have myself adapted this work several times for different learning contexts, but the fundamentals possibilities remain as follows.

Teaching the ballad 'Little Musgrave'

Resources might include recorded versions of the following:

- 'Little Musgrave' or the variant 'Matty Groves' (plenty of versions available, by Nic Jones, Planxty (my favourite), Fairport Convention or Martin Simpson).
- Printed version of 'Little Musgrave'.
- Other ballads, such as 'Rosie Anderson' (Dave Burland), 'The House of the Rising Sun' (The Animals or Joan Baez), 'Dark Streets of London' (The Pogues), 'The Dark Eyed Sailor' (June Tabor, Steeleye Span or Kate Risby).

Possible activities:
- Drama: group-based interpretations of ballads for dramatic performance.
- Reading aloud, rehearsed, in pairs to the rest of the class.
- Arranging a coherent sequence from jumbled verse order as poetry.
- Discussion of and research into the importance of oral tradition, including modern equivalents of tales, urban myths, jokes, rhymes.
- Presentation through posters, book illustrations, comic strips, music.
- Writing a ballad version of a modern story based on press cuttings.
- Writing a modern prose version (such as a tabloid newspaper article) of a traditional ballad.
- Writing based on characters and plots in ballads.
- Broader issues and extension work may include, through research, drama and discussion: study of dreams and the supernatural, the nature of the experiences often sensationally highlighted in ballads, the social and historical context of myths, the subsequent decline of the ballad form, and cross-curricular possibilities.

My most recent teaching experience of ballads focused also on the geographical location of the border ballad 'Little Musgrave', set, evocatively, amidst the dramatic scenery between Barnard Castle and Penrith – an area known to several of the (Year 9) students in the class. We started the sequence of six one-hour lessons with listening to the excellent version of the ballad played by the Irish traditional band Planxty (from their album *The Woman I Loved So Well*), whilst reading the lyrics – musically it appealed only to a small minority of the class, but on the other hand it served to bring the tale to life. Poetry, for me, is the form of language that most approximates to music, not least in its potential for emotional impact; as Abbs shows (2003: 113),

> The music of poetry has the power to free language from its general bureaucratic servitude to literal meaning, and one dimensional denotation. It opens language to the innate creativity of the speculative and questing mind and makes it a prime agent of exploration.

Subsequent discussion certainly elicited some interestingly exploratory perceptions about the narrative, its structure, the music itself (surprisingly, to me, actually liked by several), and the nature of the characters involved, focusing on the way the story progresses through shifting viewpoints and dramatic turns, and the key themes of jealousy, lust, betrayal and loyalty. We talked also about the oral tradition of which the ballad was originally part, and some of the pupils related contemporary parallels such as urban myths and jokes. The small-group-based task arising from the preliminary study was either to transfer the essentials of the *Little Musgrave* tale to the context of an episode from a modern soap, or to take a contemporary newspaper story and retell as a ballad, if possible using music as accompaniment. For example, three girls, struck by press stories centring on the Minogue sisters, began their ballad:

> Two sisters there lived, side by side,
> And one was fair, the other was dark.
> The eldest had it all, but fate would decide,
> Cancer and disease left their terrible mark.

I was struck by the results of these activities, not least by the creative energies that went into them, and by the concern for accuracies of form as a disciplined vehicle for expression.

Teaching Coleridge's *The Rime of the Ancient Mariner*

The Rime of the Ancient Mariner (1797–8: see Wordsworth and Coleridge 1967) is interesting and appropriate to teach on several counts. Significantly, it provides a ready opportunity to exemplify and teach about the historical context of the English literary 'heritage', although its study does not of course preclude a questioning of the nature and composition of such a 'heritage' – indeed, it may occasion it. In the light of any introductory discussion on the nature of poetry, there may also be a further opportunity to look at Coleridge's own views on the relationship between poetic form and content in the context of his philosophy of organic growth. As a prompt note to an 1812 lecture, he wrote

> The Spirit of Poetry like all other living Powers, must of necessity circumscribe itself by Rules, were it only to unite Power with Beauty. It must embody in order to reveal itself; but a living body is of necessity an organized one – & what is organization but the connection of Parts to the whole, so that each Part is at once End and Means! This is no discovery of criticism – it is a necessity of the human mind – and all nations have felt and obeyed it, in the invention of metre, & measured Sounds, as the vehicle and Involucrum of Poetry itself, a fellow growth from the same Life, even as the Bark is to a living Tree.
> (from Coleridge's Literary Lectures, in Holmes 1998: 321).

This passage deserves, and would repay, careful study in itself – quite something for a mere prompt note. Its insights, formulated a considerable time after the writing of *The Ancient Mariner*, seem particularly apposite to the teaching of this poem in an arts context, and these are the connections I should like to emphasise in any scheme of study, making good use of some of the following areas and general principles:

- The poem's appeal is on several levels, and successful teaching can occur from early primary school days to A level – certainly at Key Stages 3 or 4. Presentation of the poem in a form suitable for young children, for example, could draw on this wide appeal.

- It is a fine vehicle for teaching about poetic terms and techniques, not least because Coleridge himself adopted and adapted the archaic ballad form, and, as we have just seen, was acutely conscious of the fusion of form and content in verse.

- For similar reasons, the poem lends itself to exploration of language change over time, with the possibility of contemporary versions and equivalent voyages of discovery, using, for example, the genre of science fiction.

- The imagery is vividly pictorial, and there are useful resources to emphasise this, such as the illustrative engravings by Gustav Doré and Mervyn Peake. The opportunities to illustrate, display, and adapt for various media are endless.

- The poem provides ready opportunities for lively 'performance readings' and dramatic interpretations, including mime, thought tracking, and tableaux.

- It may also lead on to a consideration of the oral tradition, such as the nature of traditional ballads and possible modern equivalents like 'urban myths' and jokes.

- Following this point, the similarities between poetry and music may be further explored through listening, and through musical performance, with scope for bringing in traditional and contemporary ballads (and, of course, Iron Maiden's version of *The Rime* which has a certain appeal).

- Empathetic writing may usefully arise, exploring, for instance, the viewpoint of the hapless Wedding Guest or other stranger creatures and presences who populate the poem.

- The story of the poem's original context, including its place in the *Lyrical Ballads* with the famous *Preface* dealing with poetic language and purpose, and the nature of Coleridge's imagination, opium fed or otherwise, offers fertile ground for the cultural contextualisation of literature – now an important feature of GCSE and A level syllabus requirements.

In my own relatively recent teaching experience, I used an exploration of ballads, described above, as a prelude to study of *The Rime*. Following the impressive presentations based on *Little Musgrave*, we went straight into a reading of *The Rime of the Ancient Mariner* – a reading I performed as well as I could; despite its length, the power of the narrative held their attention effectively. In the subsequent lesson, I took the opportunity to relate something of the biographical background to Coleridge's writing of *The Rime*, using as a basis a brief clip from the film *Pandemonium*, rather contentiously (and some would say with scant regard for historical accuracy – but then maybe poetic licence is a strength in this respect). Thus emphasis on historical and biographical contexts, which may at first sight appear to be something of a hindrance to successful literature teaching of any sort, may be used fruitfully to actually increase the imaginative possibilities for teaching older literature: often, Romantic poets lived lives far more captivatingly interesting than notorious celebrities of today, and their stories are well worth telling vividly.

The imagery of the poem is also vividly pictorial, and there are useful resources to emphasise this, such as the powerful illustrative engravings by Gustav Doré and Mervyn Peake – often nightmarishly extending interpretive possibilities inherent in the verse itself. Pertinent here, too, is the musicality of the poem, and there is vast potential to use live or recorded music to enliven and broaden the scope of these activities. The opportunities to illustrate, display and adapt for various media are endless, and this provided the basis of the whole-class activity further exploring the poem, culminating in a classroom display juxtaposing images by Doré and Peake with the pupils' own artistic renditions of key scenes (with the relevant quotations) from the narrative and appropriate music playing. As well as this whole-class presentation, students in small groups had the choice of a range of shorter-term adaptations, and we found that the poem provides ready opportunities for lively 'performance readings' and dramatic interpretations, including use of music, mime, thought tracking, exploration, hot-seating, tableaux and of alternative viewpoints (especially that of the Wedding Guest). The last of these possible exploratory activities gave rise in turn to an extended piece of empathetic writing. Giving something of the flavour typical of these students' compositions, one boy started his writing:

I know he's old and desperate, and he deserves pity, but he stinks and I'm
missing my best mate's wedding. Why can't I just leave?

Several of the mixed-ability group involved in this project felt distinctly challenged by these activities, but in the end were able to rise to the challenges – and I do feel that this is largely because of the arts context of the work, enabling different students to shine in different – and perhaps differentiated – ways. After all, as Steiner says, 'teaching should focus just above the pupil's reach, rousing in him or her effort and will' (Steiner 2003: 107).

The Romantic context of music

It is, I think, no accident that many of the artists and thinkers I have cited in this chapter could be broadly termed Romantics; the advent of Romanticism two centuries and more ago signalled a spirit of creativity across human activity, with the emphasis very much on connections between the arts. The interdisciplinary venture at the heart of the present series could indeed be seen a centrally Romantic project – especially as pertains to the arts. As we saw in the outline of the spiritual, moral and religious contexts of literature teaching, this sense of history is vitally important, and the following brief summary attempts to do the same for the impact of music in context.

The Romantics tended to see value in play – and in an important sense the arts could be seen as the adult version of play. As such, strict formal boundaries within the various art forms and between them tended to be eroded – another instance of the reaction to what was increasingly perceived as narrow Classicism. The merging of and interplay between the arts was increasingly widespread, and seen as a positive virtue. The power of music began to be recognised as somehow purer, less mediated and adulterated, than other art forms during the Romantic era. Musicians and composers themselves began to throw off the yoke of servitude and aristocratic patronage (they had been little more than liveried servants for centuries) in favour of greater artistic, professional and personal autonomy – although this was certainly not a straightforward development without painful struggle and, all too often, abject poverty.

Even a cursory look at what some contemporaries said about the power of music serves to underline its growing significance. Schiller pronounced the validity of other art forms, pictorial and textual, as relative to the power of music: 'the plastic arts, at their most perfect, must become music. ... Poetry, when most fully developed, must grip us as powerfully as music does' (from *On the Aesthetic Education of Man* 1795: 155). The composer and musical critic Ernst Hoffman (1776–1822) echoed these sentiments in his appraisal of the music of Beethoven (1810); for him it 'sets in motion the lever of fear, of awe, of horror, of suffering, and awakens that infinite longing which is the essence of Romanticism' (cited in Stevens 2004: 36).

Beethoven (1770–1827) himself was keenly conscious of the nature of his genius, seeing his musical powers as a gift – if sometimes a rather malign one – from a divine source. He was reported in 1810 to have told Elizabeth Brentano, a beautiful and cultured admirer, that

> when I open my eyes I must sigh, for what I see is contrary to my religion, and I must despise the world which does not know that music is a higher revelation than all wisdom and philosophy, the wine which inspires one to new generative processes, and I am the Bacchus who presses out the glorious wine for mankind and makes them spiritually drunken. ... Music is the one incorporeal entrance into the higher world of knowledge which comprehends mankind but which mankind cannot comprehend.
>
> (ibid.)

The reliability of this witness has been questioned, and when Beethoven saw her record of the conversation he exclaimed, 'Did I say that? Well, then I had a raptus!' (ibid.). In a sense, of course, it does not matter whether he said these words or not; the sentiments typify the gathering Romantic attitudes to music and the spiritual among both musicians and their audiences. For Beethoven, music was a direct representation of spiritual feeling, and that was its whole point; writing, on the other hand, caused him often to stumble incoherently: apologising for a delay in answering a letter from a friend, he wrote, 'I often compose the answer in my mind, but when I wish to write it down, I usually throw the pen away, because I cannot write as I feel' (ibid.). The German composer Felix Mendelssohn (1809–1847) developed this crucial distinction between writing and music:

> What any music *I* like expresses for me is not *thoughts too indefinite* to clothe in words, but *too definite*. – If you asked me what I thought on the occasion in question, I say, the song itself precisely as it stands. And if, in this or that instance, I had in my mind a definite word or definite words, I would not utter them to a soul, because words do not mean for one person what they mean for another; because the song alone can say to one, can awake in him, the same feelings it can in another – feelings, however, not to be expressed by the same words.
>
> (Stevens 2004: 37)

Interesting, if controversial, here is the sense of music as being more explicit in conveying meaning than text – an explicitness that could lead directly to a sense of a community of feeling rather more easily than with text. Reading, after all, must remain a rather private activity. The statement also links interestingly with Romantic ideas about the education of feeling, in the sense I have previously alluded to that music seems to predate verbal language in its appeal to the senses of infants. For the Romantics music rarely stood alone: in many ways it is the cross-fertilisation of art forms and genres that was most significant in the development of the Romantic aesthetic sense. Thus, poetry, with its strong rhythmic sense and relatively smooth transformation into melody, was celebrated as the textual form above others, and the most akin to music.

Music journalism

Perhaps it is time now to come back to earth – or at least that earth inhabited by most of the pupils in an average English classroom.

From *Total Guitar* (March 2002 edition)

> Dublin 1997. After getting their teenage kicks from early-period Manics, Siamese Dream era Pumpkins and just, like, all of Nirvana, Mark Graeney (guitar, Buckley-inspired vocals), Hillary Woods (bass and total babe) plus Fergal Matthews (drums, joined the band because Mark 'had a jacket that was really nice') decided to form their own band. 'You shoulda been there' gigs soon followed and by August 2000 their self-titled debut was out: angsty Nirvana-isms colliding with a guitar sound that conjured up the spirit of early Manic Street Preachers and Joy Division.
>
> Greeney … is definitely in the 'less is more' school of guitar playing. But that's certainly not a polite way of saying he's a slouch in the guitar department: his richly evocative guitar harmonies on I to Sky weave a web of melodies that help bring to life the spiritual themes of the album's lyrics. Now, how cool is that?

I looked at this text with a Year 9 English class, in the context of exploring the genre and its implied characteristics, leading to the pupils themselves experimenting with writing some similarly lucid, knowing, somewhat ironic pieces about music (or other broadly cultural artefacts – but they all chose music) that they themselves liked. I was concerned principally with how media texts influence and are influenced by readers – in other words the kind of intimate complicity implied in writing of this kind. Each group was able to report back on all of these areas, presenting interesting insights gained through their own cultural literacy in an area I certainly knew very little about. I too was becoming more literate, as I freely acknowledge. We developed the themes through writing, exploring pupils' ability to write for a range of audiences and purposes through adapting the creative and aesthetic features of language they found in non-literary texts. Their ensuing journalistic pieces were certainly often sharply amusing, but also informative and occasionally affective. In a subsequent lesson each group presented their piece of writing aloud, having first played a section of the music they had chosen as their particular focus. Subsequent discussion centred on the nature of the cultural artefact of rock/pop music, its attempted manipulation by commercial interests, and its continuing ability apparently to escape such interests.

Art and English: pictures and words

For the vast majority of young children, picture books prefigure purely written texts, and the attraction of seeing pictures mingling with words – in a huge and ever-expanding series of contexts – I suspect never leaves us. As one of the most celebrated figures from these childhood picture books, Alice, protests: '… and what is the use of a book … without pictures …'. William Blake, for one, realised the compelling power of the combination, and throughout his huge *oeuvre* words and pictures assume equal status. Apart from Alice, many of the most influential commentators on arts education and the place of English within this field, including several we have already encountered in this book, have been primarily concerned with the teaching and learning of art itself. Herbert Read, Peter Abbs and Elliot Eisner, to name but three, fall into this category.

Ways of exploring John Berger's *Ways of Seeing*

Another key commentator from this stable is John Berger, whose *Ways of Seeing* (1972), a series of pertinently illustrated essays on the nature of our perceptions of the world we inhabit, has been influential in a broad cultural context, with pictures and words juxtaposed creatively throughout. Berger introduces his argument forcefully, and pertinently:

> Seeing comes before words. The child looks and recognises before it can speak. But there is also another sense in which seeing comes before words. It is seeing which establishes our place in the surrounding world; we explain that world with words, but words can never undo the fact that we are surrounded by it.
>
> (Berger 1972: 7)

Perhaps this statement is a little disingenuous: after all it takes words to explain this position. Certainly it is deliberately provocative, and, in an educational context, can stimulate productive discussion and active work on the potentially interdisciplinary relationships between art and English. For this reason, among others (it is after all a most entertaining read) *Ways of Seeing* is well worth studying in the English classroom. It is perhaps more suitable for KS4 or post-sixteen students conceivably following media studies or communications or even art courses as well as those centring on English literature or language, and as such its potential strength may well lie in its multi-faceted possibilities. The essays go on to elaborate on Berger's main idea, the centrality of image, using examples from traditional and modern art, and from the mass media. In the sense that this text echoes Blake's words 'As a man is, so he sees' (Letter to Rev. Trusler, 1799), it is part of a continuing debate concerning the relations between subjective and objective, and that debate often centres on the place of language – even if dismissive of its pre-eminence. In this general context, students could be asked to carry out a range of creative tasks, such as:

- seeking and presenting materials to illustrate the arguments of specific sections of the book, particularly drawing on knowledge and understanding of the media;
- creating collages of pictorial images to surround and exemplify carefully chosen quotations from the text;

- writing a reasoned reply – illustrated if possible – to one or more of the more contentious arguments featured;

- writing the parallel script – either expository or for the three purely pictorial essays in the book which are 'intended to raise as many questions as the verbal essays';

- creating the storyboard and script of a television version of the book, bearing in mind that it was originally conceived as the accompaniment to a BBC TV series of the same name.

Art and poetry: William Blake

As I hope has already been apparent, there are many fertile links between the two art forms, many of which are demonstrated in Michael and Peter Benton's series (as previously cited): the combination of Breughel's painting *Landscape with the Fall of Icarus* and W.H. Auden's poem, *Musée des Beaux Arts* (in Benton and Benton 1990), originally prompted by that painting, for example, is an excellent way into intertextual exploration. I have also alluded several times to the work of William Blake, notable especially for his juxtaposition of illustration and poetic text, as this brief scheme of work description shows (with reference also to musical connections).

The context for this series of activities is the AS English Language and Literature course, within which Year 12 (sixteen to seventeen year olds) activity focused on a selection of William Blake's *Songs of Innocence and of Experience* and involved a combination of art and language forms in approaching, interpreting and presenting the verse. I was concerned that notions of creative understandings and interpretations of poetry become part of the conscious repertoire of students, building on Cliff Hodges' argument that

> it is important for teachers to make their implicit understandings explicit precisely so that students can *learn* from them, not just *copy* them. To develop this aptitude, teachers need opportunities to discuss and reflect on creativity and talk about why and how students' achievements are creative.
>
> (2005: 53)

With this in mind, and forming an important part of the preliminary discussions with the group, the initial phase involved simply the informal exploration of a range of resources focused on Blake: some of the poems from *Songs of Innocence and of Experience*; on separate sheets, Blake's accompanying illustrations; some of his other paintings and prints; some postcards of London scenes roughly contemporaneous with Blake alongside modern equivalents, including some of the areas he lived in; a few of Blake's more provocative aphorisms from *The Marriage of Heaven and Hell* and elsewhere; and other artefacts touching explicitly or implicitly on Blake (including Van Morrison's *If the Slave* … and John Tavener's versions of *The Tiger* and *The Lamb* on CD, a video of Alan Ginsberg singing *The Tiger* to a harmonium accompaniment, and a recording of the traditional folk song *The Fair Maid of Islington*, alongside two more contemporary songs centred on the experience of living 'on the edge' in London – Ralph McTell's *The Streets of London* and Richard Thompson's *Sights and Sounds of London Town*. The diversity of art and language forms – text, music and pictorial arts – seemed fitting for Blake's own talents and interests (apart from writing, engraving and painting, he also apparently sang many of the *Songs of Innocence and of Experience* to a selected audience). My intention for this lesson was simply to stimulate work in small groups to collect and subsequently re-present a selection of the available resources according to taste, without attempting to analyse or evaluate the results too deeply. The results, as I had hoped, were lively – even liberating – in the imaginative resourcefulness shown by the students. They succeeded in using the images and artefacts – and each other – to spark off ideas and perceptions, and the activity certainly served its purpose in whetting the appetite for more of Blake.

A major part of my objective here was to focus on London as context (thus also involving a geographical dimension), developing towards a detailed appraisal of Blake's poem *London* and the sharply delivered social criticism so much embedded in this poem. Working collaboratively, we spent two further lessons exploring in more critical detail some of the resources listed above. Apart from these resources, I am particularly indebted to three further publications as inspiration for this teaching – and it's important in these days of strategies and dictated curricula that we as teachers discover creative inspiration too, especially if we are to present a model of inventive, interdisciplinary resourcefulness to our students: Peter Ackroyd's excellent biographies *Blake* (1995) and *London: the Biography* (2000), and Peter Whitfield's fascinating, copiously illustrated *London: A Life in Maps* (2006). I was also interested in further developing some of the teaching ideas I had first presented in an edited edition of some of Blake's writings, *William Blake: Selected Works* (Blake 1995), and I made available a copy of Tracey Chevalier's *Burning Bright*, an enjoyable novel set in late eighteenth century London and featuring William Blake himself as a significant character. I was unaware of this at the time, but the British Library (see Resources section for website) also has a wealth of appropriate resources available. Two particular learning emphases were, first, on the relationship between Blake's poems and the forms, rhythms and content of traditional song, and, second, the evocative sense of place – in this instance, London in flux. In practical teaching terms, the culmination of the activity was an afternoon of presentations to those Year 11 students (fifteen to sixteen year olds) who had finished their GCSE examinations and were seriously considering studying A Level English Literature in Year 12 – a part of the week-long induction set up by the school for their benefit.

The eventual presentations were telling in their combination of critical insight and analysis on the one hand, and enthusiastic celebration on the other. I chose to concentrate especially on *London* as the culmination of our study, as it seems particularly apt, both for my own reflections on the relevance of Blake to education, and for the needs of the students, developing a strand of the conclusion of a previous study (Stevens and McGuinn 2004: 134), in which I wrote of the poem:

> It is both worth teaching and simultaneously worth learning from in the context of pedagogy: the poet/narrator may be likened to the teacher, in effect, and in this sense the poem models positive reciprocity. Particularly striking in this respect is the dynamic combination of critical detachment from the observed situation, and passionate involvement in it – the detachment making possible a startling clarity of vision, balanced by the powerfully felt motivation to do something about it. It is precisely this combination that has been recommended throughout this book; the two qualities are complementary in an intercultural context, and neither would be

sufficient by itself. Although part of the same oppressive world he depicts in the poem, Blake, by virtue of his poetic insight, is able to penetrate it critically; by doing this he implies a way forward.

So, to return to the presentations themselves, the results were illuminating for all concerned – including the 'real' audience involved – not just because of what I was able to teach them about Blake (pretty limited, I suspect) but because the format of the exploration allowed students to use their own talents and interests in genuinely artistic and creative ways as befitted the subject matter. Among these talents, some of which I had never envisaged coming to the fore, were musicianship in the folk idiom, mime, map-drawing (one student, it turned out, was fascinated by maps following his Duke of Edinburgh Award experience), ICT research in collecting apt photographs, sculpture, pictorial art, and the selection of pieces of classical music to evoke the appropriate atmosphere for the verse. The key point here, of course, is that the arts in education have precisely this pedagogically liberating potential, in the sense that Craft maintains (2005: 44):

> A pedagogy which fosters creativity depends on practitioners being creative to provide the ethos for enabling children's creativity: in other words, one that is relevant to them and in which they can take ownership of the knowledge, skills and understanding to be learnt … ensuring … a significant amount of control and opportunities to be innovative.

Teaching *The Lambton Worm*

My final example of the interdisciplinary teaching of poetry, through the arts in this instance, explicitly involves cross-curricular collaboration: student teachers of English and art working together with a group of Year 11 pupils, although the work (true to the spirit of this book) could conceivably have occurred solely in an English (or for that matter an art) classroom. Interestingly, each of these student teachers had been given a fairly free hand in deciding how to fulfil a particular aspect of the departmental scheme of work for the year group in question: in the case of the English teacher, the brief was to teach about some of the differences between Standard and non-standard English; for the art teacher, the departmental scheme of work required her to teach the group how to construct and present a poster. Neither requirement, it seemed at first sight at least, had much to do with poetry. And yet, once the two teachers started exploring the possibilities of collaboration (at least with some of their pupils, for the art and English groups were not identical), using a poem as the way into the curricular requirements seemed to offer a feasible solution. Tellingly, Eisner (who, significantly, often cites examples from the teaching and learning of art to illustrate his ideas) observes,

> Every task and each material with which we work both imposes constraints and provides opportunities for the development of mind … It is literalism that suppresses the almost natural tendency to use language poetically, as very young children often do. Similarly, if students are to learn to see and talk about visual qualities, they need opportunities for seeing and talking.

(Eisner 2002: 12)

113

A beguilingly simple point to make, maybe, but often ignored in practice. Working collaboratively in a sense increases the kind of constraints Eisner refers to; but by the same token it also enhances the opportunities for extension of 'repertoire' in the arts field – and, as Marshall shows in her discussion focusing on an arts-based English curriculum, 'Implicit within the term is the sense of a body of knowledge acquired through exposure, experimentation and practice. It connotes technique, artistry and interpretation' (Marshall 2001: 18).

It was precisely those qualities, among others, that emerged from the English and art lessons I observed, based on exploration of the curious Wearside folk tale *The Lambton Worm*. For the English lessons, the focus was sharply on language – the distinction between varieties of spoken and written standard and non-standard Englishes, to be more explicit. In this context, it helped that the poem was set in the locality, although such is the rivalry between localities (especially as represented by football teams) that nobody in the Teesside school in question counted themselves as very familiar with the Wearside dialect ('They're all mackems up there, miss!') of the verse itself. The student teacher of English, in inspiring her class to investigate further, gave a colourful rendition of the poem herself, and went on to play recordings of modern dialect speakers from Wearside, Teesside and Tyneside, alongside Standard English as spoken on the BBC Radio 4 *Today* programme. My slight reservation, expressed during the planning stages of these lessons, that the poem was being used simply as a vehicle for language study rather than as an artistic entity in its own right (I see quite enough of this kind of thing as it is, often ostensibly occasioned by the National Strategy) was quickly dispelled by the celebratory reading aloud, and by subsequent relating by the pupils of other folk tales relating to local dialects. I was surprised at how much was known by these young people, and both I and the student teacher learned a great deal: I was reminded yet again of how the best resources in any classroom are the people present – especially, I believe, in arts education. The class went on subsequently to look at examples of Standard English, both spoken and written, exploring in depth some of the disjunctions and connections, before returning with some gusto to 'translating' Standard English news stories into dialect folk tales and ballads. A neat circularity here, I thought, in that these tales from the oral tradition in a sense preceded printed newspapers in disseminating newsworthy stories – with about the same concern for accuracy as we witness nowadays. All this, had there been time, would have made an excellent introduction to media study of journalism.

While all this was going on, the art teacher took her group of pupils through a similarly imaginative sequence of lessons, creatively complementing the activities of the English classroom. The student teacher of art in question was already an enthusiastic user of poetry in her lessons to inspire artistic activity, notably Neil Astley's excellent selection of mainly contemporary verse, *Staying Alive* (2002), and Michael and Peter Benton's various books imaginatively linking poetry and art: *Double Vision* (1990), *Painting with Words* (1995), and *Picture Poems* (1997) – alongside a wide range of other resources. Her scheme of work, designed to complement the explorations of her English colleague, comprised five stages. During the preliminary lessons, she introduced the theme by showing various posters of dragons and mythical beasts from diverse times and cultures, working towards a reading of the poem. Pupils then 'mind-mapped' their responses to the poem and the poster images, mindful of the eventual task of poster design linking images with words and collaboratively picking out key words and phrases, before sharing all these with the rest of the class ('draw your own conclusions', advised the teacher at one stage, apparently unaware of the possible meanings until pointed out to her by one of the pupils – and that is precisely what they did, in all sorts of ways). Subsequent lessons focused on some of the skills that would be involved in accomplishment of the design and execution task, including typography, colour-complementarity and composition – all this provided strong practically orientated foundations, whilst never losing sight of the poem itself (prominently displayed throughout this period). The final lessons concentrated on drafting, then completing, appropriate posters to promote the poem. The eventual posters, striking and colourful, were then displayed prominently in the school, where they occasioned a great deal of positive comment.

The place of drama

English and drama are closer, arguably and depending on local circumstances, than any two other secondary phase curriculum subjects. In terms of the National Curriculum, drama was from the start subsumed into the English orders, and in practice the two departments (if indeed they are represented by separate departments at all) often work closely together. Certainly, drama techniques have hugely influenced English pedagogy, especially in the teaching of Shakespeare since the telling influence of Rex Gibson and others of similar persuasions. Perhaps precisely because the subjects are often envisaged as so closely connected, however, drama practitioners are frequently concerned to safeguard and develop their own pedagogies – and in my view, rightly so. As with all the interdisciplinary ventures commended in this book, I am interested not in diluting subject identities but in fostering connections from positions of strength and breadth – and the relationship between English and drama is no exception. The following examples of text-based drama, briefly summarised, may show something of these fruitful connections.

Poetry and drama

One of the major advantages of working with an interdisciplinary mindset is that it keeps us as teachers constantly alert for new connections, and new ways of building on existing ones. I am myself acutely aware of this in writing the present book: ideas come to me as I write about how to develop possibilities already mentioned, and in the context of allying poetry with drama is a telling case in point. Further to teaching and learning activities already mentioned, then, are some general ways into poetry through drama, loosely defined. Activities may include:

- Performance-based interpretations of poems, including mime, music, and role-playing characters. The juxtaposition of particular pairs of poems, one each from Blake's *Songs of Innocence* and *Experience* I have found especially apt here (including, of course, his illustrations of each poem to give an artistic dimension to interpretation): for example, a dialogue between the 'Innocent' and 'Experienced' Chimney Sweep, each recounting their outlook on life and exploitation.

- A 'critics debate' triads, with two students debating opposing interpretations while a third listens carefully, takes notes and finally reports back with an attempt at consensus: a form of drama directly aiming at critical interpretations and dialogue.

- Playing the poet in role in a hot-seating exercise to face questions, perhaps with a particular teacher-given focus in mind (or indeed with the teacher playing the part of the poet in question).

- Using choral readings with echoes of key words to achieve different effects and understandings, examining through the sound of the verse stylistic features such as rhythm, rhyme and assonance (a device developed from active dramatic work on Shakespeare in education).

- 'Behind the picture' activity, through which pupils, either individually or in pairs, interpret given (or self-selected) pictures of people as poems, then combine into small groups to plan and present dramatic renditions of these poems, with the original pictures projected above.

- Having groups/pairs construct their own questions, both open and closed, to ask each other on the text, subsequently summarised by the teacher.

- Selection of quotations to give weight to an interpretation, using them constructively in the context of many of the above activities and others.

Emerging from this thorough preparation must be a creative combination of close reading, fully endorsed by references and quotations, with a freshness of subjective response. The vital principle, kept in sight throughout the range of activities undertaken, is to return always to the text itself – hopefully with new insights and understanding.

Teaching Penelope Lively's *The Whispering Knights* through drama

I was interested here in connecting a drama sequence to the reading of Penelope Lively's novel *The Whispering Knights* (2008) for a mixed-ability Year 7 group. Clearly reading here is a springboard for diverse activities, such as media-based reporting of the controversy and the meeting itself, and research-based work on local issues of genuine concern. The two points made at the end of the sequence description are vital, however, if the connection between drama and reading is to remain the focus: first, that the group be returned to the text itself for enhanced understanding; and second, that subsequent discussion concentrates on how reading relates to its dramatic contexts and purposes.

- The novel itself, briefly, centres on three children who arouse the malevolent spirit of Morgan le Fay, who then mischievously causes changes to a motorway building project so that it would go through the children's home village, Steeple Hampden, and its surrounding picturesque countryside.

- The focus of the teaching and learning was a role-played public meeting to discuss the routing of the motorway, chaired by the teacher in role (a useful drama teaching device). In previous lessons, alternative routes, based where possible on close reading of the text, had been drawn up and a map produced (geography again).

- The class then divided into appropriate pressure groups for particular views and enacted propaganda campaigns. In a subsequent lesson, still in anticipation of the public meeting, pupils were given explicit (but reasonably flexible) role cards for characters in the novel and others invented for the project, including at least one representative from each pressure group.

- A lesson was then spent researching and developing these characters, with interim presentational activities built in, with some discussion also as to the nature and form of public meetings.

- For the public meeting role play itself, skilful chairing is essential so that each voice is heard, and if need be prompted, and that evidence from the text is adhered to. It is also important that the meeting is not simply allowed to drift, so that properly feasible conclusions are reached, including if need be elements of conflict resolution, and that these inform subsequent teaching and learning of the novel itself.

Teaching Tennessee Williams' *A Streetcar Named Desire*

Generally taught at A/AS Level, but feasibly adaptable for Key Stage 4, *A Streetcar Named Desire* is a play containing a mixture of passion, sex and raw energy, occasionally spilling over into violence. As with the reading of any play (including Shakespeare's plays, taught throughout the secondary years), it is effective to conjure an atmosphere of a theatre group working towards a shared understanding essential for some sort of performance. The text then becomes a working script; the preliminary group reading raises questions, displays possibilities of interpretation and enactment, and progresses towards a thorough acquaintance with the play itself. During this reading it may be best to avoid too much detailed note-taking in favour of jotted marginalia (although an issue here might be whether the students own their own texts or not). During a second, more detailed reading the group should be discovering what works in terms of the drama, acting sections out and receiving guidance towards the key themes, characterisations, and the twists and turns of the plot: this would be the appropriate time for a more extensive accumulation of notes after each session, with the possibility of additional short-term writing tasks. On completion of this reading, probably taking up to a half term of study, the group should be ready to adopt a variety of approaches to the whole play. There may be options available at this stage, and the activities are often best summarised on a handout such as this:

1. Presentations (working in groups of three) given to the rest of the group on themes within the play, with each using a minimum of six carefully chosen quotations to illustrate the presentation. The themes are:
   • class conflict and the battle between old and new;
   • gender conflict and notions of sexuality;
   • psychological issues and the question of (in)sanity; and
   • setting and atmosphere throughout the play.

2. Tableaux: eleven 'frozen moments', each introduced by the appropriate line(s) – one tableau for each scene, enacted to the most minute detail of facial expression, and open to interpretive questioning from the rest of the group.

3. Theatre programme design (working in the groups established for (1)) to include:
   • biographical information;
   • themes of the play;
   • historical, social and geographical contexts;
   • symbolism and staging;

- art and design presentational work; and
- imaginary cast list and pen portraits of the actors involved.

4.   Hot-seating: another drama-based activity which involves each character, played in role, facing investigative (possibly hostile) questioning from everyone else. Preparation in researching the nature of each character has to be thorough and imaginative.

7

Cross-curricular approaches: English and modern foreign languages

English and modern foreign languages: an intercultural perspective

It may seem, at first glance, that English and modern foreign languages (henceforth MFL) are ideal bedfellows: after all, both are centrally concerned with language, and language as used in the contemporary world at that. There is, of course, much truth in this observation, and, at least since the Bullock Report urged language across the curriculum from the 1970s onwards, there have been several worthy (and often successful) attempts to build on the cross-curricular connection in secondary schools. However, forging a working model of collaboration has not always been straightforward. The pedagogies of English and MFL have developed in contrasting ways, which has tended to mean that although, potentially at least and if handled sensitively, each has been able to illuminate the other, there have been practical problems in implementing co-operation except on a fairly superficial level. MFL teachers have been known (often with some justification) to complain vociferously that their pupils were ill-prepared by English colleagues in terms of any sort of detailed knowledge of grammar or even language workings more generally, whilst the standard English teachers' response that this is precisely the role of MFL teachers, as grammar knowledge is not needed for English teaching and may actually inhibit spontaneity, simply will not do any more (and probably never did). The reality in most schools, I suspect, lies somewhere in between these poles. However, when English and MFL departments attempted to plan and realise a 'language awareness' scheme of work at a school I taught in during the 1980s, we rapidly found each other's lesson plans so alien to the spirit of our respective subject teaching and learning methodologies (for MFL, meticulously planned to the smallest detail of each pupil-teacher exchange; for English, typically open-ended and far more flexibly exploratory) that the scheme pretty quickly ground to a halt – although some interesting and imaginative work had emerged, and we were able to continue cross-curricular activity in other ways.

The model of the consciously interdisciplinary English teacher commended throughout this book is, I hope, more appropriate to working in a cross-curricular spirit. The diversity of cultural and linguistic backgrounds now represented in school classrooms has also changed considerably since Bullock: a challenge, certainly, in terms of teaching pupils whose first language is not English, but also a huge opportunity to explore the breadth of language experience and its cultural contexts. In English classrooms the length and breadth of the country this opportunity is being seized resourcefully, as I have often witnessed at first hand, and emerging surely from this situation is, I feel, a new kind of English teacher: essentially, an interdisciplinary English teacher. Broadly, I believe we need to focus here on language awareness within and beyond the English language itself, and on the nature of intercultural education (a pedagogical school deriving directly from MFL teaching, in recognition of the realisation that to teach a foreign language separately from its cultural context is something of a nonsense). Inevitably, both of these areas have already featured prominently in previous chapters, and both are fundamental to the interdisciplinary project; we need now to look at them in a little more detail.

In 1921 George Sampson's seminal book on English teaching in British schools *English for the English* was published. Sampson was primarily concerned to establish the subject English – native-language teaching, in effect – as the mainstay of the English school curriculum, and to point the way forward for literature-based English teaching as a humanising force in that curriculum. In so doing, Sampson was very much part – indeed he was one of the main instigators – of what might be termed the 'cultural heritage' model of English teaching we have already encountered in Chapter 1: a way of transmitting, reinforcing and renewing the national culture in a time of increasing secularity and spiritual uncertainty. Charges of national exclusivity and intellectual elitism have been frequently levelled against such a position, and yet, in practice, this model remains a powerful influence, although now in need of re-evaluation and in my view redirection in the light of gathering concern for intercultural (and interdisciplinary) identities in education. This section, then, will focus on the central position of native-language English teaching for intercultural awareness, based on a slightly ironic reworking, or amplification, of Sampson's 1921 title of *English for the English*. In the present context of a book drawing upon interdisciplinary practices and points of view, perhaps a further word of explanation, if not quite apology, is necessary. For me, there is a sense in which native-language teaching (in this instance, English) ought to stress intercultural concerns precisely because it may seem likely to avoid it. The alternative is to have a narrowly conceived and ultimately ethnocentric native-language education as the cornerstone of each nation's school curriculum. This would be wholly inappropriate as we move into the information/communications obsessed world of the twenty-first century; there are already quite enough nationalistic and ethnocentric influences at work, and I feel we have to counter them in a coherent and principled way.

We need first to consider the nature of intercultural pedagogy, even if this means blurring the focus, initially, on the relationship between English and MFL. Essentially, intercultural teaching acknowledges and embraces difference, whilst simultaneously suggesting connectivity, in terms of language and cultural identities. This is its intercultural core: a recognition and celebration of negotiated, complex relationships of teaching and learning. To cite the metaphor of place, recurrent in this argument, Gregoriou (2001: 135) notes that

a philosophical investigation of place from a pedagogical perspective asks how we *make place* for others: how we receive what is abstract and unintelligible, how we expand the borders of our localities and soften the ligaments of our ethnic, historical and cultural identities so that we can envelope new discursive idioms and narratives in the genealogies of our cultures.

Especially noteworthy here is the emphasis placed on pluralities – of identity, of culture, of others – suggestive of a definitively intercultural classroom. The particular flavour of the subject English, I suggest, derives partly from the same sources, especially the cultural, and partly from the proposed envelopment of specifically discursive idioms and narratives – the very stuff of an imaginatively conceived and interdisciplinary English curriculum. Perhaps we are beginning with these kinds of perception to form a tentative answer to the challenge of how to see language study in ways which are both realistic for the classroom, and profoundly radical – the challenge provocatively mounted put by commentators like Hoyles a generation ago:

> Most of the time we don't question the purpose of literacy. In school its function so often seems simply one of social control. If it is to be liberating, the problem is how to *change* the context. … The problem is how to revolutionise the *total* context
>
> (Hoyles 1977: 30)

In order to offer some sort of working resolution of this question, there needs to be genuine pedagogical reflection, and this again is part of the intercultural world view – in the sense that Dewey first suggested as the basis of his theory of democratic education:

> … reflective thinking, in distinction from other operations to which we apply the name of thought, involves (1) a state of doubt, hesitation, perplexity, mental difficulty, in which thinking originates, and (2) an act of searching, hunting, inquiring, to find material that will resolve the doubt, settle and dispose of the perplexity
>
> (1933: 12)

Again the similarity to Romantic thought is striking; and again such a perception seems particularly relevant to the teaching of English, frequently alone among the core curricular subjects in its emphasis on the processes of perception in learning as opposed to the acquisition of a vast body of information in the guise of 'knowledge'. As Medway (2002: 6) elaborates,

> The needed epistemology of English … must go on to specify that English doesn't teach about the world in the way that Biology does. Rather than accounts that aspire to be objective in the sense that they record what is potentially available to any investigator, English typically deals with phenomenological knowledge; knowledge of the world *as it enters experience*. This is Bruner's point about the 'subjectivisation' that is characteristic of literary texts, novels and films.

It is interesting to discover how often education may be conceived of in triangular terms (borrowing from the discipline of mathematics, of course), thinking back to C.K. Stead's analogy we considered earlier. John Dewey himself emphasised the dynamic triangular nature of learning, involving knowledge-as-perception, experience, and reflective thinking. Guilherme elucidates (2002: 28):

Dewey saw the relationship between theory and practice as a web that is continuously made and remade. Furthermore, he saw the connection between experience and learning as part of a wider democratic project that linked education and society. … This triangular mode of learning would provide young individuals with the attitudes and skills necessary for the reinforcement of a democratic way of life and would also empower them to take advantage of all the possibilities they have access to while living in a democratic society.

Subsequent radicalisation and extension of Dewey's arguments, to encompass political and social as well as pedagogical dimensions of radical activity, by Williams, Freire and Eagleton among many others, have further strengthened their validity in the intercultural and interdisciplinary contexts. The fusion of intercultural and pedagogical insights is indeed striking: issues of culture and issues of the classroom tend to model, complement, but also frequently create friction between each other. In the following perceptive quotation from Williams, for example, the word 'teaching' could quite easily – and tellingly – be substituted for 'culture', and the reciprocity serves to illuminate both:

We have to plan what can be planned, according to our common decision. But the emphasis of the idea of culture is right when it reminds us that a culture, essentially, is unplannable. We have to ensure the means of life, and the means of community. But what will then, by these means, be lived, we cannot know or say. The idea of culture rests on a metaphor: the tending of natural growth. And indeed it is on growth, as metaphor and as fact, that the ultimate emphasis must be placed.

(in Eagleton 2000: 119-120)

It is precisely this sort of formulation which provides a key to unlocking the nature of the interdisciplinary culture of the classroom.

From a broad perspective like this, the urgent need to keep reinvigorating language teaching and learning is hardly a luxury. It is, rather, at the very core of our professional identities as English teachers – and this is our return route to the MFL connection. As George Orwell realised and illustrated so frighteningly in *Nineteen Eighty-Four*, control over language means power. The 'Ingsoc' tyranny portrayed in the novel developed 'Newspeak' (a term that, interestingly, has entered popular consciousness, along with 'Big Brother' and 'Room 101') precisely so that 'a heretical thought – that is, a thought diverging from the principles of Ingsoc – should be literally unthinkable, at least so far as thought is dependent on words' (Orwell 1949: 312). For many, inside and outside our classrooms, this is not simply an academic matter, as Kureishi observes:

It is always illuminating to think of those groups and individuals who are denied the privilege of speaking and of being listened to, whether they be immigrants, asylum seekers, women, the mad, children, the elderly, or workers in the third world. It is where the words end, or can't go, that abuse takes place, whether it's racial harassment, bullying, neglect, or sexual violence.

(2003: 4)

Having established something of a radical intercultural context for interdisciplinary teaching and learning focused on native and foreign languages, let us now consider some practical curricular opportunities for enhanced language awareness.

Language awareness through language study

Language teachers have an invaluable ally here in what seems to be the intrinsically fascinating nature of language, precisely because it denotes so many things and is open to so many interpretations. It is at once intensely personally subjective in how it feels, and dynamically social in its communicative uses. Class, age, personal identity, peer group membership, locality and nationality all contribute to this fascination, and all of these provide excellent starting points for the examination of language in the English classroom. Such is the overwhelming power of the human propensity for language that it may be described as instinctive (although this word itself is problematic in meaning). Pinker (1994: 21) suggests:

> The workings of language are as far from our awareness as the rationale for egg-laying is from the fly's. Our thoughts come out of our mouths so effortlessly that they often embarrass us, having eluded our mental censors. When we are comprehending sentences, the stream of words is transparent; we see through to the meaning so automatically that we can forget that a movie is in a foreign language and subtitled … The effortlessness, the transparency, the automaticity are illusions, masking a system of great richness and beauty.

Language awareness should be geared towards uncovering this 'system of great richness and beauty', while at the same time enhancing celebratory spontaneity. This is a challenging task, and requires careful thought and sensitivity – across the curriculum, certainly, but with special significance for English and language teachers.

Varieties of English

To speak of language awareness in the singular is in some respects misleading, for we all use, and know about, many different languages – even those of us who could define ourselves as 'monolingual'. Language activities, some of which we shall look at below, can explore these different forms of English and other languages, depending as they do on context and purpose, and even without the aid of good teaching children are impressively adept at functioning in a vast range of linguistic circumstances and switching painlessly from one to another. As interdisciplinary language teachers, we need to build on this 'natural' ability, and we need to pay particular attention to formal and informal modes – to describe them somewhat simplistically. As with so much else, there is nothing especially new in this. It is illuminating, for instance, to consider Hardy's 1891 presentation (in *Tess of the D'Urbervilles*) of his heroine Tess, in part at least the product of the new national education system, in contrast to her relatively unschooled mother:

> Mrs Durbeyfield habitually spoke the dialect; her daughter, who had passed the Sixth Standard in the National School under a London-trained mistress, spoke two

languages; the dialect at home, more or less; ordinary English abroad and to persons of quality.

(Hardy 1985: 58)

Hardy, presumably, intends irony here: Tess's ability to converse in Standard English opens the way to two 'persons of quality' in particular, who between them destroy her. Interestingly, Hardy, in his first edition of the novel, wrote of Tess using the local dialect form of English not merely 'at home, more or less' but 'only when excited by joy, surprise, or grief'.

At the functional 'adult needs' level, of course, we need as language teachers to ensure that our pupils can function and flourish in the full range of language forms manifested in a pluralist society – meeting the challenge implied by equality of opportunity, in effect. However, the more we probe the nature of language in a social context, the more we are likely to discover that the reality is far more complex than implied by the purely functional model: potentially liberating, certainly; but also, as Tess found to her cost, potentially dangerous. The relationship between language, emotions ('joy, surprise, or grief') and social reality is complex and often problematic, and any worthwhile attempt to educate pupils in language awareness must fully acknowledge this. Neither should the relationship be conceived as static, but rather as dynamic and dialectical, with social opportunities and constraints both influencing and in turn being influenced by the nature of the language(s) involved. In practical terms, as in so much else concerned with English teaching, this is an argument for a fully integrated interdisciplinary curriculum both within the subject itself and in relationship with other curricular areas, all of which assuredly deal with manifestations of social reality. One of the particular strengths of English, however, is its potential use of literature as language in action and in this sense all literature, including *Tess of the D'Urbervilles*, is centrally concerned with (and of course expressed through) language, whatever else may be its subject.

Language study based on what is read as 'literature' is only one approach to enhanced language awareness. We need now to consider in more general terms what shape the integration of language knowledge into the interdisciplinary English curriculum could begin to take. There are many questions to answer, all of which revolve around the central tensions of knowledge about language outlined above:

- How exactly can knowledge about language be integrated into the other aspects of the English curriculum, for example those dealing with literature?

- How may we respect, and encourage respect for, pupils' linguistic experience while preparing them for the realities of language in society?

- How do we deal with the tension between 'correctness' in terms of Standard English and 'appropriateness' as preferred by most linguists?

- In seeking to improve pupils' language use, either written or spoken, should we rely principally on a 'remedial' approach, tackling faults and shortcomings as they arise naturally in English activities?

- Should we rather be 'proactive' in teaching methodically aspects of language which we know through experience often give problems, such as speech punctuation, certain spellings, the use of semicolons or sentence structure?

- Whichever of the last two approaches is used – and they are not, of course, entirely mutually exclusive – what sort of metalinguistic vocabulary is needed in order to teach effectively about language?

- How should this metalinguistic vocabulary itself be taught?

- What opportunities are there for cross-curricular collaboration in terms of language in society (the humanities), expressive forms of language (the arts), language as a communication system (modern foreign languages), etc.?

- What opportunities are there also for cross-phase collaboration, so that the often impressive knowledge about language developed in primary schools may be further built on in the secondary phase, and any omissions made good?

These questions and the issues sitting behind them may helpfully inform professional practice, and like the most useful questions in teaching itself they are intended to be open, suggestive of exploratory ways forward rather than implying 'correct' answers given by us or anyone else. Brian Cox's descriptions of his Committee's investigations into English teaching as they worked on the original National Curriculum in the mid-1980s form a useful reminder here too. He noted that while there was often little formal teaching of knowledge about language in English classrooms, metalinguistic terms such as 'sentence', 'verb' or 'full stop' were constantly and unavoidably being used. This, of course, relates to two of the key questions posed above concerning metalinguistic terminology, with some implications for other points also. This is just one rather narrow aspect of knowledge about language, but a vital one (and perhaps even more so in the MFL teaching and learning context) which may provide a very practical focus for explicit planning of language teaching. Consider, for example, this brief list concerning language terminology as featured (or not) in the classroom:

- the metalinguistic terms commonly used;
- whether there is likely to be a shared or widespread understanding of them;
- how they are used (orally, in marking, remedially, prescriptively, descriptively, etc.);
- how these terms are taught or explained;
- which, if any, may be discarded; and
- which other terms may be usefully added to the list.

The resulting list could provide a useful starting point for cross-curricular development, but it is the process through which it is arrived at that may well throw up similarities and differences in approach. Cox (1991: 57) is again helpful in providing a broader context here:

> Two justifications for teaching pupils explicitly about language are, first, the positive effect on aspects of their use of language and, secondly, the general value of such knowledge as an important part of their understanding of their social and cultural environment, since language has vital functions in the life of the individual and of society … Language is not merely a neutral medium for the conveying of information; it can trigger emotional responses which may spring from prejudice, stereotyping or misunderstanding. Such attitudes need to be laid open to examination and discussion.

In practical terms, this suggests that the sort of language analysis we are concerned with developing in the classroom, and the attendant terminology, should not be conceived as neutral, decontextualised or static. To help further in this process it may be useful to go back a little further, to the Kingman Report (DES 1988) which (as we have seen in Chapter 1) was intended to provide the theoretical framework for the teaching of language but because it failed to provide a narrowly prescriptive model never really gained the official approval it deserved. Ironically, perhaps this has been its strength: certainly there is a great deal of value in it and it is well worth referring back to. Selective quotations give a flavour of the Report:

> We believe that for children not to be taught anything about their language is seriously to their disadvantage … pupils need to have their attention drawn to what they are doing and why they are doing it because this is helpful to their language ability.

> Awareness of the forms of language is an entirely natural development.

> Teaching language must involve talking about language since learning without that activity is slow, inefficient and inequitable (in that it favours those whose ability enables them to generalise without tuition).

> Nor do we see it as part of our task to plead for a return to old-fashioned grammar teaching and learning by rote.

> We reject the belief that any notion of correct or incorrect use of language is an affront to personal liberty. We also reject the belief that knowing how to use terminology in which to speak of language is undesirable. There is no positive advantage in such ignorance. It is just as important to teach about our language environment. The skills, perceptions and knowledge that we are advocating will be of value to all pupils, and should in no way be the exclusive privilege of the more able.

We have met some of these arguments before, and some – like language itself – may remain somewhat contentious. In many schools, even now, MFL teachers bemoan the absence of language awareness (generally in the field of grammar) in pupils, asking why their English teaching colleagues had not done more to address this aspect of the subject. There is also a certain anxiety involved: most English teachers remain educated primarily in literature rather than language (although this is changing), and, if our annual PGCE subject knowledge audits are anything to go by, it is grammar teaching that causes most consternation for practical teaching purposes. However, I am not suggesting here that English teachers need to be professional linguists; rather that the interdisciplinary turn requires an understanding of what is needed for pupils to make the kind of progress we should like. It is, I think, essentially a matter of exploring the possibilities of legitimising and subsequently developing the fascination for and considerable knowledge of language brought into any English classroom by the pupils – and, for that matter, their teacher (lest we forget!). This development requires conscious decision making about language use; and as Davies (1996: 52) has pointed out,

This is what English teaching should provide especially well: opportunities for learning about the choices that can and must be made in the use of language, and help for learners in developing explicit understandings and vision of what they can make language do for their own varied and complex needs.

In this context of making informed choices we do need some sort of structure within which to develop the teaching of language. Kingman's four-part model for the consideration of language – its forms; communication and comprehension; its acquisition; its variation – makes a great deal of sense and has been used, in its more detailed form as presented in the Report itself, by some English departments as a convenient model to ensure entitlement.

Language awareness beyond the secondary English classroom

A central message of this book is that we should be ready as English teachers to look around us as well as examining closely the detail of our own subject teaching. Particularly, I have in mind here the possibilities for cross-curricular and cross-phase co-operation, both of which should serve to emphasise the nature of language awareness. For the former, there is a wealth of excellent practice going on in primary schools about which secondary colleagues are sometimes only dimly aware. Pressures of time and curriculum crowding, together with the shrinking of INSET courses, have made it more difficult to share ideas and practices, although the current literacy initiative and the emphasis NATE is placing on attracting primary-based English teachers may do something to alleviate the worst effects in our subject. Successful cross-phase partnerships depend on the willingness of whole school staffs, with the impetus often coming from senior management, but there is still a fair amount achievable by English teachers to build bridges to enhance language teaching. With the continuing policy of emphasising foreign language teaching in primary schools, there is a distinct opportunity here too for an interdisciplinary dimension. Some possibilities specifically on knowledge about language include:

- cross-phase meetings to discuss which aspects of knowledge about language are taught – including the appropriate terminology – and when;
- projects involving research and interviews on aspects of language, perhaps focusing particularly on acquisition, development and variation;
- teaching specific lessons across the phase divide, perhaps for secondary teachers as 'tasters' of what is to come, and for primary colleagues addressing areas of expertise relevant to a secondary English curriculum such as early years language development;
- sharing of relevant resources, many of which are deliberately cross-phase in nature;
- the keeping by pupils of a language scrap-book or journal to be carried on from the primary school into the secondary phase;
- pupils in both phases using each other as audiences for language-based activities, such as code making and breaking;
- mutual project study of language as used in either phase, such as teachers' language or the language of school brochures and publicity material.

Practical implications for language teaching and learning

Davies (1996) offers a very useful overview of recommended topics intended as a programme of study that would last the whole of compulsory secondary education at least:

The history of the English language:
- the development of dialects of English;
- the development of Standard English;
- language change.

Language structures:
- an introduction to descriptive linguistics.

The nature of language variation:
- variation according to user: social class and locality;
- variation according to use: register (discourse analysis);
- attitudes to language variation;
- language development and learning;
- language and power: gender, race, class and education.

This appears to be a comprehensive framework, and could easily be adapted for specific school circumstances – not least for the kinds of activities outlined in the rest of this chapter. Resources are many and varied: language is all around us, often unnoticed because of its very ubiquity, and the language teacher needs to cultivate a 'magpie' attitude towards collecting linguistic resources: junk mail, instruction booklets, tourist guides, health information leaflets, digitally photographed signs and advertisements, labels, fliers and the like. The resounding popularity and success of so many A and AS Level English Language courses indeed testifies to English teachers' imaginative resourcefulness here, and of course such approaches strongly imply interdisciplinary breadth, especially across diverse languages and their cultural contexts.

In previous chapters I have already alluded to teaching and learning activities focusing on aspects of language awareness (for example, in geographical or artistic contexts). Possible further practical illustrations of these approaches to language could include:

1. An exploration of language structures through the invention of 'new' languages and codes. This exploration could touch on:
    - the 'invention' of Esperanto and its rationale, history and characteristic features;
    - invented languages in fiction (including 'Newspeak' in *Nineteen Eighty-Four*, as mentioned above);
    - forms of English featured in fiction: novels such as *Trainspotting*, *A Clockwork Orange*, or
    - study of codes and how they have developed and been used.

2. Translation studies, loosely conceived:
    - study of instruction booklets featuring the same basic instructions translated (or mistranslated) into several languages – pupils could start with foreign language

examples and work out basic vocabulary and structures before getting to the English version;
- basic (and perhaps more sophisticated) translations to and from English as featured in popular Internet sites;
- translations (again, to and from English) of media texts, especially soaps, songs and films – looking at dubbing, for example;
- the availability of more 'literary' texts in diverse languages through translation – especially poetry.

3. Broadly based language awareness studies:
- the etymology of key everyday words, and what such knowledge may tell us about meaning, reception and response;
- study of the derivation of names, especially interesting and valuable in multi-ethnic classrooms;
- further creative investigating and celebrating the languages (and cultures) featured in the classroom – and not forgetting that most indigenous 'English' people have more interestingly diverse ancestries than is immediately obvious.

4. Further explorations, including
- different cultures and languages as presented in advertising; TV ads can be especially fertile here, as barometers of the age – for example, a comparison between car ads featuring French (accentuating flair, perhaps femininity) and German ('Vorsprung durch Technik' efficiency) products;
- as above, but as presented in tabloid newspapers ('Up Yours Delors') – especially fertile ground during international football tournaments;
- construction of guidebooks or phrasebooks for foreign visitors, explaining key words and cultural artefacts and conventions (this could be combined with a 'Martian' approach);
- investigation of rhythm and stress in languages (including names – how they become unrecognisable with different syllable stress, for example) – what these may tell us about cultural stereotypes.

Throughout these practical explorations, and the theoretical underpinning we glanced at previously, it behoves us as interdisciplinary English teachers – language teachers in effect – to acknowledge and build on the languages brought into (and of course developed) in the classroom. As Street (1997: 47) reminds us, language and literacy should be envisaged as

> social practices rather than technical skills to be learned in formal education. …The research requires language and literacy to be studied as they occur naturally in social life, taking account of the context and their different meanings for different cultural groups. The practice requires curriculum designers, teachers and evaluators to take account of the variation in meanings and uses that students bring from their home backgrounds to formal learning contexts.

CHAPTER

8

Cross-curricular approaches: English, mathematics, the sciences, and physical education

General context

These, for me and many other English teachers, are the tricky subjects. As I hope I have demonstrated, building on my own and colleagues' pedagogical experiences, there are many and diverse links between English and the humanities, arts and other languages – indeed, in many ways, the subject may be defined by its relationship to them. The challenge lies now in seeking, exploring and developing approaches that relate to some of the remaining subjects on the usual secondary school curriculum. I am of course aware that this curriculum itself is constantly changing – both expanding and contracting in various directions, including the interdisciplinary turn vindicated here – and there are some subjects that receive little if any attention from me in this book. Nevertheless, I hope that, by attending to the subjects I have explored, English teachers with characteristically resourceful adaptability may be able to forge yet more links across the curriculum and see our subject from even more perspectives in so doing. Certainly a book purporting to support an interdisciplinary conception of the subject English that failed to acknowledge its relationship to mathematics, science or physical education would be sadly deficient. In primary schools, of course, the practical development of such links is bread and butter to teachers, and, again, there is a great deal to be learned from their experiences.

English and mathematics

'Bring out number, weight and measure in a year of dearth' wrote William Blake over two centuries ago, presumably (and provocatively – the quotation is from his *Proverbs of Hell*) implying that we only need to measure things when we're short of them. This sentiment has informed Romantic thought over two centuries, including (arguably) the formation and development of English as discipline and subject. And of course there is a kernel of truth in Blake's words: measurement can certainly distract from holistic engagement and enjoyment. However, I feel too that Blake is being deliberately disingenuous to some extent – after all, Blake himself, like all artists, had to be able to purchase the appropriate quantities of materials for his engravings and paintings, and to estimate numbers and combinations of pages in his illuminated books. However, perhaps we need now, as interdisciplinary English teachers, to re-evaluate our conceptions of each other's subjects and ways of working: mathematics, I have heard it said by colleagues from that curriculum area (we do speak occasionally) is not really about calculations and arithmetic, fundamentally – rather, it's about ideas and concepts. This was brought home to me recently when I heard on the radio that the concept of zero is a human invention, necessary for disciplinary progress in mathematics; I was quite shocked, for I had always considered mathematics to be 'out there', entirely objective – that is, when I had considered it at all. So maybe it could be through an appreciation of some of these ideas that cross-fertilisation, beneficial to both subjects, could occur.

Practically orientated possibilities for interdisciplinary English teaching and learning, drawing on mathematics, include:

- Explorations of rhythm and metre in poetry, summarised mathematically as essential aspects of poetic structure and effect. Once summarised, different rhythmic patterns could be tried and tested, often with interesting effects, and the way is opened for an exploration of whether such structural devices help or hinder creativity – what happens, for example, when the conventions are momentarily departed from, or broken altogether?

- Lexical proportionality in texts offers fertile ground here. For example (using the 'search' and 'find' facilities in Word™), the number of occurrences of key words in texts, and, by the same token, the number of words not included – the postmodern emphasis on the silences of texts and their speakers. Interestingly, this technique is often used in analysing media texts such as politicians' speeches, with the key words (or their lack) uncovering the basic message (for example, Tony Blair's speeches whilst leader of the Labour Party rarely mentioned the word 'socialism'). Literary texts also offer great opportunities here: the number of times 'fair' and 'foul' are mentioned in *Macbeth*, for instance.

- Some texts are particularly apt for cross-fertilising English and mathematical approaches – all the more so when they are both entertaining and thought provoking at the same time. *The Curious Incident of the Dog in the Night-time* (2002), that marvellously inventive short novel by Mark Haddon, is especially good for opening up interdisciplinary discussion and activity here.

- Proportionality, further, may hint at more elusive structural matters. The great film maker Sergei Eisenstein, for example, asserted that his films should follow a basic pattern of thirds: two thirds activity to one third inactivity, in one particular instance (*The Battleship Potemkin*). He based this notion of proportionality in nature, as evidenced in the structure of pine cones and other natural phenomena. The study of structural patterns in any text (including what happens in lessons), using mathematical notions of proportionality and representations through number, algebra or geometry, can be highly illuminating.

- A particular aspect of proportionality relevant to language study is to do with how much of any given text need be displayed for meaning to be apparent, and how

131

variation in how much is displayed may alter reader response. The 'Consequences in writing' game (alluded to previously as a painless way into writing activity) builds on this way of looking at texts: the (pro)portion of an opening sentence available to the next writer in the game will inevitably inform him or her of what sort of genre it is, and largely determine what comes next.

■ I am indebted to Francis Spufford, in his inspiring book *The Child that Books Built* (2002) for another possible adaptation of textual proportionality, which he himself developed from Claude Shannon's 1948 book *Mathematical Theory of Communication,* and his own experience of learning to read independently by hazarding meaning to unknown vocabulary – surely a universal learning experience from all reading histories. As Spufford explains: 'I was able to do this because written English is an extremely robust system. It does not offer the user a brittle binary choice between complete comprehension and complete incomprehension. It tolerates many faults, and still delivers some sense'. Spufford then acknowledges his debt to Shannon in this respect, pointing out that:

> Ignorance is just a kind of noise; and Shannon was interested in measuring how much of a message could be disrupted by the noise that's inevitable on any channel of communication, before it became impossible to decipher it. … The person receiving the message – Shannon concluded – would be able to understand it adequately if noise removed any amount of the message up to the maximum redundancy built into the message by its structure. He … calculated that … up to half of an English text could be deleted before doing such critical damage to its message that you'd give up and say Eh?
>
> (Spufford 2002: 72–4)

It strikes me that there is much potential in this realisation for interdisciplinary English teaching, especially using ICT as a way of conducting the necessary calculations. A huge variety of texts – written, spoken, media-based and others – could be subjected to potentially illuminating scrutiny in this respect: effectively an investigation into the relationship between generic form(s), specified content, and reader response, but using the language, and perhaps the strategies, of mathematics to conduct it.

■ The possibility of using mathematical ideas and language to construct new 'languages' or codes: apparently, when scientists were sending out signals into space, hoping to make contact with other forms of intelligent life, they would not send out messages in English (or French or Spanish for that matter). Instead they would be sending out numbers like 'pi' (3·1415 …) which is a universal constant. Furthermore, they would send out these messages not in base ten, but in base 'e' ('e' being the 'natural' base). If there was any other intelligent life out there, they would then draw the conclusion that only intelligent beings could have sent them such a message. I find this intriguing, and potentially helpful in exploring the nature of precision in language.

■ Finally, as has become fairly widespread English practice, it can be a helpful aid to literary study to construct graphs, flow diagrams and the like to summarise and demonstrate the developments of plot and character. Graphs tracing the emotional journeys of characters are quite widely used, but it would also be feasible to look at relationships between characters in a similar way, or to trace other aspects such as relative status, physical well-being, financial success or self-awareness.

English and the sciences

'Science states meanings; art expresses them' wrote John Dewey (1934: 84), and in this formulation lies the potential for fruitful connection. Much of the potentially helpful relationship between English and sciences hinges, I think, on the question of values. If we consider three examples from the (relatively) recent history of scientific discovery and invention, this may be readily apparent (and incidentally shows how, as an English teacher first and foremost, I immediately go for a narrative exposition). Just over a hundred years ago, Thomas Edison, keen to demonstrate the power of his preferred version of electrical current (and, incidentally, the effectiveness of moving-picture photography) did so by publicly electrocuting a captive circus elephant, having already left in his wake a series of electrocuted stray dogs and cats. At about the same time the Wright brothers developed manned flight towards hitherto unimagined capability, confident in the knowledge – or so they thought – that such a machine would never be used in warfare, and in fact its potential for destructive power would force nations to seek ways of avoiding any sort of armed conflict in the future. Einstein thought much the same, a couple of decades later, when investigating and subsequently actually conducting the splitting of the atom: far too terrible a power for it even to be considered as a weapon. No doubt there are countless further examples, many far more extreme than these, and they have combined in the popular imagination to establish a certain stereotype of the scientist as either disinterested and unworldly, even if benevolently, or deliberately exploitative of life to the point of obsessive madness. Stereotypes of course are themselves cultural artefacts, constructed broadly through language and imagery, and as such they deserve critical study in the English classroom – again, an instance of interdisciplinary exploration. Evidence comes not only from the history of science, but in fiction too: perhaps the most vivid example of this is Mary Shelley's all too prescient novel, *Frankenstein* (1818).

Teaching Mary Shelley's *Frankenstein*

Mary Shelley, the young author of the novel (amazingly, she was only twenty when it was first published), like many of her contemporaries, was fascinated by the accelerating discoveries and inventions of contemporary science. At the same time, she was acutely aware of the dangers of a scientific outlook conceived of as beyond humane values, a quest for knowledge and power over nature that could so easily become self-destructive. In this insight, modern feminist criticism has found an interpretive lens for reading the novel, focusing on it as an exploration of and exposure of the folly of masculine posturing – in the role of the ambitious scientist intent on the domination of nature. As such, the character of Frankenstein echoed contemporary scientific discourse; Humphrey Davy, for example, a pioneering scientist read and admired by both Mary and her husband the poet Percy Shelley, enthused about science enabling 'man' to change and modify the beings surrounding him, and by his experiments to interrogate nature with power, not simply as a scholar, passive and seeking only to understand her operations, but rather as a master, active with his own instruments.

(from *A Discourse, introductory to a Course of Lectures on Chemistry*, 1802, cited in Stevens 2000)

Striking here is the concept of mastery, and the male principle is conventionally emphasised by the use of gendered pronouns. In the novel, even before Frankenstein begins his story, the 'framing' narrator Walton speaks of his quest for 'the dominion I should acquire and transmit over the elemental foes of our race', thus setting the tone for Frankenstein's own scientific (and both Faustian and Promethean) ambitions. Mary Shelley subtly undermines and questions such male assumptions throughout the novel, using the text as a prophecy in the sense that William Blake meant when he wrote of a true prophet not foretelling a predetermined future, but rather warning: 'Thus: if you go on So, the result is So' (from *Marginalia* 1798). The character Frankenstein in the novel goes a step further: not only does he seek to impose his will on passive and characteristically feminine 'nature', he actually usurps the female maternal role in his quest to create life. But of course he cannot, and the result is a disastrous distortion of the ostensibly feminine principle of creativity, and of the investigative role of science too.

Consideration of the nature of the scientific quest, both in Shelley's time and ours, offers an exciting way into the novel, and the novel itself (or of course extracts from it, or film versions) serves as a vivid introduction to the theme of science and values. Possible approaches include:

- A consideration the subtitle of the novel, *The Modern Prometheus*, and research on the nature of the Prometheus myths.

- An exploration of key questions relating to the broad topic of science and values: how do these Promethean myths relate to Mary Shelley's novel, or to the history and values of science? Does the Prometheus figure stand for Frankenstein, his creature, or, somehow, both? How might the novel illuminate the paradoxes of scientific progress, or the quandaries that scientists find themselves facing?

- In the sense that, with the immense progress in genetics since Shelley's time, the Frankenstein story is now far more plausible than then, what modern parallels may there be? The Internet and media should be able to provide plenty of resources here.

- Pupils, following the kind of discussions prompted by the points above, could go on to write contemporary versions of the novel, possibly through different genres. There is of course no shortage of film versions of *Frankenstein*, including, in recent times, Kenneth Branagh's *Mary Shelley's Frankenstein*, which is reasonably faithful to the original, and Marcus Nispal's 2004 adaptation, *Frankenstein*, featuring a 200-year-old Dr Frankenstein, genetically modified, terrorising New Orleans with a few of his manufactured creatures assisting.

- Study of the novel could lead into exploration of science fiction (to take the term literally – fiction based on science): pupils could write narrative accounts based around possible impacts of modern scientific ventures, as does the best of science fiction as an established genre.

- Exploration of the excitement of scientific thought and activity as the basis for creative writing. Something of this excitement come across, for example, in Anne Wroe's biographical description of Mary Shelley's husband Percy, for whom it seems 'Chemistry ... was the key to truth. The crowding batteries and jars were his "philosophical apparatus". From chemistry to philosophy was but a small step for him: changing substances, minds, the world, by the agency of fire' (Wroe 2008: 302).

The aesthetic context

Another helpful meeting place for English and scientific viewpoints and ways of working is through the aesthetic experience – although here again the issue of values is fundamental. *All Our Futures* (1999: 73) contends, appropriately enough, that

> the difference between the arts and sciences is not one of subject matter ... The difference is in the kinds of understanding they are pursuing: in the questions they ask, the kind of answers they seek and in how they are expressed. An important common factor is aesthetic appreciation. ... A feel for aesthetics can be a driving force in creative processes in any field including scientific research. Scientists typically speak of the beauty of ideas and experiments, of the elegance of a theory or proof.

Discussion in this context may centre on the nature of the aesthetic experience, and in particular the distinction between analytical (scientific) modes of appreciation and understanding, and more holistic approaches (commonly accepted as those dear to the arts). I have touched on this tension in the context of media education in Chapter 3, and hinted then at possible synthesis – but the tension remains widespread in human experience and the language used to present it, well worth tapping into in the interdisciplinary English classroom. Do we, as Wordsworth had it, 'murder to dissect'? or is that question itself only appropriate to a mode of scientific enquiry now well past its prime, replaced by far more humane and indeterminate models? Two excellent recent books, Richard Holmes' *The Age of Wonder*, subtitled, aptly enough, *How the Romantic generation discovered the beauty and terror of science* (2009) and Richard Dawkins' *Unweaving the Rainbow: science, delusion and the appetite for wonder* (2006) address these questions from different, contrasting perspectives: Holmes is essentially a literary biographer with a specific interest in the Romantic era, Dawkins an eminent scientist.

For Holmes, for all their differences of approach, the worlds of science (or 'natural philosophy' as it was generally known during the period he is writing about) and creative arts had and have much in common, and certainly could each benefit from cross-fertilisation. He expertly traces their relationship through the Romantic era of the late eighteenth and early nineteenth centuries, vividly illustrating his initial thesis:

> Romanticism as a cultural force is generally regarded as intensely hostile to science, its ideal of subjectivity eternally opposed to that of scientific objectivity. But I do not believe this was always the case, or that the terms are so mutually exclusive. The notion of *wonder* seems to be something that once united them, and can still do so. In effect there is Romantic science in the same sense that there is Romantic poetry, and often for the same enduring reasons.

(Holmes 2009: xvi)

Significantly, coming at this theme from precisely the opposite direction, Dawkins makes a similar point, and elaborates throughout his own study of the same relationship. Interestingly, in the light of areas I have touched on in earlier chapters, Dawkins cites the 'Martian' conceit as a pertinent approach to the wonder he feels is central to scientific enquiry, in a serious attempt to counter what he terms 'the anaesthetic of familiarity' (Dawkins 2006: 6–7), continuing,

> a sedative of ordinariness, which dulls the senses and hides the wonder of existence. For those of us not gifted in poetry, it is at least worth while from time to time making an effort to shake off the anaesthetic.

Despite the Romantic poet John Keats' reservation about science damaging his wondrous perception of a rainbow by analytically explaining how it comes about (thus providing Dawkins with his subtitle), Dawkins argues '…that poets could better use the inspiration provided by science and that at the same time scientists must reach out to the constituency that I am identifying with, for want of a better word, poets' (op. cit.: 17).

As both Holmes and Dawkins maintain, there is a debate to be had, with copious evidence to hand, about the nature of the relationship between science and English (specifically the Romantic conception of English, centrally important to my own thesis). As interdisciplinary English teachers, it behoves us to open up this debate as vividly and resourcefully as possible – and of course one of our prime resources here is fiction (as we have already seen with regard to *Frankenstein*). Another apt novel in this respect, in a sense updating the discussion, is Ian McEwan's *Enduring Love* (1998), frequently taught on A and AS English Literature courses. *Enduring Love* scrutinises the scientific mind of its main protagonist Joe Rose, and, simultaneously and seamlessly juxtaposes different ways of thinking in the range of other characters. The principal intellectual antithesis of Joe, his partner Clarissa, is a Keats scholar, and on one level at least the novel could be read and explored as an important and timely contribution to the science and art debate (although there are many other levels too). The following passage illustrates the relationship between the two main protagonists neatly:

> We were having one of our late-night kitchen table sessions. I told her I thought she had spent too much time lately in the company of John Keats. A genius no doubt, but an obscurantist too who had thought science was robbing the world of wonder, when the opposite was the case. If we value a baby's smile, why not contemplate its source? …That smile must be hard-wired, and for good evolutionary reasons. Clarissa said that I had not understood her. There was nothing wrong in analyzing the bits, but it was easy to lose sight of the whole. I agreed. The work of synthesis was crucial. Clarissa said I still did not understand her, she was talking about love.
>
> (McEwan 1998: 71)

There are many other literary texts dealing with the nature of science – Aldous Huxley's *Brave New World*, for example, or Kazuo Ishiguro's *Never Let Me Go* – and the significant point here, in the context of the interdisciplinary project, is to read and explore them through the appropriate lenses.

Further practical explorations

- As befits the English classroom, there is great potential in exploring the contrasting languages of science and English, within the school and elsewhere. A starting exercise might be to exchange genres: describing a scientific experiment in poetic terms, for example, and giving a poetry appreciation the form of a scientific observational write-up. This kind of encounter could lead to a close evaluation of how language is used for different purposes, and also how the type of language chosen tends not just to describe, but also to close off other possible interpretations.

- The mysteries of science provide fertile ground for activity, and incidentally also help to dispel the myth that all science is based on a hard-edged objectivity. Consideration of black holes, for example, or such contentious phenomena as 'Schrödinger's Cat' (a famous thought experiment through which the Austrian physicist presented the idea of a cat in a box that might be alive or dead, depending on an earlier random event) can lead to wide-ranging discussion and – especially, in my experience – vivid writing.

- In the same way as I earlier considered artistic and historical contexts for literature, the much-neglected scientific contexts should be brought to bear on literary study. Again, *Frankenstein* offers a pertinent example, and the other texts I alluded to above, but in fact scientific context is relevant to *any* text – even those which ostensibly have nothing to do with science. John Donne's poetry provides excellent ground for contextual work here, as does the work of many other poets such as Seamus Heaney in *Death of a Naturalist* – all that's really required is the opening of our interdisciplinary eyes.

- The stories attached to scientific discoveries, too, can be usefully exploited to humanise that world, and yet again *Frankenstein* gives us a good example: textual comparison of Frankenstein's first encounter with his invention contrasted to accounts of real-life scientific discoveries. As so often, so much hinges on the language used.

- Education for sustainable development is a crucial cross-curricular strand in the National Curriculum, as we have seen, and rightly so. There is considerable scope here for looking closely at scientific debates and positions, and in particular at how these are presented. Questions concerning the validity of climate change theories, for example, are frequently in the public domain, and deserve our closely critical attention as English and media teachers.

English and physical education

Language is as central to the teaching and learning of PE as it is with any other subject, and as such it provides yet more fertile ground for interdisciplinary adventure – as I hope the examples below illustrate.

The descriptive language of sports

An exploration of the language that attaches itself to sports, particularly in radio, television and newspaper sports journalism, is perennially interesting (and by the way often especially involving for boys), with the media providing a vast range of suitable examples. Some of these can be taken humorously – the infamous 'Colemanballs' for instance – whereas others verge on the poetic: the radio commentaries of Stuart Hall or Dickie Bird's cricket commentaries to name but two. A few examples may give a little flavour here.

First, a selection of 'Colemanballs' collected by the satirical magazine *Private Eye* (responsible for the term, of course):

- 'We've had cars going off left, right and centre'.
- 'Do my eyes deceive me, or is Senna's Lotus sounding rough?'
- 'With half of the race gone, there is half of the race still to go' (all from Murray Walker, motor racing commentator).
- 'He's pulling him off. The Spanish manager is pulling his Captain off!' (George Hamilton, Irish football commentator).
- 'That's cricket, Harry, you get these sort of things in boxing'. (Frank Bruno).
- 'He's 31 this year - last year he was 30'. (David Coleman).
- 'Here they come, every colour of the rainbow: Black, White, Brown'. (Anon.).
- 'When your back's against the wall it's time to turn round and fight' (John Major, showing cross-genre ingenuity here).

And some comments to do with the newly 'popular' sport of curling:

- 'It's not just a rock. It's forty-two pounds of polished granite, with a beveled underbelly and a handle a human being can hold. Okay, so in and of itself it looks like it has no practical purpose, but it's a repository of possibility. And, when it's handled just right, it exacts a kind of poetry - as close to poetry as I ever want to get. The way it moves … Not once, in everything I've done, have I ever felt the same wonder and humanity as when I'm playing the game of curling'. (Paul Gross, John Krizanc and Paul Quarrington in the film *Men with Brooms.*)
- 'Curling is not a sport. I called my grandmother and told her she could win a gold medal because they have dusting in the Olympics now'. (Charles Barkley.)
- 'My drinking team has a curling problem'. (As seen on a shirt.)
- 'If curling were easy, they'd call it hockey'. (Author Unknown.)
- 'When Hell freezes over, I'll curl there, too'. (Author Unknown.)
- 'Curling is sweeping the nation'. (Author Unknown.)

Further lively use of language for sporting commentaries can be found, for instance, in the long-standing work of Stuart Hall; extracts from interviews with this celebrated sports journalist are available at:

- www.abc.net.au/rn/sportsfactor/stories/2006/1527862.htm
- www.markhodkinson.com/pages/journalism_stuart_hall.htm

All three of these examples give a different account of sport and language, and of course this is merely a small sample: the range available is huge. The potential for language-based activity is similarly huge, including adaptations of many of the approaches we have already encountered in previous chapters. In my experience, one especially successful way in is to focus on cross-genre adaptations: using the language of football commentary, for example, to describe a school assembly (ensuring of course that colleagues' sensitivities aren't too ruffled).

Another possibility centres on the often quite subtle differences between the language (and, more broadly, the media imagery) that adhere to different sports: a comparison between rugby union and rugby league, for example, or darts and cricket. The Internet, particularly through blogs, football club fan sites and the like, is bristling with lively instances of sport-in-language: I have been especially struck, for example, by the wealth of good writing about football that now appears (among a great deal that isn't so good, of course, but that's part of the story too), much of it written by men and boys who (I imagine) would probably not have taken pen to paper about such matters – or anything else – in pre-Internet days. There is a distinct opportunity here for exchange between pupils as sports writers within and across schools – including a possible international dimension.

The 'issue' of boxing

There are clearly many serious issues around sport, and any of these offers opportunities for interdisciplinary English teaching, based on the language and media imagery through which the various positions are presented. Money in sport is one such issue, as is the use of stimulants, animals in sport, over-competitiveness for young sports people, gender in sport, bribery – the list goes on. I have chosen here to look at the nature of boxing, abhorred by many as brutalising, exploitative and dangerous to its participants, and loved by others as liberating for the disadvantaged, a 'safe' outlet for natural aggression, and simply entertaining. Three quite different texts provide appropriate starting points: Bob Dylan's song *Who Killed Davey Moore?* (Dylan 1987), extracts from F.X. Toole's popular novel *Rope Burns* (2001), and Leslie Norris's poem *The Ballad of Billy Rose* (see Wired Shire (n.d.) for this and other related poems and lyrics). An excerpt from each gives a sense of their messages:

From *The Ballad of Billy Rose* (Leslie Norris)

Billy Rose fought there. He was top of the bill.
So brisk a fighter, so gallant, so precise!
Trim as a tree he stood for the ceremonies,

He had no chance. Courage was not enough,
Nor tight defence. …

From *Who Killed Davey Moore?* (Bob Dylan)

Who killed Davey Moore,
Why an' what's the reason for?

'Not us,' says the angry crowd,
Whose screams filled the arena loud.
'It's too bad he died that night

But we just like to see a fight.
We didn't mean for him t' meet his death,
We just meant to see some sweat,
There ain't nothing wrong in that.
It wasn't us that made him fall.
No, you can't blame us at all.'

From *Rope Burns* (F.X. Toole)

I stop blood.
    I stop it between rounds for fighter so that they can stay in the fight.
    Blood ruins some boys. It was that way with Sonny Liston, God rest his soul. Bad as he was, he'd see his own blood and fall apart. …
    And it's not my job to hospitalize a boy for brain damage. My job is to stop blood so the fighter can see enough to keep on fighting. I do that, maybe I save a boy's title…

(Toole 2001: 13)

All three texts are in one sense critical of boxing, focusing on its destructiveness, but also emphasise the excitement and energy (especially the F X Toole stories). To provide a balanced exploration, clearly, texts professing strong opinions on any given theme should be juxtaposed with others professing different views. A point worth making, I think, however, is that 'balance' is not always desirable, and as the interdisciplinary English teacher selects resources from an ever-widening pool, careful sensitivity to the issues, their presentation, and their reception by the pupils in question has to be observed. If looking at 'Kick Racism out of Football' text, for example, I should not be seeking to counter with a racist text to provide a spurious 'balance', but I would be probing, through discussion and textual study, to uncover and understand the nature of any racism in sport. Interestingly too, from a generic standpoint, both cited texts work within the ballad form we looked at previously (and the Dylan song borrows specifically from the 'Who Killed Cock Robin?' traditional verse); in my own teaching I have successfully followed a thematic exposition of the texts by asking pupils to write their own ballads on a sporting event of their choice. Constructive links are of course possible with other curricular approaches too: music, especially, through playing the Dylan song, and a more recent musical version of 'Billy Rose' by '16 Second Stare'. All three texts also suggest and portray a number of different participants, and would lend themselves admirably to drama activity addressing themes of citizenship and social responsibility.

9

The future potential of cross-curricular teaching and learning in English: a sense of direction

'We hope that the classrooms of tomorrow will not be about control but about space', wrote Julia Davies and Kate Pahl (2007: 102). I couldn't agree more, and such a formulation is absolutely apt for the vision of the future encapsulated in the present book.

Interdisciplinary education, specifically when focused on English teaching as in this context, has a powerful role to play in making sense of the welter of confusing impressions, requirements and predilections, making connections where possible and by the same token distinctions where not. As well as forging an idea of self-identity, such an education should provide the opportunity to understand, tolerate and empathise with other possible identities, both for oneself (whether teacher or pupil, for the boundaries inevitably dissolve) and for the other. As befits the nature of the subject English, and in particular my essentially Romantic conception of it, we have over the course of this book encountered a number of poems, and for a purpose. The experience of reading literature – perhaps especially poetry, language distilled – gives us cause to reflect on these areas, holding up a mirror to our own cultural identities in order that this reflection may occur. In a rather more complex way, too, it allows for multiple reflections in so far as each reader, in the collaborative conditions of the creative classroom, brings new meanings and interpretations. It is perhaps, as ever, best to leave it to a poet to say this more succinctly and suggestively: Percy Shelley, describing the intercultural power of poetry in his passionately argued *A Defence of Poetry*:

> A poem is the image of life expressed in its eternal truth. ... the creation of actions according to the unchangeable forms of human nature, as existing in the mind of the creator, which is itself the image of all other minds. ... [It] is universal, and contains within itself the germ of a relation to whatever motives or actions have place in the possible varieties of human nature. ... Poetry is a mirror which makes beautiful that which is distorted.
>
> (Wroe 2008: 106)

The interdisciplinary perspective in teaching and learning, as I hope I have shown, lends itself particularly to this sort of aesthetic, ordering and enlightening experience: creating appropriate connections and breadth of understanding. Although what we are talking about here is an intensely personal experience, it is also intensely interpersonal – intercultural, in fact. As Imison puts it (in DfEE 1999: 50),

> If you only understand one culture it is like seeing with one eye only, but if you add the dimension of other cultures, you become binocular and things can be seen in perspective. It allows you to appreciate much more.

With these interdisciplinary (binocular) lenses firmly in place, I should like to explore several more poems, in the hope that they may provide yet more illumination. Firstly, a clear message from the eponymous central figure in Khalil Gibran's *The Prophet* (1923):

> Then said a teacher, 'Speak to us of Teaching.'
> And he said:
> No man can reveal to you aught but that which already lies half asleep in the dawning of our knowledge.
> The teacher who walks in the shadow of the temple, among his followers, gives not of his wisdom but rather of his faith and his lovingness.
> If he is indeed wise he does not bid you enter the house of wisdom, but rather leads you to the threshold of your own mind.

I find that reading this poem is a necessarily humbling, but simultaneously liberating, experience, and the types of understandings offered here are, of course, inextricably connected – as indeed are all understandings: an interdisciplinary message for all teachers.

And now for a different kind of prophecy. Over ten years ago, in 1997, Sally Tweddle and colleagues discussed the possible future directions of the secondary school-based curriculum for English in their aptly titled *English for Tomorrow*, concluding, in their final chapter 'Into the Twenty-first Century', with some interesting prospects:

> So far we have been discussing English as if it will remain a separate subject in the curriculum even if its subject matter ceases to be purely literary. However, it may well be, under pressure of mixed and merged media and in response to the richness of provision of textual types on the circuits, that … English will merge with, or incorporate, other areas, such as music and art. In recent years, teachers of English have been eclectic, borrowing methods and materials from other disciplines to illustrate, in an intuitive way initially, the process of meaning-making in various genres, outside the purely language based. Yet at the same time other teachers have similarly been reaching into areas historically reserved for the English teacher. Both movements show every sign of accelerating further.
>
> (Tweddle *et al*. 1997: 89–90)

More than a decade on, we have the benefit of hindsight, but the picture is still unclear. Certainly there have been many and influential moves in the directions suggested by Tweddle, but, as we saw in the survey of the recent history of English teaching in this context in earlier chapters, the developments have been far from smooth – two steps forward, one step back, cynics might say – and it may well only be now, with new official and unofficial curriculum initiatives everywhere gathering momentum, that the time has come for the interdisciplinary turn. Certainly this book, and the entire series it is part of, testifies to a sense of genuine change.

As I have tried to demonstrate, the momentum of change is motivated by a certain convergence of various agendas and pedagogical movements. Many of these – as indeed Tweddle and her colleagues demonstrate – are not new. It has become something of a truism to say that in the field of education nothing is ever new, and that if you wait around long enough without changing your practice your time will come round again. It's a cynical view, perhaps, and certainly not one I endorse; and yet, I do have a sense of important ideas (like the interdisciplinary venture at the centre of this book's thesis) flowing as a stream, at times underground, at times clearly visible. Merely citing this geographical image has reminded me yet again of the interdisciplinary, metaphorical nature of language, the ultimate focus of the English curriculum. The seminal educational philosopher John Holt, several decades ago, emphasised the interconnectedness of experience, educational and otherwise:

> people who have been mis-schooled into thinking that life, the world, human experience, are divided up into disciplines or subjects or bodies of knowledge, some of them serious, noble, important, others ignoble and trivial. It is not so. The world and human experience are one whole. There are no dotted lines in it separating History from Geography or Mathematics from Science or Chemistry from Physics. In fact, *out there*, there are no such things as History or Geography or Chemistry or Physics. Out there is – out there. But the world, the universe, human experience, are vast. We can't take them in all at once. So we choose, sensibly enough, to look at this part of reality, or that; to ask this kind of question about it, or that. ... But these different ways of looking at reality should not make us forget that it is all one piece, and that from any one place in it we can get to all the other places.
>
> (Holt 1972: 95)

This appraisal, it seems to me, is sanely apposite, and its sense of insight coupled with realism needs to be kept firmly in mind.

Further impetus, as we have seen, comes from a contemporary radical perspective: intercultural teaching and learning (itself originally derived from MFL in an interdisciplinary spirit), critical pedagogy (CP), and a related growing awareness of the international dimension of education. One of the foremost exponents of CP, Henry Giroux, maintains that, with CP, there is a distinct 'emphasis on breaking down disciplines and creating interdisciplinary knowledge' (Giroux 2006: 5), and much of the work he and others, following the pioneering philosophy and practice of Paulo Freire, has been precisely along these lines. Alex Moore (Moore 2000: 168) has taken up the interdisciplinary challenge, realistically suggesting a way forward through '...a possible 'transitional' curriculum, that might facilitate and characterise the link between 'traditional' subject-based curricula and new, experience-based curricula'. The thinking behind such an initiative, and the practical experiences involved, would, Moore feels, engender a radical, critically questioning approach:

> It calls into serious question ... the fragmented, subject-based curriculum, which offers such 'a poor basis from which to frame courses of transforming social action

that stand a reasonable chance of being effective' (Lankshear 1993: 55). Through questioning definitions of subject areas, and focusing on making sense of the world through interrogations of the representations by which we experience it, it concentrates less on 'what is' than on 'what might be' – or 'what ought to be'.

(ibid.)

There is, then, a distinctly radical challenge at the centre of the interdisciplinary project, or at least the potential for activating this dimension. The intercultural aspect of the curriculum is given an especially sharp edge for the subject English, dealing as it does not only with the nature and effects of language in all its broad manifestations, but in particular with the *English* language and its global implications both positive and negative. The radical challenge is thus at once complicated – 'problematised' is the term CP practitioners would I think prefer – and made yet more influential. How this challenge is taken up has a great deal to do with the future potential of cross-curricular teaching and learning in English within schools and, increasingly, beyond into local and national communities. Richard Andrews, in his helpful survey of research centred on English, takes up the point:

'English' as a term locates the source of the subject … in the English language. To study English in, say, a school in Saudi Arabia or a university in Australia entails the cultural baggage that comes with the term. In its liberal versions, then, 'English' becomes a misnomer for what is actually being taught (e.g. literature in languages other than English, translations, Australian Media Studies). More conservatively, what looked like a simple solution to a core education in the classics at the beginning of the twentieth century – Sampson's proposals as couched in *English for the English* (1921) – looks overly simplistic at the beginning of the twenty-first. … 'English' might be the best umbrella term for the time being, but the subject is rapidly breaking out from under that umbrella.

(Andrews 2001: 3)

Quite what breaks out from under the umbrella and what form it then takes is the subject of the present book, of course, but it is important to remember that, despite the apparently overwhelming influence of global and national social, linguistic and educational factors, teachers themselves will also have an important say. There is an important debate going on, which must be allowed to continue, about the entire nature of education: learning for its own sake, for the sheer enjoyment of gaining knowledge and understanding, pitted against a learning that is purely instrumental. Both have their place, of course, as Robert Frost sensed in this excerpt from his poem *Death of the Hired Man* (1914), in which a farmer and his wife discuss whether to re-employ their hired man from long ago, as his days of useful labour are by now behind him:

Harold's associated in his mind with Latin.
He asked me what I thought of Harold's saying
He studied Latin like the violin
Because he liked it--that an argument!

He said he couldn't make the boy believe
He could find water with a hazel prong--
Which showed how much good school had ever done him.

In a sense it is difficult – indeed maybe undesirable – to prophesise what will happen when so many complexities are involved. If teachers and their pupils (and their parents) are to have a real influence over events, as a radical democratic agenda would surely insist upon, it would in any case be mistaken to provide at this stage too detailed a blueprint. Nevertheless some sort of vision is essential – some kind of overarching purpose in education, as we witnessed in the pleading of yet another poet, Thomas Traherne, cited in Chapter 1.

Two key practitioners in and commentators on contemporary education, Tim Brighouse and David Woods, revisiting and revising Brighouse's important 1991 book *What Makes a Good School?* for an updated edition renamed *What Makes a Good School Now?* (2008) have some helpful and interesting things to say about the possible directions for education in the early twenty-first century and beyond. The most significant point, perhaps, in the interdisciplinary context, is that the secondary school curriculum, having 'enjoyed' relative calm and stability for the best part of two decades (and I do stress the word 'relative' here – I know what initiative fatigue feels like), is again undergoing rapid development. Brighouse and Woods signal this in subtitling part of their final chapter 'The Return of the Curriculum', maintaining that 'As for the secondary curriculum, we believe it is already undergoing enormous change and will experience yet more as a result of three initiatives' (Brighouse and Woods 2008: 137). The three initiatives in question are, first, the 'relatively modest' Royal Society of Arts project *Opening Minds* 'which seeks in Key Stage 3 to challenge 'subject'-dominated thinking' through initiating and sustaining a wide range of school- and community-based projects broadly based on creativity across the curriculum. The second and third initiatives posited by Brighouse and Woods are more top-down in nature, and have already been explored in earlier chapters of the present book: the revisions of the National Curriculum at Key Stages 2 and 3 in favour of more generic cross-curricular dimensions, and the overhaul of the fourteen to nineteen curriculum to give far greater flexibility of approach through emphasis more on appropriate skills that extensive content. 'In such a world of increasing uncertainty', Brighouse and Woods conclude, 'we want youngsters to feel the future is theirs to seize and make sense of. It's why, therefore, secondary schools include thinking about the curriculum on their agenda in a way they haven't since 1988' (op. cit.: 139).

There are many interested parties in fostering change, some of which we have already encountered in earlier chapters. In a sense, any topical theme may be usefully explored through cross-curricular teaching and learning, and in all of these, language – and thus English teachers – will play a pivotal role. Increasingly, as one trawls the Internet to find examples of such practice, the healthy diversity of experience is readily apparent. The roles of the arts and creativity, of environmental awareness and global sustainability, of education for citizenship and democracy, of international understanding in a global educational context: there are indeed almost infinite possibilities. For example, the broadly based teaching resources network *Teaching Expertise* is persuasive in its introduction:

Young people in our Secondary Schools encounter a compartmentalised day with pre-determined blocks of unrelated subjects. In any one day they can move from lessons in Maths to English (maybe a break) then Science, Geography (maybe lunch) to Design Technology and then RE. What a lot of mixed messages they may get during the day. Unless this can be co-ordinated kids today may have to move from algebra to Shakespeare to energy forms ..., without any coherence in the messages received before a nourishing (or not) lunch. ... Pilot schools have shown how cross-curricular topics can be introduced so that the pupils can study a global issue in sustained and co-ordinated work.

Teaching Expertise (n.d.)

The part played by the teacher in keeping a sensitive eye on the wood in the midst of a sometimes bewildering forest of trees is quite a challenge, but a challenge worth rising to, as I hope has become apparent. I shall leave the last word to another poet, W.B. Yeats, in his aptly titled *Among School Children*, describing his visit, as an eminent man of letters, to a small Irish school:

I walk through the long schoolroom questioning;
A kind old nun in a white hood replies;
The children learn to cipher and to sing,
To study reading-books and histories,
To cut and sew, be neat in everything
In the best modern way — the children's eyes
In momentary wonder stare upon
A sixty-year-old smiling public man.

But it is in Yeats' final verse that the sense of the inseparability of experiences is paramount, borne of struggle, perhaps, but in the end enjoyed with pleasure. I have never heard this feeling of connectedness more eloquently and suggestively celebrated:

Labour is blossoming or dancing where
The body is not bruised to pleasure soul.
Nor beauty born out of its own despair,
Nor blear-eyed wisdom out of midnight oil.
O chestnut-tree, great-rooted blossomer,
Are you the leaf, the blossom or the bole?
O body swayed to music, O brightening glance,
How can we know the dancer from the dance?

Appendix: helpful websites

www.bbc.co.uk/learning
The BBC's education website.

www.bfi.org.uk/education
British Film Institute education website.

www.bl.uk/learning
British Library education resources.

www.centreforglobaleducation.org
Resources for teaching and learning about global issues.

www.classroom-resources.co.uk
General resources, particularly film-based.

http://curriculum.qcda.gov.uk/key-stages-3-and-4/index.aspx
The National Curriculum for secondary schools.

www.englishandmedia.co.uk
English and Media Centre resources and teaching ideas.

www.findyourtalent.org
A useful website dealing with creativity for young people.

www.le.ac.uk/engassoc
The English Association: a long-standing subject based association.

www.literacytrust.org.uk
The National Literacy Trust: focus on literacy teaching and learning.

www.oxfam.org.uk/education
The Oxfam website: excellent resources pertinent to global issues.

www.nate.org.uk
The principal organisation for English teaching, the National Association for the Teaching of English: a wealth of resources, publications and education topics centred on the

teaching of English, especially at secondary level. The Spring 2000 edition of the magazine *Classroom*, for example, is dedicated to cross-curricular initiatives involving English.

www.nationalstrategies.standards.dcsf.gov.uk/secondary/english/framework
The English Framework within the National Strategy.

www.poetryarchive.org *and* www.poetrysociety.org.uk
Both websites provide wide-ranging poetry resources.

http://schools.becta.org.uk
Technology within education.

www.teachingexpertise.com/articles/19-developing-citizenship-sharing-our-experiences-891
Citizenship/global awareness website.

www.teachers.tv
Information and follow-up discussion on Teachers TV programmes across a wide range of educational topics.

www.teachit.co.uk
Practically orientated teaching ideas and resources.

www.tes.co.uk/resources
The *Times Education Supplement* resources and discussions.

www.thersa.org/projects/education/opening-minds-old/opening-minds-framework
The Royal Society of the Arts 'Opening Minds' project and other resources.

www.ukla.org
UK Literacy Association: a wealth of resources and ideas, focused on literacy, with a generally primary slant, but useful for secondary English teachers also.

References

Abbs, P. (1976) *Root and Blossom: Essays on the Philosophy, Practice and Politics of English Teaching* London: Heinemann.

—— (1982) *English within the Arts: A radical alternative for English and the arts in the curriculum* London: Hodder & Stoughton.

—— (2003) *Against the Flow: education, the arts and postmodern culture* London: RoutledgeFalmer.

Ackroyd, P. (1995) *Blake* London: Sinclair-Stevenson.

—— *London: The Biography* (2000) London: Chatto & Windus.

Alred, G., Byram, M. and Fleming, M. (eds) (2003) *Intercultural Experience and Education* Clevedon: Multilingual Matters.

Amis, M. (1991) *Time's Arrow* London: Penguin.

Andrews, R. (1997) 'Editorial: Electronic English' *English in Education* 31(2): 1–3.

—— (2001) *Teaching and Learning English: A Guide to Recent Research and its Applications* London: Continuum.

Astley, N. (2002) 'Introduction' in Astley, N. (ed.) *Staying Alive: Real Poems for Unreal Times* Tarset: Bloodaxe Books.

Barnes, D. (1976) *From Communication to Curriculum* Harmondsworth: Penguin.

Bazalgette, C. (ed.) (1989) *Primary Media Education: A Curriculum Statement* London: BFI Education.

Benton, M. and Benton, P. (1990) *Double Vision* London: Hodder & Stoughton.

—— and —— (1995) *Painting with Words* London: Hodder & Stoughton.

—— and —— (1997) *Picture Poems* London: Hodder & Stoughton.

Braithwaite, E.K. (1969) *Limbo* in *Islands* Oxford: Oxford University Press.

Buckingham, D. and Sefton-Green, J. (1994) 'Making Sense of the Media: From Reading to Culture', in S. Brindley (ed.), *Teaching English* London: Routledge.

Bearne, E. and Marsh, J. (eds) (2007) *Literacy and Social Inclusion: closing the gap* Stoke on Trent: Trentham.

Berger, J. (1972) *Ways of Seeing* Harmondsworth: Penguin.

Black, J. (2000) *Maps and Politics* London: Reaktion Books.

Black, P. and Wiliam, D. (1998) *Inside the Black Box* Occasional paper, London: King's College online, available at: www.collegenet.co.uk/admin/download/inside the black box_23_doc.pdf

Blake, W. (1995) *Selected Works*, D. Stevens (ed), Cambridge: Cambridge University Press.

Boden, M. (2001) 'Creativity and Knowledge' in Craft, A., Jeffrey, B. and Leibling, M. (eds) *Creativity in Education* London: Continuum.

Brighouse, T. and Woods, D. (2008) *What Makes a Good School Now?* London: Network Continuum.

Brindley, S. (ed.) (1994) *Teaching English* London: Routledge.

BECTA/NATE (2009) *Secondary English with ICT: A Pupil's Entitlement to ICT in English* online, available at: www.becta.org.uk and www.nate.org.uk [both accessed 15 February 2010].

Britton, J. (1972) *Language and Learning* Harmondsworth: Pelican.

—— (1994) 'Vygotsky's Contribution to Pedagogical Theory' in Bridley, S (ed.) *Teaching English* London: Routledge.

Brooker, P. (1994) 'Key Words in Brecht's Theory and Practice of Theatre' in Thomson, P. and Sacks, G. (eds) *The Cambridge Companion to Brecht* Cambridge: Cambridge University Press.

Brontë, E. (1997 [1847]) *Wuthering Heights*, ed. R. Hoyes, Cambridge: Cambridge University Press.

Carlyle, T. (1915 [1843]) *Past and Present* Boston: Richard D Altick.

Carr, D. (2003) *Making Sense of Education* London: RoutledgeFalmer.

Carr, W. (2004) 'Philosophy and Education' in Carr, W. (ed.) *The RoutledgeFalmer Reader in Philosophy of Education* London: RoutledgeFalmer.

Carroll, L. (2007 [1865]) *Alice's Adventures in Wonderland* London: Vintage.

Chambers, A. (1985) *Tell Me: Children, Reading and Talk* Stroud: Thimble Press.

Chanan, G. and Gilchrist, L. (1974) *What School is For* London: Methuen.

Chevalier, T. (2008) *Burning Bright* London: HarperCollins.

Chomsky, N. (2003) *Chomsky on Democracy and Education*, ed. P. Otero, London: RoutledgeFalmer.

Cliff Hodges, G. (2005) 'Creativity in Education', English in Education 39(3): 47–61.

Coleridge, S.T. (1977) *The Portable Coleridge* ed. I.A. Richards, Harmondsworth: Penguin.

Council of Europe (1996) *Modern languages: Learning, Teaching, Assessment. A Common European Framework of Reference* Strasburg: Council of Europe.

Cox, B. (1991) *Cox on Cox: An English Curriculum for the 1990's* London: Hodder & Stoughton.

—— (1995) *Cox on the Battle for the English Curriculum* London: Hodder & Stoughton.

Craft, A., Jeffrey, B. and Leibling, M. (eds) (2001) *Creativity in Education* London: Continuum.

Csikszentmihalyi, M. (1990) *Flow* London: Harper Collins.

D'Arcy, P. (2000) *Two Contrasting Paradigms for the Teaching and Assessment of Writing* Sheffield: NATE.

Davies, C. (1996) *What is English Teaching?* Milton Keynes: Open University Press.

Davies, I. (ed.) (2000) *Teaching the Holocaust* London: Continuum.

Davies, I., Gregory, I. and McGuinn, N. (2002) *Key Debates in Education* London: Continuum.

Davies, J. and Pahl, K. (2007) 'Blending Voices, Blending Learning: Lessons in Pedagogy from a Post-16 Classroom' in Bearne, E. and Marsh, J. (eds) *Literacy and Social Inclusion: closing the gap* Stoke on Trent: Trentham.

Dawkins, R. (2006) *Unweaving the Rainbow* London: Penguin.

De Bernières, L. (1998) *Captain Correlli's Mandolin* London: Vintage.

Defoe, D. (1998 [1722]) *A Journal of the Plague Year* Oxford: Oxford World Classics.

DES (1975) *A Language for Life* London: HMSO.

—— (1988) *Report of the Enquiry into the Teaching of English: Language* (The Kingman Report) London: HMSO.

—— (1989) *English for Ages 5-16* (The Cox Report) London: HMSO.

Dewey, J. (1933) *How to Think* Boston: D.C. Heath.

—— (1958 [1934]) *Art as Experience* New York: Capricorn.

DfEE (1998) *The National Literacy Strategy: Framework for Teaching* Sudbury: DfEE Publications.

—— (2001) *Key Stage 3 National Strategy: Framework for Teaching English Years 7, 8 and 9* London: HMSO.

DfEE/QCA (1999) *English: The National Curriculum for English* London: DfEE and QCA Publications.

Doherty, B. (1991) *Dear Nobody* London: Orchard Books.

Dylan, B. (1987) *Lyrics 1962-1985* London: Jonathan Cape.

Eagleton, T. (1983) *Literary Theory: An Introduction* Oxford: Basil Blackwell.

—— (2000) *The Idea of Culture* Oxford: Blackwell.

Eisner, E. (2002) *The Arts and the Creation of Mind* New Haven CT: Yale University Press.

Fanthorpe, U.A. (n.d.) *Dear Mr Lee*, online, available at: www.wonderingminstrels.blogspot.com/2000/07/dear-mr-lee-u-fanthorpe.html

Fenton, J. (1978) 'Of the Martian School' in *New Statesman* (20 October 1978: 520–6).

Filipovic, Z. (1994) *Zlata's Diary: A Child's Life in Sarajevo* London: Penguin.

Fleming, M. (2007) *The Challenges of Assessment within Language(s) of Education* Council of Europe (Strasbourg) conference paper online, available at: www.coe.int/t/dg4/linguistic/source/prag07_LPE_Evaluation_Fleming_EN.doc [accessed 15 February 2010].

Forster, E.M. (1962 [1927]) *Aspects of the Novel* Harmondsworth: Penguin.

Fowles, J. (1969) *The French Lieutenant's Woman* London: Jonathan Cape.

—— (1981) *The Aristos* Reading: Triad.

Frank, A. (1995) *The Diary of Anne Frank* Basingstoke: Macmillan.

Freire, P. (1996 [1970]) *Pedagogy of the Oppressed* London: Penguin.

Freire, P. and Macedo, D. (1987) *Literacy: Reading the Word and the World* South Hadley MA: Bergin & Garvey.

Friel, B. (1981) *Translations* London: Faber and Faber.

Frost, R. (1914) *Death of the Hired Man* online, available at: www.online-literature.com/frost/752/

Fullan, M. (2010) *The New Meaning of Educational Change* Columbia: Teachers College Press.

Fullan, M. and Hargreaves, A. (1992) *What's Worth Fighting for in Your School?* Milton Keynes: Open University Press.

Gale, T. and Densmore, K. (2000) *Just Schooling: Explorations in the Cultural Politics of Teaching* Buckingham: Open University Press.

Gardner, H. (1993) *Frames of Mind: The Theory of Multiple Intelligences* New York: Basic Books.

Ghose, Z. (n.d.) *Geography Lesson*, online, available at: www.drainchild.blogspot.com/2009/09/three-poems-by-zulfikar-ghose.html.

Gibran, K. (1923)*The Prophet*, online, available at: www.leb.net/~mira/works/prophet/prophet.html.

Gibson, R. (1986) *Structuralism and Education* London: Hodder & Stoughton.

Giroux, H.A. (1997) *Pedagogy and the Politics of Hope: Theory, Culture and Schooling* Boulder CO: Westview Press.

—— (2001) *Theory and Resistance in Education: Towards a Pedagogy for the Opposition.* Westport CT: Bergin & Garvey.

—— (2006) *America on the Edge.* New York: Palgrave Macmillan.

Glazier, J. (2007) 'Tinkering Towards Socially Just Teaching: Moving from Critical Theory to Practice' in *Changing English* 14(3): 375–82.

Gold, J. (n.d.) *From a Distance*, lyrics online, available at: www.lyricsfreak.com/b/bette+midler/from+a+distance_20016990.html.

Goodwyn, A. (1997) *Developing English Teachers* Milton Keynes: Open University Press.

Goodwyn, A. (ed.) (2000) *English in the Digital Age: Information and Communications Technology and the Teaching of English* London/New York: Cassell.

—— (ed.) (2002) *Improving Literacy at KS2 and KS3* London: Paul Chapman.

Goodwyn, A. and Findlay, K. (2002) 'Secondary Schools and the National Literacy Strategy' in Goodwyn, A. (ed.) (2002) *Improving Literacy at KS2 and KS3* London: Paul Chapman.

Gregoriou, Z. (2001) 'Does Speaking of Others Involve Receiving the Other?' in Biesta, G. and Egéa-Kuehne, D. (eds) *Derrida and Education* London: Routledge.

Griffiths, M. (2003) *Action for Social Justice in Education: Fairly Different* Maidenhead: Open University Press.

Guilherme, M. (2002) *Critical Citizens for an Intercultural World* Clevedon: Multilingual Matters.

Habermas, J. (1970) *Towards a Rational Society* Boston: Beacon Press.

Haddon, M. (2002) *The Curious Incident of the Dog at Night-time* London: Jonathan Cape.

Hargreaves, D. (1999) 'The Knowledge-Creating School' in *The British Journal of Educational Studies* 47(2): 122–44.

Harber, C. (2004) *Schooling as Violence* London: RoutledgeFalmer.

Hardy, T. (1985 [1891]) *Tess of the D'Urbervilles* ed. D. Skilton, London: Penguin.

Harrison, B. (1994) *The Literate Imagination: Renewing the Secondary English Curriculum* London: David Fulton.

Harrison, C. (2002) *The National Strategy for English at Key Stage 3: Roots and Research* London: DFES.

Harrison, M. and Stuart-Clark, C. (eds) (1989) *Peace and War: A Collection of Poems* Oxford: Oxford University Press.

Hart, M. (1999) *Spirit into Sound: The Magic of Music* Los Angeles: Grateful Dead Publishing Company.

Heaney, S. (1966) *Digging*, online, available at: www.bbc.co.uk/schools/gcsebitesize/english_literature/poetheaney/diggingrev1.shtml.

Hodgkinson, W. (2009) *The Ballad of Britain: How Music Captured the Soul of a Nation* London: Portico.

Hoggart, D. (1998) 'Critical Literacy and Creative Reading' in Cox, B. (ed) *Literacy is Not Enough* Manchester: Manchester University Press.

Holbrook, D. (1979) *English for Meaning* Windsor: NFER.

Holt, J. (1972) *Freedom and Beyond* Harmondsworth: Penguin.

Holmes, R. (1998) *Darker Reflections* London: Harper Collins.

—— (2009) *The Age of Wonder: How the Romantic Generation discovered the Beauty and Terror of Science* London: Harper Press.

Hoyles, M. (1977) *The Politics of Literacy* London: Writers and Readers Publishing Cooperative.

Hunt, G. (2002) 'Classroom literacy and everyday life' in Goodwyn, A. (ed.) *Improving Literacy at KS2 and KS3* London: Paul Chapman.

Johnson, D. (2008) 'Obituary for Alain Robbe-Grillet' *The Guardian*, Tuesday 19 February 2008.

Keane, F (1996) *Letter to Daniel* London: Penguin (and as a BBC Radio Collection audiotape: BBC Worldwide 1997), also available online at: www.pbs.org/wgbh/pages/frontline/shows/rwanda/todaniel/.

Kenneally, T. (1982) *Schindler's Ark* London: Hodder & Stoughton.

Kenny, A. (ed) (1994) *The Wittgenstein Reader* Oxford: Blackwell.

Knight, R. (1996) *Valuing English: Reflections on the National Curriculum* London: David Fulton.

Kress, G. (1994) *Learning to Write* London and New York: Routledge.

—— (1995) *Writing the Future: English and the Making of a Culture of Innovation* Sheffield: NATE.

Kureishi, H. (2003) 'Loose Tongues and Liberty' in *The Guardian* 7 June 2003.

Lankshear, C. (1993) 'Curriculum as Literacy: Reading and Writing in 'New Times' in Green, B. (ed) *The Insistence of the Letter: Literacy Studies and Curriculum Theorising* London: Falmer Press.

Lawrence, D.H. (2007 [1913]) *Sons and Lovers* London: Wordsworth Classics.

Lewis, M. and Wray, D. (eds) (2000) *Literacy in the Secondary School* London: David Fulton.

Littlefair, A. (1991) *Reading All Types of Writing* Milton Keynes: Open University Press.

Liveley, P. (2008 [1971]) *The Whispering Knights* Oxford: Oxford University Press.

Lucas, B. (2001) 'Creative Teaching, Teaching Creativity and Creative Learning' in Craft, A., Jeffrey, B. and Leibling, M., (eds) *Creativity in Education* London: Continuum.

Lunzer E. and Gardner, K. (1984) *Learning from the Written Word* Edinburgh: Oliver & Boyd.

McEwan, I. (1985) *Rose Blanche* London: Jonathan Cape.

—— (1998) *Enduring Love* London: Vintage.

Mahy, M. (1989) *Barnaby's Dead* London: Heinemann.

Marcuse, H. (1969) *An Essay on Liberation* London: Penguin.

Marshall, B. (2001) 'Creating Danger: The Place of the Arts in Education Policy' in Craft, A., Jeffrey, B. and Leibling, M. (eds) *Creativity in Education* London: Continuum.

Matthewman, S. (2007) 'But What About the Fish? Teaching Ted Hughes' *Pike* with Environmental Bite' in *English in Education* 41(3): 67–77.

Medway, P. (2002) 'Show Him the Documents: Teaching and Learning the English Method' in *The English and Media Magazine* 47: 4–7.

Meek, M. (1991) *On Being Literate* London: Bodley Head.

Michaels, A. (1998) *Fugitive Pieces* London: Bloomsbury.

Moore, A. (2000) *Teaching and Learning: Pedagogy, Curriculum and Culture* London: RoutledgeFalmer.

Morgan, W. (1997) *Critical Literacy in the Classroom: The Art of the Possible* London: Routledge.

Morpurgo, M. (2007) *From Hereabout Hill* London: Heinemann.

NACCCE (1999) *All Our Futures: Creativity, Culture and Education* London: DfEE.

National Writing Project (1990) *Perceptions of Writing* Walton on Thames: Nelson.

Nobel, A. (1996) *Educating Through Art: The Steiner School Approach* Edinburgh: Floris Books.

Ofsted (2009) *English at the Crossroads: An Evaluation of English in Primary and Secondary Schools 2005/08*, online, available at: www.ofsted.gov.uk/Ofsted-home/News/Press-and-media/2009/June/English-at-the-crossroads [accessed 15 February 2010].

Orgel, D. (1991 [1978]) *The Devil in Vienna* London: Heinemann.

Orwell, G. (1949) *Nineteen Eighty-Four* Harmondsworth: Penguin.

Owen, W. (2004) *The Poems of Wilfred Owen* ed. J. Stallworthy, London: Faber and Faber.

Peel, R., Patterson, A. and Gerlach, J. (2000) *Questions of English: Ethics, aesthetics, rhetoric, and the formation of the subject in England, Australia and the United States* London: RoutledgeFalmer.

Peim, N. (2003) *Changing English? Rethinking the Politics of English Teaching* Sheffield: NATE.

Pinker, S. (1994) *The Language Instinct* London: Penguin.

Poe, E.A. (1981[1843]) 'The Black Cat' in E.A. Poe *Tales of Mystery and Imagination* London: Octopus.

Praedl, G. (1982) *Prospect and Retrospect: Selected Essays of James Britton* London: Heinemann.

Pullman, P. (2002) *Perverse, All Monstrous, All Prodigious Things* Sheffield: NATE

QCDA (2007) *The Secondary Curriculum*, online, available at: http://curriculum.qcda.gov.uk/key-stages-3-and-4/index.aspx [accessed 15 February 2010].

—— (2010) *A Big Picture of the Secondary Curriculum*, January 2010, online, available at: http://curriculum.qcda.gov.uk/uploads/BigPicture_sec_05 _tcm8-15743.pdf [accessed 28 June 2010].

Raine, C. (1979) *A Martian Sends a Postcard Home*, online, available at: www.mit.edu/people/dpolicar/writing/poetry/poems/martian.html.

Ransome, A. (1930) *Swallows and Amazons* London: Jonathan Cape.

Read, H. (1958) *Education Through Art* London: Faber and Faber.

Richter, H. (1991) *Friedrich* London: Heinemann.

Ross, M. (1985) *The Aesthetic in Education* Oxford: Oxford University Press.

Sachar, L. (2003) *Holes* London: Bloomsbury.

Safran, L. (2001) 'Creativity as "Mindful" Learning' in Craft, A., Jeffrey, B. and Leibling, M. (eds) *Creativity in Education* London: Continuum.

Said, E. (2003) 'A Window on the World' in *The Guardian* (2 August 2003).

Sampson, G. (1921) *English for the English* Cambridge: Cambridge University Press.

Schiller, F. (2002) 'On the Aesthetic Education of Man' in Bernstein, L. *Classic and Romantic German Aesthetics* Cambridge: Cambridge University Press.

Schlink, B. (1998) *The Reader* London: Phoenix.

Searle, C. (1998) *None but Our Words: Critical Literacy in Classroom and Community* Buckingham: Open University Press.

Sefton-Green, J. (2000) 'Introduction: Evaluating Creativity' in Sefton-Green, J. and Sinker, R. (eds) *Evaluating Creativity* London: Routledge.

Sefton-Green, J. and Sinker, R. (eds) (2000) *Evaluating Creativity* London: Routledge.

Shelley, M. (1997 [1818]) *Frankenstein* ed. D. Stevens, Cambridge: Cambridge University Press.

Sinker, R. (2000) 'Making Multimedia: Evaluating Young People's Creative Multimedia Production' in Sefton-Green, J. and Sinker, R. (eds) *Evaluating Creativity* London: Routledge.

Spufford, F. (2002) *The Child that Books Built* London: Faber and Faber.

Stead, C.K. (1964) *The New Poetic: Yeats to Eliot* London: Hutchinson.

Steiner, G. (2003) *Lessons of the Masters* Cambridge MA: Harvard University Press.

Stevens, D. (2000) *Contexts in Literature: The Gothic Tradition* Cambridge: Cambridge University Press.

—— (2004) *Contexts in Literature: Romanticism* Cambridge: Cambridge University Press.

—— and McGuinn, N. (2004) *The Art of Teaching Secondary English: Innovative and Creative Approaches* London: RoutledgeFalmer.

——, Cliff Hodges, G., Gibbons, S., Hunt, P. and Turvey, A. (2006) 'Transformations in Learning and Teaching Through Initial Teacher Education' *Literacy* 40(2): 97–105.

Stoker, B. (1993 [1897]) *Dracula*, ed. D. Rogers, London: Wordsworth Classics.

Street, B. (1997) 'The Implications of the "New Literacy Studies"[THIN]' for Literacy Education' in *English in Education* 31(3): 45–59.

Swindells, R. (1993) *Stone Cold* London: Heinemann.

Tate, A. (1994) *Core skills and Cross-Curricular Initiatives in Secondary Schools* Slough: NFER.

Teaching Expertise (n.d.) online, available at: www.teachingexpertise.com (accessed 4 March 2010)

Thomas, P. (1997) 'Doom to the Red-eyed Nyungghns from the Planet Glarg: Boys as Writers of Narrative' *English in Education* 31(3): 23–31.

Thompson, R. (1986) 'How Will I Ever Be Simple Again?' from *Daring Adventures*, lyrics online, available at: www.lyricsdownload.com/thompson-richard-how-will-i-ever-be-simple-again-lyrics.html.

Tomlinson, T. (1987) *Flitherpickers* London: Walker Books.

Toole, F.X. (2001) *Rope Burns: Stories from the Corner* New York: Ecco.

Townsend, S. (1982) *The Secret Diary of Adrian Mole Aged 13¾* London: Methuen.

—— (1999) *Adrian Mole: The Cappuccino Years* London: Michael Joseph.

Traherne, T. (1960 [c. 1660]) *Centuries* ed. H. Marglioth, London: Mowbray.

Treece, H. (n.d.) *Conquerors*, online, available at: www.pkwy.k12.mo.us/west/teachers/gerding/hpoempacket.pdf.

Tripp, D. (1993) *Critical Incidents in Teaching: The Development of Professional Judgement* London: Routledge.

Tweddle, S. (1995) 'A Curriculum for the Future – A Curriculum Built for Change', *English in Education* 31(2): 5–13.

Tweddle, S., Adams, A., Clarke, S., Scrimshaw, P. and Walton, S. (1997) *English for Tomorrow* Buckingham: Open University Press.

Van Gogh, V. (1885) *Peasant Woman Digging*, online, available at: www.paintinghere.com/painting/Peasant_Woman_Digging_1266.html.

Verma, G. and Pumfrey, P. (eds) (1993) *Cross-Curricular Contexts: Themes and Dimensions in Secondary Schools* London: Falmer Press.

Walker, A. (1983) *The Color Purple* London: Women's Press.

Warnock, M. (1976) *Imagination* London: Faber and Faber.

Watson, G. (1975) *Coleridge* London: Dent.

Whitfield, P. (2006) *London: A Life in Maps* London: The British Library.

Williams, H. (1987) *Autogeddon*, online, available at: http://cfu.freehostia.com/Members/colin/autogeddon/.

Williams, T. (2009 [1947]) *A Streetcar Named Desire* London: Penguin.

Wired Shire (n.d.) *The Ballad of Billy Rose* and other boxing poems, online, available at: www.wiredshire.org.uk/professional/support/csg/english/documents/Copiesofpoems.doc

Wordsworth, D. (2002 [1897]) *The Grasmere and Alfoxden Journals* ed. P. Woof, Oxford: Oxford World Classics.

Wordsworth, W. and Coleridge, S.T. (1967) *Lyrical Ballads* ed. W. Owen, Oxford: Oxford University Press.

Wroe, A. (2008) *Being Shelley: The Poet's Search for Himself* London: Vintage.

Wu, D. (ed.) (1994) *Romanticism: An Anthology* Oxford: Blackwell.

Index

(For abbreviated entries please see abbreviation list, p. xi.)